The Power of the Object

The Power of the Object

Museums and World War II

Edited by Esben Kjeldbæk

MUSEUMSETC, EDINBURGH

Contents

8   Introduction

       What is the Power of the Object?
22   ESBEN KJELDBÆK
       Head of the Museum of the Danish Resistance
       1940-1945, National Museum of Denmark

       Interpreting the Second World War
52   JAMES TAYLOR
       Head of Research & Information
       Imperial War Museum, London

       The European Forum of Contemporary Conflict
82   ANNE GODFROID
       Exhibition Curator
       Musée Royal de l'Armée, Bruxelles

       The Exhibition: Between Book and Film
100   HANS HENRIK APPEL
       Senior Researcher,
       Royal Danish Arsenal Museum, Copenhagen

       The Breendonk Memorial
138   PATRICK NEFORS
       Former Head of Scientific Activities & Publications,
       Musée Royal de l'Armée, Bruxelles

Challenges of a Memorial
170   HENRIK SKOV KRISTENSEN
Head of the Frøslev Camp Museum,
National Museum of Denmark

The Jersey War Tunnels
200   CHRISTOPHER ADDY
Collections Manager, Jersey War Tiunnels

Showing Rather Than Telling
232   HEIKI AHONEN
Managing Director
Museum of Occupations, Tallinn

Exhibiting Secrecy
250   OLIVER BENJAMIN HEMMERLE
Visiting Professor
Masaryk University, Brno

Objects and the Power of their Stories
282   MARCEL WOUTERS
Director, Marcelwoutersontwerpers BV

The Dilemma of Exhibiting Heroism
298   CLEMENS MAIER-WOLTHAUSEN
Director, History-Memory.eu, Berlin

Post-Communist Museums:
Terrorspaces and Traumascapes

324 LENE OTTO
Associate Professor of European Ethnology,
University of Copenhagen

How Museums Speak

362 ESBEN KJELDBÆK
Head of the Museum of the Danish Resistance
1940-1945, National Museum of Denmark

394 About the Authors

400 References

422 Also from MuseumsEtc

423 Colophon

Introduction

ESBEN KJELDBÆK

Head of the Museum of Danish Resistance

1940-1945,

The National Museum of Denmark

Museum people have at least one thing in common: they work with historical objects, and therefore many of the problems and opportunities in museum work can be clarified if one takes the object as a point of departure. At least this was the idea behind a small conference entitled *The Power of the Object: Showing World War II through Objects*, which took place at the Museum of Danish Resistance and at the Danish National Museum on 10–11 November, 2008. The articles in this anthology are written by participants in this conference. Three more writers (Hemmerle, Otto, Wouters) were afterwards invited to join the anthology.

With the notable exception of the representative from The Imperial War Museum in London, all the participants spoke of countries that were small and on the periphery in the world war. This is particularly the case with Denmark, which, though occupied, was not even formally at war with Germany, and which arguably suffered the smallest number of war dead and other losses. Why, when we are still not certain exactly how many perished at the Eastern Front, should we discuss the "museumisation" of the war in countries, where the losses were so much smaller?

One reason is that even here World War II continues to loom large as a referent to current history. Also the nature of historical explanation is much more evident when we are working from a micro-perspective. It becomes possible to see real people and trace the background and outcome of their actions. And thus we are able to follow and discuss how these stories have been transmitted from the war-generations to us, and how we, today, think they should be transmitted by us to the younger generations.

Furthermore, military museums everywhere now seem to be in a process of transformation. They are no longer just repositories of guns, uniforms and armour, but are becoming museums of cultural history as well. But as their main topic is still the connection between war and society, they have a particularly complex explanatory role that should be of interest to other fields of museology. War is a supreme effort of a society, and military museums, with their huge, often quite unique collections, now have to find ways to use them to explain the mentalities of the past as well as their material basis. This creates a whole new set of challenges – which are also new opportunities.

Finally, a more general reason to look at the role of museums, even small museums, in the transmission of history is the recent death of the so-called *Linguistic Turn*. The Linguistic Turn has for two or three decades dominated much thinking in the humanities under names such as post-modernism, de-construction, and post-structuralism. An important idea here was that language itself constructed the facts it was supposed to convey.

In February 2009 the president of the American Historical Association, Gabrielle M. Spiegel, felt it was time to take a closer look at the origins of The Linguistic Turn, and that: "The reason for doing so now is that we all sense that this profound change has now run its course". Spiegel quotes Michael Roth as saying that "...the linguistic turn that had motivated much advanced work in the humanities is over" and she quotes Nancy Partner's remarks on how the new fields of interest, now being discussed, "...share a common desire to escape language, restore a pure and immediate connection with the past or at least some central aspect of experience and generally deny the power of language to contaminate history with its own uncontrollable meanings". (Spiegel 2009).

Could this mean that the objects found in museum magasines and exhibitions may now attract new interest because of their materiality, the feeling they give of direct access to the past?

If so, the articles in this anthology can also show some of the pitfalls, insights and joys of working with the solid remnants of the past.

Here is a survey of the articles in this anthology:

THE POWER OF THE OBJECT

Esben Kjeldbæk in *What is the Power of the Object?* tries to define the difference between objects of art, archaeology and history, and looks at a number of museum objects from three different perspectives: how they can document the past, inform or fascinate visitors. The question of *contaminated resurrection* is touched upon, and objects are finally seen as presenting a challenge to the curator, because they are subversive.

The next three articles discuss how large European military museums have been dealing with their permanent exhibitions.

James Taylor in *Interpreting The Second World War* takes a critical look at the permanent WWII displays and collections of the IWM, beginning with a short history of the museum and the policies of its directors. Britain was "the most mobilised of all the fighting countries" and consequently "people see in the wars an identity, both personal and national". To an institution that had 860,000 visitors in 2008 to its London branch alone, focus on these guests must be a crucial concern. But the museum is "visitor centered, not visitor driven". Instead it tries to work with their knowledge, attitudes and expectations, and is now planning to make possible individual "creative journeys" through the exhibitions planned for 2014. In this the role of objects with a personal history behind them is seen as crucial. Taylor notes that the institution is now more ready to deal with contested historical issues, but also that there is a difference between this and becoming revisionist. Rather the way to deal with such issues seems to be to admit that they are contested and to ask questions of the visitors.

Anne Godfroid in *The European Forum of Contemporary Conflict* describes how a successful temporary exhibition (*I Was Twenty In 1945*) gave impetus to a big project to display WWII from an international perspective, rather than a Belgian one, and housed in the impressive Bordiau Gallery, a building 40 metres wide, 60 metres long and 30 metres high, made for industrial exhibitions in 1879-1880. So far, two phases of the new exhibition have been completed. It was put together by museum experts, not by academic historians or veterans, and a main focus has been to fulfil the obligation that a huge collection puts on a museum by including, for example, objects from inter-war Estonia, Latvia and the Ukraine. The difficulties of combining chronological and thematic perspectives are noted, as well as the political problems that can arise from putting on display busts of the three great dictators, Mussolini, Hitler and Stalin.

Hans Henrik Appel of the Royal Danish Armoury Museum in *The Exhibition – Between Book and Film* presents the challenge of changing a 100-year old and 160 metres long permanent exhibition with 8.000 pieces demonstrating the evolution of hand weapons into something that could also interest non-experts. Appel points to the shortcomings of academic discourse in telling the stories that can make history relevant to normal museum guests. He explores instead the methods of the film and takes a critical look at three exhibitions at the Imperial War Museum (one, to him, inspiring, one successful, one failed). His suggestion of how to use the minimal space (18 square metres) in the planned exhibition on the occupation of Denmark is to focus on the history of the Armoury Museum itself. It was a boom-time for the acquisitions of weapons!

The next three articles explore the special problems of mounting exhibitions in historical surroundings which are themselves large objects.

Patrick Nefors in *The Breendonk Memorial* shows how they tackled the problem of telling the story of an historical place within the place itself. Nefors describes the *Patriotic Memories*, the power-struggles that had been going on among veterans from the camp, and other special interests right up to the present, where the demand for an explicit message from the camp-exhibition could lead to strange results! Nefors also deals with the interesting question of how photographic evidence can sometimes be more suitable than historical objects in such a context. The giant object of the Fort itself has been stripped of the many, smaller objects that were competing for attention. Instead, authentic photographs and maps now document the fate of the prisoners on the very spot where they were incarcerated.

Henrik Skov Kristensen in *Challenges of a Memorial* deals basically with the same problem: the buildings are the most powerful object in the museum, and here, too, the camp was used after the war to intern collaborators. This has given rise to two challenges. One is that the condemned collaborators, mostly members of the German minority still living in Southern Jutland where the camp is situated, demand that their story should be told too. The other is that the two authentic buildings (owned by the National Museum of Denmark) are situated in a larger camp-landscape of barracks which has been reconstructed by the local authorities, a landscape that is supposed to pay its own way, somehow. This has lead to grotesque results, culminating when in 1994 a private entrepreneur offered German tourists the possibility of a *Vacation in the Past – with Freedom and Democracy*. Kristensen, manoeuvring between three categories of historical culture: cognitive demands, political demands and commemorative demands, now plans to make an exhibition about the collaborators, but rejects the expectation that an historical institution should play a political role in promoting certain values. However, he sees commercialism as the bigger threat to the authenticity of the museum.

Christopher Addy in *The Jersey War Tunnels*, on the other hand, represents a privately owned, profit-making institution that, despite its constitution, subscribes to the Museums Association's definition of a museum and hence aspires to meet the values of their *Code of Ethics for Museums*. His museum is located in the Channel Islands - the only piece of British territory that was actually occupied by the Germans. He, too, has to deal with an historical framework - the German tunnels of Jersey - and like the Fort Breendonk or the Frøslev Camp, the site is also really the core of the institution. It has to be humanised without compromising its integrity; thus Addy's paper deals with how visitors can learn about Occupation history through active participation where the intention has been to establish a balance between the use of words, artefacts, graphic material and other mutually supporting interpretative elements, in order to meet the requirements of a diverse audience.

Heiki Ahonen in *Showing rather than Telling* raises the question of how mass culture has influenced the status of the museum as a place of learning. Like Appel, he finds the book obsolete as an exhibition format, except when the book itself can be a museum object - such as a mass-produced book, banned by the authorities and cut up for destruction. The task of the museum is to say something, but to say it visually. And here authenticity is paramount. Ahonen, who himself has spent time in Soviet labour camps, is the kind of curator who (unlike most of us) on visiting the crematorium in a German KS-museum, will yank out the contraption supposedly feeding bodies to the oven to demonstrate that it is a reconstruction. And to point out how this gives fodder to the revisionists.

Oliver Benjamin Hemmerle in *Exhibiting Secrecy*, with a provocative opening saying how easy it is to exhibit WWII, recounts how Intelligence (spying) is now becoming a new museum subject. He analyses the development of intelligence-related collections and exhibitions and then discusses the items of such collections "and their relevance for the story these objects could, should and sometimes pretend to tell". Hemmerle divides his examples into categories, among them museums and memorial sites related to the Cold War and to Eastern bloc intelligence agencies and political police. Surprisingly, many of these seem to be in former East Germany. Hemmerle mentions the problems of "museumisation" of historical locations like the former headquarters of the SS and German police (RSHA) in Berlin, or the code-breakers' buildings in Bletchley Park, Britain. The paper defines a secret object as something that was kept secret by its user, but says also that such objects (the iconic Minox camera or an Enigma code-machine) cannot be shown in isolation. Their influence and meaning must be demonstrated, which is just as difficult to do as with other historical objects, despite their seemingly easy-to-understand "functionality".

Marcel Wouters in *Objects and the Power of Their Stories* presents the viewpoint of an exhibition designer. Daring to say what we curators seldom do, that objects "emanate historical sensation", and that the most impressive exhibitions are those which embody "the force and mysticism of authenticity", he observes that exhibiting an object and interpreting it in a certain way can "produce a permanent added-value for the identity of the object". He also states that today the focus in museums "is on reflection and interpretation", and he gives examples of how this was done in the National Museum Camp Vught, and in the Hideout Museum Markt 12 Aalten (both in the Netherlands).

The three final contributions deal with the social and ideological role of museums.

Clemens Maier-Wolthausen, who in 2007 wrote a thesis about the politics of remembrance in postwar

Norway and Denmark, in *The Dilemma of Exhibiting Heroism*, points out that memorial museums is a post-WWII trend that has been gaining ground particularly in the last decades – and also that this development has an inherent, in-built contradiction. The memorial proper was a "refuge from history", whereas a museum is concerned with contextualisation, interpretation and critique. When a museum is merged with a memorial they form a symbiotic relationship where "the museum lends its scientific authority to the memorial feature which in turn pays back by giving significance to the museum". The problem is that this might "freese" the development of the museum. Maier-Wolthausen gives examples from The Canadian War Museum, the *Enola Gay* controversy at the Smithsonian, the *Wehrmacht* exhibition in Germany and the Museum of Danish Resistance. He cites the discussion about whether the museum should be a "Temple or a Forum", but suggests it should be neither. Instead the memorial museum should go in the direction of contextualisation.

Lene Otto in *Post-Communist Museums: Terrorspaces and Traumascapes* analyses post-Communist museum ways of narrating, visualising and exhibiting trauma and violence in the framework of politics of memory and culture of memory. These are contested subjects, and her cases are *The House of Terror* in Budapest, Hungary, *The Museum of Genocide Victims* in Vilnius, Lithuania, and the *Memorial of the Victims of Communism and of Resistance* in Sighet, Romania. Even though memory is a contested concept, the author believes that it can be useful in articulating the connections between the cultural, the social and the political, between representation and social experience.

Esben Kjeldbæk in *How Museums Speak* says that museums can be classed as belonging to one of three generations, where the objects work differently in each according to its stage of development. Examples are given from Calais, Brussels, Lyons, Amsterdam, Paris, Budapest and Vienna and the museographic features of the new reliance on photographs and films are discussed.

But these different types of museums also speak to their visitors each in a different voice. Seen in terms of traditional rhetoric they either focus on ethos (tradition), logos (learning) or pathos (design). They should be aware of this difference and use them consciously in combination.

The conference sessions, held in November 2008, were recorded on video. After some of the articles, excerpts from the discussions have been added. The conference was supported by the Frihedsmuseet's Venners Fond.

Esben Kjeldbæk, June 2009

MUSEUMS AND WORLD WAR II

1

What is the Power of the Object?

ESBEN KJELDBÆK

Head of the Museum of Danish Resistance

1940-1945,

The National Museum of Denmark

In 2005, when working on an exhibition about daily life in occupied Denmark 1940-1945, we were looking in the store for objects to go into the section about the occupying German forces. Among other things we came up with a rather plain German officer's jacket. It had no provenance to speak of, and we could not work out the meaning of its military badges. We consulted a young expert, who sent us a memo that we thought worthy of inclusion in the catalogue as a caption for a photograph of the uniform. It ran:

This German officer's uniform has light-blue edging braid on the collar badges and shoulder straps, which shows that it has been worn by an officer in the transportation corps. The two stars on the shoulder straps show that he held the rank of a captain, and the number 18 refers to the 18th regiment. The uniform jacket is a M/36 service uniform, that is, in use from 1936 and onwards. The collar badges are of the special type that one normally sees only on parade uniforms. This, compared with the silver threading of the shoulder boards, which are of the shiny, not the dull kind, reveal the owner as having been fond of finery. He certainly has not been strutting around anywhere near the front in this outfit. This combined with the fact that he has received no distinctions for combat leads one to assume that he could have been stationed in Denmark or other "comfortable" areas during the war. The ribbons he is wearing are mostly given for service in World War I on the Austrian side. None of the ribbons say anything concrete about whether he has distinguished himself in battle or not. But the grey underlay of the shoulder straps tells us that he is a reservist and has been called up again for service, which can be seen from ribbon number two (from the right) which shows that he took part in the preparation for, or the actual carrying out of, the occupation of the Sudeten area in 1938. (Lundbak, 2005)

So, up from the store came not a jacket, but a middle aged, somewhat vain, Austrian officer, who never saw serious combat in World War II, but probably spent his military life, safe in occupied Denmark. And as it happened his jacket was a good object for the exhibition in the sense that he was typical of the German forces that were stationed in this military backwater.

Types of objects

But if one wants to say something in general about the objects one finds in museums, it seems obvious that the jacket is not very typical as an historical object. Usually the historical objects we collect, find in the store or put on display are mute, and need extra information to make them intelligible to the public and, indeed, to ourselves. This jacket is, so to speak, designed with the purpose of providing information about the person who wears it (as long as you can get hold of someone who knows how to read it). In this sense the jacket is more comparable to a work of art. For is it not a defining characteristic of art that is was created with a viewer in mind? That art is always a visual statement from the beginning? If so, we have a fundamental difference between objects of art and the historical objects which we have somehow torn out of their past and which now confront us with questions about their interpretation, relevance and how to give them visual life in the exhibition.

And so also with another group of museum objects: the archaeological ones. These, and the circumstances in which they were dug up, are often in themselves the main source for our knowledge of the period they stem from. In some cases they are the only source, if there are no written sources to go along with them. This, for instance, is the case with Danish prehistory, objects from which were turned up for centuries in the fields by ploughmen working behind their pair of horses: axe-heads of stone, knives and finery of bronze; and in the bogs: spears and swords of iron, sometimes a human body, well-preserved but clearly long dead.

Some of these objects were sent to the King's collection of artifacts and oddities, and from 1807 they began to be registered and studied as something more than curiosities. Round about 1825 the head of the emerging Danish National Museum, Christian Jürgensen Thomsen, realised that one could distinguish between objects made of stone, bronze and iron, and that there must have been consecutive periods in which each of these materials was central to the making of tools and weapons. Jürgensen Thomsen's discovery made sense out of the hitherto meaningless jumble of things, and his "three-period system" was soon adopted outside Denmark as well. Systematic digging now had a starting point and a framework for the interpretation of the objects that were found.

Archaeology has long since turned into a science with its special techniques and vocabulary. But as exhibitors of objects the archaeologists have the great advantage – and challenge – that the knowledge and insights they are expected to share with us spring from the very objects they put on display. (Gaynor Kavanagh, I find, reached this same conclusion years ago (Kavanagh, 1996).

Types of use
So the historical museum has to work with objects that are mute, and what such objects end up saying is very dependent upon what other knowledge we have and the way we put the objects to use. For my purpose here I shall look at some objects from three different per-

spectives: how they can help provide documentation, information and fascination, within in an exhibition. The examples are mostly from the Museum of Danish Resistance 1940-45, but it is likely that you will find similar examples in all collections on display.

The bullet-riddled topcoat
Ever since its opening in 1957 the Resistance Museum has been showing a bullet-riddled black topcoat, originally displayed neatly buttoned and on a coat-hanger as if it had just come out of a closet. The bullet-holes were marked with one red and several white circles, and a brief text told the bare facts about the coat: a young saboteur was arrested by the Gestapo but managed to sneak his hand into the inner breast pocket from where he fired his gun, wounding but not killing the arresting officer. The saboteur fled and the shots of the wounded Gestapo man hit his coat in several places but did not harm the young man, who got away. Although displayed at the back of a large showcase where the text was difficult to read, it was a very popular object. It made a good story on guided tours. Paul Celan, one of the great European post-war lyricists, must have seen it before writing a poem which, although in German, was entitled with the Danish word *Frihed* (freedom - the museum is called *Frihedsmuseet* in Danish). The central

part of the poem speaks about: *The saboteur's coat with the red, the white rings around the bullet-holes.* On one occasion, a group of Kurdish refugees was shown around the museum. Seeing the coat, one of them asked if it had belonged to the Danish president (evidently he did not yet know Denmark is a monarchy). But what his question implied was that to him bullet-riddled coats were nothing out of the ordinary, so surely this one must belong to a prominent person in order to be put on display? A good question, actually. The answer would be that Denmark suffered very few casualties compared to other occupied countries, so that bullet-holes were something out of the ordinary, and important to preserve in order to document that armed resistance had really taken place.

But when an object is put into a documentary role, the problem of authenticity may arise, which it did in this case. When preparing a total renewal of the exhibition in 1994-95, I held the coat in my hands for the first time and eagerly turned out the inner pocket to see the damage done by the saboteur's outgoing shot. There was no trace of any damage. The pocket looked original, and of the same cloth as the lining. And worse: the in-coming shots from the German's gun in several places had only penetrated the outer cloth but not the lining! Was the coat a fake?

The saboteur, Jørgen Jespersen (1926-2003), was still alive, and as he was still slim, the coat fitted him perfectly, even his long arms. His war-time exploits as leader of several groups in the BOPA sabotage organisation are well documented, so it was not a case of his reputation hanging on this particular object. But he insisted that this was the original coat. He had been asked to donate it to an exhibition taking place in the immediate post-war period, and from there it had entered the collections being brought together for the planned Museum of Resistance.

We sent the coat to the conservation department of the National Museum. They photographed the inner pocket with a high-definition camera, and it turned out that the pocket had in fact been repaired but by invisible mending that the naked eye could not see. Slowly it dawned on us what must have happened. The shooting incident took place in February 1944 and was mentioned in an illegal newspaper. But obviously Jespersen did not at the time see his bullet-riddled coat as a future museum object. Woollen coats were scarce and much-needed by illegals living underground. So he must have had it repaired. When it was going on exhibition after the war, the exhibitors were former members of the resistance, not museum professionals. One of them must have solved the problem of the missing bullet-holes by going over the coat with a screw-driver, adding a few extra ones for good measure. In the new exhibition we have mounted the coat so that it is open, not buttoned, explaining how Jespersen could have survived the shots. And the number of bullet-holes has been reduced to those which penetrated the outer as well as the inner cloth. It is nearer, but not identical, to the look it must have had after the episode in 1944 (Kjeldbæk, 1998).

But by being displayed unbuttoned, it has also been changed from being a tragic object that (falsely) denotes "death", to one that is about getting away and staying free.

Contaminated resurrection

Now, the problem of authenticity is seldom really about whether an object is a fake or not. The problem is rather in what condition an object should be exhibited, because objects have a history in terms of use and physical decay apart from when they were freshly made and apart from the historical moment you want them to bear witness to. At the *Musée de L'Armée* in Paris they display a taxi of the type that was used when, in September 1914, the German army was closing in on Paris and the front was so near that the troops who were rushed in to stop them could be transported in taxis to fight the Battle of the Marne, which halted the German advance for the first time. So this taxi is an icon, a *Marne-Taxi*, and it looks the part, being beautifully restored, gleaming with green and red paint and new tyres. But did it look like that in September 1914? The problem, which also faced us with Jespersen's coat, has been called contaminated resurrection (Dechow, Leahy, 2006), and there is, I believe, no solution to it except to make the compromises that seem necessary, and be open about it.

In the open inner court-yard of the Resistance Museum, for example, stand three concrete pillars, part of the electric fence around the concentration camp of Neuengamme, from where former Danish prisoners brought them back right after the war, compliments of the American driver of a military flat-bed truck. The pillars had been cast on the spot using low-grade floodsand from the Elbe, and they are fragile. Acid rain was breaking down their curved tops, so the conservation department covered them in lead foil. Later some of the porcelain insulators holding the electrical barbed wire started cracking up from the winter frost. They were replaced by copies cast in brownish plastic, but by then the head of the conservation department told me earnestly that from a professional point of view they could not go on like this. Either we had to move the pillars indoors where they could be safe long-term, or we would simply have to give them up. We did neither, they are still there, out in the open, and a local bricklayer has repaired the worst ravages of frost on the pillars. In theory, someday nothing will be left of the original pillars but their form.

The rescue of the Danish Jews
One of the problems of the use of objects to document historical events is that these events do not necessarily reproduce themselves in objects in proportion to the importance we later attach to them. A case in point would be the rescue of the Danish Jews in October 1943. As a consequence of Denmark's dubious position as occupied but still neutral, Nazi racial policies had not been implemented in Denmark, since the Danish government had made it clear that this was not acceptable. But when the government gave up in August 1943, the German Reichsplenipotentiary in Denmark, Werner Best, proposed taking action against the 7000 Jews in Denmark. When it happened on the night of 1st October 1943 it was a failure. Less than 500 were caught, the remaining 90% or so escaping across the strait of Øresund to neutral Sweden. There were reasons for this result. The action came late in the war, there was a neutral country close by, a warning was given by the

Germans themselves, and their military forces were not doing much to catch the Jews. Modern research has also pointed out that the Danish fishermen, who transported the Jews to safety, did so for a price. Still, thousands of Danes were spontaneously active in hiding and helping the Jews escape, and so this incident has been seen as a *Small light in the blackness of the Holocaust*. Even the 481 Jews who were caught and taken to the camp of Theresienstadt, were protected. The Danish authorities made a deal with Adolf Eichmann that they were not to be transported Eastwards (that is, to their death). They also received packages of food and clothing from Denmark, and only about 50, mostly the old and sick, perished, the rest returned, being driven back by Swedish Red Cross buses in April 1945.

A few photographs from the rescue in October 1943 exist, but the best of them, under close scrutiny, have sadly turned out not to be authentic, being instead reenactments from after the war.

The available objects at the museum to tell the story of the rescue can be counted on the fingers of one hand: a broken-off piece of an oar, a flask of powder that could supposedly defeat the noses of German sniffing-dogs, religious objects left by a fleeing Jew (who was later identified by the museum), and a wad of illegal pamphlets recording the protests against the action by students, bishops and other professional organisations. And there is a return ticket Copenhagen-Hillerød, stamped with the very date 2 October 1943 and clipped once by a conductor. The last is arguably the best object. A fleeing Jew bought the ticket to Hillerød, which was the gateway to the small ports North of Copenhagen where fishermen might take him to Sweden. Not to arouse suspicion he bought a return ticket, and as the single clip in it shows, he was successful.

But, curiously, we have more than a hundred objects, small pieces of paper mostly, but also a torn jacket with a yellow Star of David sewn on it, a pair of cloth dolls from the 481 Jews deported to Theresienstadt. They were able to bring them back because of the relief action by the Swedish Red Cross. But these objects also have a sinister story to tell.

Theresienstadt was built in 1780, in what is now the Czech Republic, as a city of military barracks. In early 1942 it was turned into a ghetto for "prominent" Jews whom it was uncomfortable for the Nazi authorities to let disappear outright in the system of death camps. Invalid German-Jewish war veterans, prominent scientists, artists, businessmen – and the Danish Jews – were placed here, ostensibly living in a system of self-government by a council of Jewish Elders. Actually the camp was an integral part of the greater system of death camps. All told about 140,000 Jews from Germany and occupied Europe were sent there. After a while 88,000 were sent further East to their death, while about 33.000 died in the camp from illness, cold and exhaustion. 17,000 were alive in the camp at the end of the war. From September 1943, by a high-level decision, the camp underwent a *Verschönerung* (beautification) in order to make it presentable to the outside world as an example of Nazi policy towards the Jews. The place, until then known as *Ghetto Theresienstadt*, was renamed *Jüdisches Siedlungsgebiet Theresienstadt* (Jewish Territory of Theresienstadt), the bank of the self-government issued its own currency, *Theresienstadt-Kronen*, and the inmates were given bank-books where a monthly salary would be written down (though you could not actually buy much with the money). Flowerbeds were constructed, grass sown, a music pavilion, a sports grounds and cultural institutions were fitted out. There was a café. It was all set-pieces, but on 23 June 1944 a commission with members of the Danish and the International Red Cross were shown around in the camp, and were duly impressed. Immediately before their visit 7,500 inmates had been sent to death camps in order that the town should not appear overcrowded and that no cases of tuberculosis should be visible to the commission. In the Autumn of 1944 a film was made about *the town given by the Fuehrer to the Jews*. Some of the Danish Jews can be seen in it acting along with the others as happy town dwellers. After the film was finished, the actors and the director of the film were sent to death camps.

The small notes brought back by the Danish Jews reflect this huge hoax. We have an identity card printed *Ghetto Theresienstadt* and the same person's new card titled *Siedlungsgebiet...* There are bank books, Theresienstadt currency (with a severe admonishment against forgery printed on them), and a whole system of file cards with their names, home address, nationality and address in Theresienstadt, the last reflecting how the angular streets in the town, that originally were identified just by a number and a letter, had been given cosy, Austrian names during the *Verschönerung*.

Dictatorships have much greater respect for history than our liberal democracies have. So they take care to shape it the right way. The *Verschönerung* did not only serve a particular purpose in the context of the commission from the Red Cross. After a Nazi victory the film, the piles of personal documents, identity cards, applications for this and that, would have been proof, undeniable authentic proof, of the humanity of Nazi policy towards the Jews.

Some objects document a possible outcome of history that never happened. And we museum people, or somebody like us, would have accepted them and put them on display as the truth. Only the Allied victory in real life prevented that. (Kjeldbæk, 1984)

The communist posters
Sometimes you need to inform visitors about ideological questions and policies and find that suitable objects are scarce or non-existant. Only a lucky find in the archives, for instance, made it possible to illustrate the changing ways during 1939-1941 of the Danish Communist Party, which was among the pioneers in the Resistance. During the 1930s the Communists had followed the changing policies of Moscow. One of their poets had underscored the party's internationalist perspective by writing a poem that called for the *ugly white cross* in the Danish flag to be struck out so that the flag would be *made red*. The small and widely unpopular Communist party had the unusual position in Europe of being legal in Denmark, even after the German occupation in April 1940. This was due to the Hitler-Stalin pact of 1939, and so in this period Communist propaganda explained the war as simply an "imperialist" contest that had nothing to do with the working class. This all changed when Hitler attacked Soviet Russia on June 22, 1941. Danish police acting on

a German instruction interned the Communist leaders and the party was outlawed, driving the members underground. In this precarious situation the party called for a "National front" against the German occupiers, now suddenly embracing, for instance, historical national heroes.

The archival find was two Communist posters that were lying apart among many others. Both showed a muscular working man's arm holding a waving flag. They were clearly printed from the same source. On one poster the flag was plainly a luminous red. On the other a white cross had been added turning it into the *Dannebrog*, the Danish national colours, and thus also dating it as post-June 1941. Never mind what the poet of the 1930s said.

Himmler's eye-patch

While such a find may make it possible to visualise a complicated point in an exhibition, it is more difficult to define what makes an object fascinating, especially to the casual visitor. Perhaps one of the qualities called for is that the object should have multiple layers of meaning, and perhaps also that it should be connected to a person we can recognise. A case in point might be Heinrich Himmler's eye-patch. At the end of the war the *Reichsführer-SS* was chief of all German police, was responsible for what happened in his empire of concentration camps, as well as military leader of multiple SS-divisions fighting at the front. Unlike Nazi leaders like Goebbels or Hitler himself, he at first tried to survive the defeat, masking himself in the uniform of a non-commissioned officer and wearing an eye-patch. Allied soldiers picked him up as a prisoner-of-war, and at first he passed inspection. But when British interrogators were beginning to undress him, he gave up, said who he was and chewed on a cyanide capsule that quickly killed him. A Danish officer had been seconded to help the British identify wanted Germans from Denmark, and someone gave him Himmler's eye-patch as a souvenir. When he later rose in the ranks of Danish intelligence, the eye-patch went on the wall of his office, framed, as part of the small personal museum many such men keep. His successors let it hang there until one decided it was time to do away with it. An older subordinate proposed to give it instead to the Resistance Museum, where it now sits, still in its frame with the photograph of the dead Himmler, in a showcase dedicated to the total defeat of the Nazi system (Kjeldbæk, 1998).

No doubt it is a fascinating object if only for its connection with Himmler in his last days

But was he merely a coward who wanted to prolong

his life, or did he have a plan with his masquerade? He knew that the coalition of the Anglo-Saxon powers and Soviet Russia was not stable, and that a confrontation between them was likely to follow the defeat of Nazi Germany. During the last months of the war he made several attempts to make contact with the Western Allies, bartering, for instance, with the fate of the surviving Hungarian Jews. The general idea was to make a separate peace on the Western front in order to go on fighting the Red Army on the Eastern front. He also held a secret meeting with the Swedish Count Bernadotte, making it possible for the Swedish Red Cross to drive the Danish and Norwegian concentration camp prisoners through the hail of Allied bombs to neutral Sweden in white painted buses before the final capitulation of Germany. He seems to have had serious hopes that the Western powers would find use for his skills as a fighter against Communism, and it was only at the point of disclosure that he realised the impossibility of this in his case. So perhaps Himmler's eye-patch does not only point back to the crimes of Nazism. It might also be an early, perhaps the earliest, object from The Cold War.

Historical objects v. objects of cultural history
Objects like Himmler's eye-patch or Jørgen Jespersen's

bullet-riddled coat represent particular historical events, and even individual historical persons whom we know. They have a unique, historical functionality. But in the stores and exhibitions of history museums we are likely to find many more objects that have no such definite connections. These objects are, to us, the products of a particular period denoting certain techniques, living-conditions, or lifestyles. As World War II recedes into history, we increasingly need such objects, otherwise the great battles, the acts of resistance or collaboration, the deportations will have no background against which to unfold. They may end up being incomprehensible as just a catastrophe with no understandable historical roots. A period where heroes fought villains without any explanation of how they ended up in those roles. And what it meant living through that period if you were neither one or the other. It is true that to the populations of Eastern, and Central Europe the war was a pervasive influence on their lives, and that some of what happened there remains difficult to really understand to-day. But even here there was also, to large sections of the population, a daily life with intermittent periods of peace. In occupied Western Europe life sometimes went on almost as if the war was happening a long way off. This was particularly the case in Denmark, where in fact few of us are the descendants of either resistance heroes, Nazis or victims of deportation.

When doing the above-mentioned exhibition in 2005 on daily life during the occupation, we discovered that the founders of the Resistance Museum had also collected items from "daily life" that had no connection to the Resistance. They registered them in one single group (no. 25 with some subheadings), and some of them were clearly collected as curiosities. Shoes made out of fish-skin, cigars and cigarettes produced from Danish-grown tobacco, gas-saving home-made stoves, synthetic types of seasoning, clothes made of synthetic wool, a "producer" which was a kind of stove you screwed onto a car and filled with chips of wood, and which could then produce wood-gas that would drive the car. Although Ersatz-products like these were in common use, it was just as common to simply de-modernise and go back to older techniques. In many cases the replacement for a gasoline-driven car was not one with a producer mounted on it, but simply a vehicle drawn by a horse. But as Denmark never (unlike many other occupied countries) suffered a life-threatening decline in living standards, these replacements become interesting from a psychological angle: what were they really trying to replace? Why did some build cars out of plywood that looked like real sports-cars but were propelled by bicycle-pedals? Why was jazz-music suddenly popular everywhere, when all right-thinking citizens had despised it as *nigger-music* just a few years earlier? Why did Danish cigarettes have to appear in packages with quasi-American names and designs? It seems that the primary purpose of such products was not to fill an immediate material need, but to keep alive the dream of a future with peace, freedom and affluence, as symbolised by sports-cars, modern music and smoking-habits which were (however strange it may seem today) then a statement of coolness, modernity and equality between men and women. This was not resistance, but it was definitely non-Nazi, and Danish SS-men cut the long hair of young jazz-fans in the streets and blew up dance halls where Jazz-music filled the floors.

Even in the very basic question of fuel, its "materiality" can make a point that ought to interest the descendants of the war generations. The normal way of heating was with coke, and when this grew scarce, peat was used as a replacement. You can even to-day get hold of blocks of peat (or Danish low-grade brown-coal) and display it, for peat is exotic. But so is coke really. The point is that the extraction of peat or brown-coal, along with work on German fortifications and the general de-modernisation of methods required many more workers, and so the unemployment of the 1930s, which had grown sharply at the beginning of the occupation, almost disappeared by 1944. There was a war on, but in personal, economic terms, life was suddenly safer. The result was that people now had the babies they had postponed in the years of economic uncertainty. Suddenly the Danish population was reproducing itself for the first time in many years. The same happened in the USA where war-production wiped out unemployment and produced the baby boom.

So the children and grandchildren of the war-generation should look with respect on an old block of peat. In a sense, it is the reason that they themselves are here at all.

Explaining the objects
But if an object is suitable for documentation, information or the fascination of visitors, how do you actually do that in an exhibition? How articulate should you be?

In the case of a traditional British regimental museum, the arms displayed there cannot, as Simon Jones has observed, explain the reasons and complexities of conflict on their own. They would need to be accompanied by the bags of tea or the bales of cotton that were the tangible background and results of many British wars in the 19th Century (Jones, 1996).

Objects, as Peter Vergo has said, are brought together because they are part of a story one wants to tell. But perhaps best not in the simplistic way proposed by the American Brown Goode, who defined the *efficient* educational exhibition as *a collection of instructive labels each illustrated by a well-chosen specimen*. Instead one should challenge oneself to achieve this using the objects themselves in juxtaposition to each other and in a setting of other visual media like photographs, films and posters that can reduce the need for texts and still, as Vergo says, *coax... the reticent object into loquacity*. (Vergo, 1989)

This, of course, is easier said than done.

In 2006 Douglas R. Dechow and Anna Leahy wrote in *Curator* that American aviation museums were more than just collections of aircraft. They were also *the collective 'hangar' of our commemorations*. Often they seem to convey a consistently constructed narrative of World War II, where American technology triumphs. Examples of labels are given, and it is said that: *The prevalence of numbers (weight, range, horsepower, number of crew, speed, and so on) in aircraft labels... implies progress, significance, universal criteria and objectivity*. (Dechow, Leahy, 2006)

In the same issue of *Curator*, Tom Crouch of the Smithsonian answered by pointing out that some exhibitions countered this proposed master narrative of US technological superiority by way of the objects they put on display. At the Udvar-Hasy Center a lot of Allied WWII military planes can be seen, but: *While those machines carried the fight to the enemy, and prevailed, they represented the end of the line for conventional, piston-engine, propeller-driven fighters and bombers. The lineup of German aircraft, on the other hand, includes such advanced designs as the Arado 234, the world's first operational jet bomber and reconnaissance aircraft; the twin-engine Dornier 335, the fastest piston-engine fighter ever built; the HE 219A, one of the best night-fighters of the war; and the revolutionary swept-wing Horton Ho IIH, Ho IIIF and jet powered Ho 229 V3, as well as a full array of Axis rocket-propelled missiles. Surely perceptive visitors must be struck by the fact that the German aircraft on view are more technologically advanced than their American adversaries.* (Crouch, 2006)

But do they really get struck by the objects themselves?

The 1995 exhibition at the Resistance Museum has been criticised for not debunking the myths about occupied Denmark – chief among them that nearly all Danes stood shoulder to shoulder against the occupying enemy. And it does not really help to reply that some objects have now been included that could do just that. There is the figure, prominently displayed, of a

Danish volunteer in the *Waffen-SS* with the information that more than 6,000 Danes fought on the Eastern front for the Nazis. There is the showcase about the occupying German forces entitled *The Cream Front*, dispelling the idea that the Resistance did serious battle against the German military proper. And there are the two very significant hand guns that demonstrate the consequences of accepting (albeit under protest) the German occupation in return for their letting the parliamentary Danish government continue to run internal politics. The precarious position this put the government and its officials in was demonstrated when in 1942 the British SOE started to drop Danes trained as their agents into the occupied country. When on 5 September 1942 the Germans traced one of their clandestine radios, Danish police were sent to arrest the operator. There was an exchange of shots and the chief arresting officer, his small 6.35mm gun jamming, was killed by the 7.65mm Colt pistol of the Danish agent, who then committed suicide, taking his cyanide pill. Later the same month Danish police tried to arrest the head of the British agents in Denmark. Again there was a shoot-out, the Danish agent's single bullet penetrated the coat, jacket, and wallet of the arresting officer, ending up by cracking his belt-buckle but doing him no other harm. The Danish police officers subsequently put a dozen bullets in the body of the agent. The Danish police never considered itself an auxiliary force to the occupiers (as was the case in some occupied countries), but merely loyal civil servants doing the bidding of the government. In September 1944 the force was disbanded by the Germans and 2000 of them deported to a camp in Germany. Still, their role in 1940-1944 highlights the general dilemma of the Danish policy of "co-operation" with the occupiers, and therefore the relics of these shoot-outs in peaceful Denmark are important objects.

The two pistols from the first incident, and the coat of the arresting officer of the second, wallet, cracked belt-buckle, and the cases of the spent bullets (numbered), were mounted by the Police themselves in small showcases along with police sketches of the events, and were placed among other artefacts in the internal *Kriminalmuseum* (Crime Museum) of the Police. When this museum was closed down for reasons of economy in 1977, the police passed many of the objects to museums, and those dating from 1940-1945 ended up at the Resistance Museum, where some, like these, eventually went into the exhibition. Here they are explained and presented in a rather neutral way as an illustration of the precarious position of the Danish authorities vis-a-vis the occupiers.

The new exhibition of 1995 did provoke criticism from some veterans in the museum's original group ("too much war and Nazism, not enough Resistance"), but the protests focused on post-war symbols that had been taken down, not the new objects that referred to internal Danish strife or cooperation with the enemy. None of the protests went into the media. And nobody has ever complained or taken special notice of these meticulously explained objects, politically speaking.

This is not very surprising. Most museum people will remember what happened in 1995 when the *Enola Gay*, the first aeroplane to drop an atomic bomb, was taken out of its store and reassembled in order to go on show at the Smithsonian, where the setup would question the necessity and morality of dropping the bomb on Japanese civilians. Protests prevented the planned exhibition, and today the *Enola Gay* sits at the Udvar-Hasy Center among other WWII aircraft where, according to Dechow and Leahy, it is exhibited primarily as a piece of technology, and does not stand out.

But there was another bomb, the one over Nagasaki, which effectively ended World War II, and the B-29 that dropped it, the *Bockscar*, had been on exhibition for decades at the National Museum of the United States Air Force when the *Enola Gay* controversy broke out (Dechow, Leahy, 2006)

So it would seem that the curator does not really have to choose between showing or not showing a particular, dangerous object. He has to choose how to show it and thereby choose how much controversy he wants to generate (although one might guess that most curators who get themselves in hot water do so out of naïveté rather than by design!).

The power of the object
Objects can document, inform and fascinate, but they do so in tandem with the external knowledge and experience, usually contributed by an exhibition's creators.

Objects can interact with each other in an exhibition in a way that is different from a book or a film, because these latter are the product of one creator, speak with a single voice, and have to be listened to from beginning to end. Objects, standing apart from each other, all have their own "otherness" as autonomous time-capsules, and this they impose on the others around them. But as a group they are all captured within a museum, which was the last thing intended for them when they were first created. It is still us who put them in position and put labels next to them.

Does this mean that in the end objects are really like clay and can be moulded to serve any purpose we want them to? I think definitely not. In his 1960s song

Visions of Johanna Bob Dylan says that *inside the museums, infinity goes up on trial*", and quite right. There are any number of ways we can exhibit objects, but there are also an equally large number of ways we cannot exhibit them if we are to stay true to what they are and what they represent. Infinity is at work from both perspectives.

Facing an object, you are facing a challenge. It is a thing torn out of a bygone past, yet the thing is still here and can be measured and weighed. Objects are to be respected, even feared, because they are simultaneously in the past and in the present. When you put them on exhibition, your visitors will look at them, using their own competences and experience which – never forget – can be considerable. And they will also look at you, as will your colleagues, and worst of all, you yourself, to see how you chose to present this relic of the past. If it was too wrong the object will knock you off your feet, for objects are subversive.

And that is their greatest power.

2

Interpreting the Second World War

JAMES TAYLOR

Head of Research & Information,

Imperial War Museum, London

In just one week in February 2009, Imperial War Museum London received 40,000 visitors, a record for the institution. Figures for the year 2008-2009 show that IWM London received 860,000 visitors, an increase of 120,000 on the previous year. And this largest London branch of the IWM is just one of five branches which make up the Imperial War Museum family. Total visitor figures for the organisation as a whole are 2 million annually, when we include IWM Duxford, HMS Belfast, the Churchill Museum and Cabinet War Rooms and IWM North. Clearly, the Museum is doing something right. Yet we cannot be complacent. The Museum's continued and increasing popularity – especially when much lighter museums and heritage sites are on offer elsewhere in the capital and beyond – has always relied upon the organisation's ability and willingness to change. With that in mind, our key priority at IWM London is to re-examine our First and Second World War permanent displays and their interpretation. Some of these exhibitions, which were groundbreaking when they opened and won a number of awards, are now twenty years old. The wear is showing in terms of their balance, and our historical understanding of our subject matter, not least the Second World War, has moved on. More importantly, these galleries need to centre upon visitor needs and expectations which have changed in the course of two decades. They must actively engage new and ever diversifying audiences. In this paper, I will take a critical look at our permanent Second World War displays in Imperial War Museum London, the nature of our collections and how we might seek to interpret those collections to ensure that the Museum remains a key site of learning.

First of all, I should explain something about the history of the Museum. The Imperial War Museum is Britain's national museum of conflict. Its terms of reference cover all wars involving British and Commonwealth forces from the First World War to date. There is some irony in writing about the Museum's interpretation of the Second World War. It was a conflict which the Museum was never intended to cover. Conceived in 1917 and opened to the public three years later, the Museum's terms of reference were not intended or expected to go beyond the First World War. As founding Chairman Sir Alfred Mond said in his opening address on 9 June 1920, at the Museum's first site at the Crystal Palace, the IWM would serve as: *a lasting memorial of common effort and common sacrifice...and an inspiration for future generations.* (IWM: Third Annual Report, 3)

Further, the new Museum was to record the: *immeasurable sacrifices and supreme national effort which not only saved the Country from dire catastrophe, but, as we all hope, laid firm and deep foundations of a better world.* (IWM: Third Annual Report, 3)

Less than twenty years later, with another world war looming, the Museum's 21st Annual Report (IWM:1) lamented that the institution created to make an historical record of the war *that was to end war* was faced with covering *a series of world wars, each more terrible than the last.*

The Museum was closed for much of the Second World War, with some weapons in its collection even being taken back into service. It reopened in November 1946, but for the next fifteen years, the *Great War* remained the Museum's *raison d'être*, if not in the mind of its visitors, then certainly in the thinking of its director from 1937 to 1960, Mr LR Bradley. His successor, Dr Noble Frankland, recalled that Bradley, a First World War veteran, retained an: *empathy... almost wholly with the First World War... to him the Second World War was a nuisance which deposited masses of material in the Museum, squeezing its already restricted space and disrupting such order as its exhibitions had earlier had.*

As the Great War receded from public memory, wrote Frankland, Bradley *gave the impression of hoping, as he approached the grave, that the Museum, which he had served for so long, would do the same.* (Frankland 1998: 164)

As my colleague Terry Charman has observed (Charman. 104),that the Museum did not expire was due to the vision of Dr Frankland, a Second World War Bomber Command navigator who recruited professional museum staff to revitalise the institution. Frankland put his "own" war squarely in the Museum's terms of reference. He was modest about his achievements: *I recognise that the exhibitions in the Imperial war Museum for which I was responsible did fall far short of the ultimate in historical truth. I claim, all the same, that they made a substantial contribution to a better historical understanding of the subjects with which the Museum was concerned.* (Frankland:175)

Major temporary exhibitions like Colditz (1973-1974), about the Second World War prisoner of war camp in central Germany, saw long queues. The IWM also collaborated with Thames Television on the hugely popular, award-winning TV series *The World at War*. First broadcast in 1973 and still a staple of British TV schedules, this series remains a benchmark in television documentary and raised the Museum's profile enormously.

Dr Frankland's own successor, Dr Alan Borg embarked upon a major redevelopment programme, with new, permanent exhibitions, which were completed incrementally from 1989. These are the permanent displays which our visitors still see today. By far the greatest space in them is given over to the First and Second World Wars, rather than to the postwar and present day conflicts which also fall within the Museum's terms of reference. The two global conflicts exert a powerful draw on our visitors. Each involved millions of men and women in Britain, the Empire and Commonwealth, both in the armed forces and on the 'Home Front'. King George V was talking about the Great War, but might equally have been referring to the Second World War, when he said in his address at the Museum's opening in 1920: *we owe our success ... not to the armed forces alone, but to the labours and sacrifices of soldiers and civilians, of men and women alike. It was a democratic victory... organised as never before for a great national struggle.* (IWM. Third Annual Report. 4)

Indeed, in the Second World War, Britain was the most mobilised of all the fighting countries. Today, few have to search hard for ancestors or even living family members who lived through it. Family history, the search for one's roots, has seen an explosion of interest in the last fifteen years and it is no exaggeration to say that people see in the wars an identity, both personal and national. With the increased social and geographical mobility of recent years, and a decline in religious belief, people are in search of belonging and identity.

THE POWER OF THE OBJECT

The Museum provides for them evidence of "what it was like" for an ancestor in extraordinary times.

The visitor first confronts the Museum and its Second World War collections in the Atrium, a large space which awes the visitor with a display mainly comprising larger weapons – tanks, aircraft and artillery, either on the floor or suspended from the ceiling. One of the reasons for placing the larger objects here was that the floor loading could bear their weight. Visible from the Atrium floor are further large objects, on a mezzanine, which invite the visitor another floor upstairs and therefore place them two levels above the main, permanent First and Second World War narrative displays, which I shall move onto shortly. The effect of this array of industrial weaponry in the Atrium is without doubt striking. But at the same time it can disorientate the visitor. It is almost like a sculpture park. There is no discernible order to the exhibits and the Second World War objects jostle for visitor attention with pieces from the First World War and postwar periods. Moreover, the Atrium display can confuse as to the scope and purpose of the Imperial War Museum. These large weapons of war suggest a military or service museum, not a <u>war</u> museum. One of my colleagues described the Atrium as *the biggest boys' bedroom in London.*

As regards the objects, there is no clear commonality to them, other than their size. Some are iconic in themselves, or because of an association with an individual. In the first category one could put, among others, a Mk1 Spitfire, 25 pounder field gun, Sherman tank, a V-1 Doodlebug, a T-34 tank and a fuselage section from a Lancaster bomber. In the second category, one might place General Bernard Montgomery's command tank from the 1942 Battle of El Alamein and another fuselage section, this one from the Messerschmitt 110 flown to Britain in 1941 by Rudolf Hess on his abortive peace mission. In addition, there are large objects whose significance is arguably clear only to the military history enthusiast, such as the Focke Wulf 190 fighter, the *Jagdpanther* tank destroyer, and the 20mm German antiaircraft gun. There are also some fascinating oddities such as the German Biber one man submarine and Italian *Human Torpedo*. As for the interpretation of these large objects, there are short captions complemented by a series of audio-visual stations relaying film of the objects in question. The emphasis is very much on type, performance – how high and fast it went – and destructive power. The truly key pieces are not given any treatment which identifies them as such and so they are lost in this forest of metal and wood. The fact that the order in the phrasing of the caption heading for Montgomery's tank - *M3A3 Grant Tank: Monty's Tank*

- illustrates that point.

From the Atrium, the visitor reaches the permanent, narrative First and Second World War galleries down a flight of stairs, and then goes through a wide corridor. On either side are large photographs each with an accompanying quotation. Some of these are surprisingly pacifist in tone: *In every parting there is an image of death* (George Eliot); *Only the dead have seen the end of war* (Plato).

As with the Atrium, the Second World War permanent exhibition was completed in 1989. It consists of eleven spaces, each themed by campaign, from the 1939 outbreak of war and Phoney War, through the 1940 Blitskrieg campaign in France and the Low Countries to the 1941-1945 War in the Far East. Each themed area contains, by turn, large showcases. These are crammed with exhibits – uniforms, equipment, small arms, letters, diaries and photographs huddling together and competing for space and attention. One of the express intentions behind the permanent exhibition was to put on show as much of the Museum's collection as possible. This was a laudable aim but, today, the impression is one of the regimental museum, the *Traditionskabinett*. Some object groupings are arranged by type. As with the Atrium, it is difficult to judge which are the key pieces. As with the Atrium, it is clear that the exhibition was planned and written by military historians. The "sharp end of war" on land, at sea and in the air, prevails. Lead texts give brief histories of each campaign. Interpretation of each object, such as it is, is short – rarely more than 25 words. Technical specifications of the weaponry loom large. Yet the causes and consequences of war for Britain are scarcely represented. Wider political and social context is lacking. While the texts may be factually accurate, historical myths and falsehoods go largely unchallenged and controversial episodes are not acknowledged as such – the Strategic Bomber Offensive against Nazi Germany being a case in point. Crucially, this framework hardly allows for the human impact of war to come through. The one area where this was attempted is the Blitz Experience, a recreation of what it was like to be in a shelter during an air raid, complete with smokey, bombed street and accompanied by an actor playing an Air Raid Warden. As Sir Noble Frankland wrote in his memoirs: *the Blitz Experience is… not history. The Air Raid Warden is not an Air Raid Warden; he is an actor giving an impression of what an Air Raid warden might have said but probably never did. The crunch of the bombs does not impinge on the ear drums, the aftermath of dust does not penetrate the lungs, and the warning of broken glass littering the street can safely be disregarded.* (Frankland:175)

But the *Blitz Experience* remains hugely popular with

THE POWER OF THE OBJECT

our visitors, such is the thirst to experience what so many had been through in Britain's bombed cities.

In their defence, these displays were hugely relevant when they first opened. In creating them, the Museum historians who led the interpretation of the galleries could assume some prior knowledge of the Second World War and its material culture on the part of many visitors. This was a time when many people who had experienced the Second World War, either on the fighting fronts or on the Home Front, were still alive and a key purpose of the exhibition spaces was, clearly, to provoke memory. Visitors could use the objects in the Museum to take children, grandchildren and friends on personal journeys through the exhibition spaces – this was the type of ration card we used, this is the type of rifle I fired...

Indeed, these visitor-guides' audiences were likely to have known something about the war themselves, even if they had no direct experience of it. When I visited the Museum as a boy, I was already enthused with the subject matter, through my own parents and grandparents' stories of their "own" wars. The objects themselves were familiar too, through making Airfix plastic kits and playing with Second World War toy soldiers. As small boys, my generation's appetite for literature was largely confined to trashy war comics and classic war books such as Paul Brickhill's *The Dam Busters*, our viewing habits determined by the rash of wartime feature films released in the 1960s and 1970s such as the *Battle of Britain*, television dramas such as *Secret Army* and the documentary series *The World at War*. With the passage of time, the knowledge and memory of the Second World War and its material culture is now passing and we must make a fundamental reassessment of our approach and interpretation to the permanent galleries, which was aimed at a now dwindling audience. That knowledge, on which we could rely in the past, is now rapidly disappearing.

Today, British collective memory of the Second World War is clouded by nostalgia. It remains a national triumph in British minds. In our collective memory, it was a time when we as Britons all pulled together in adversity, the last time that time that Britain truly was Great Britain. The war, and when one talks about *The War* in Britain it always means the Second World War, is held up as our Finest Hour, a time when what we fondly imagine to be very British qualities of pluck, resourcefulness and the stiff upper lip won the day. The two years when Britain stood "alone" against Hitler (and before Russia and the United States entered the conflict and muddied the issue as to who the real "winners" were) are the key edifices in this national memory. Its cornerstones are the *Miracle of Dunkirk*, the *Spitfire Summer* of 1940, and the German bombing of London in the Blitz. Indeed the phrases *Dunkirk Spirit* and *Blitz Spirit* are still used to describe doggedness and triumph in the face of adversity. We hold up Winston Churchill as the embodiment of that spirit, the man who gave the lion its roar to paraphrase our wartime Prime Minister.

So, with these factors in mind, how are we now tackling these crucial issues for the Museum? How are we to make the Museum more relevant? Firstly, we have readdressed our mission. This has been revised as follows: *Enabling people to understand human behaviour through the lens of war and conflict.*

This means we will explore world conflict from contemporary perspectives, with a focus on Britain and its former empire. The mission is now to be supported by five key messages:

- War reveals people at their best and their worst
- War amplifies human dilemmas
- War is the most destructive force in history – but can be immensely creative
- War is the most extreme human experience
- War drives people to bear witness to their experiences

Our aim is to be visitor-centred, based upon extensive evaluation of their needs and expectations, but not visitor-driven. The move will be from passive to active narratives, that is from didactic *telling* to *showing*, encouraging our audiences to engage in debate and to providing a framework for them to understand the impact of conflict.

Thorough evaluation of our audience, to ensure that we are truly visitor-centred, will be critical to the process of reinterpreting our long-term exhibition spaces. That said, our experience over the past twenty years, both with these galleries and through temporary exhibitions has helped us to understand more what our visitors respond to as their relationship to conflict changes over time and will go to inform our approach to our new galleries. We have, over time, moved from the regimental cabinet to exhibitions led by clear narratives and fed by multiple perspectives. Key to this development has been to use personal stories, which either follow selected historical witnesses throughout an exhibition, or alternatively give them small, single areas of their own, supported by personal artefacts and other supporting documentation. An example of the former is our permanent *Holocaust* exhibition, completed in 2000, which makes a very strong feature of using the experiences of twelve survivors, whose individual experiences are woven throughout the exhibition. Again, these survivors act almost as guides, helping the visitor through an extraordinarily difficult episode of history while the IWM voice comes in the form of supporting, contextual information and evidence. Single, individual personal stories now form the backbone of all IWM temporary exhibitions, such as *In Memoriam* (2008-2009), which looks at the experience of the First World War and acts as a foil to the displays of weaponry in the First World War permanent display. The online exhibition *Through My Eyes* has also made a strong feature of individual human experiences.

Personal stories, often emotive, not only enable visitors to understand human behaviour through the lens of war and conflict, they also connect us and give us insights into often complex episodes in history where a Museum historian's "objective" voice would fail.

This new "human" approach is well supported by the Museum's collections. The collections are the engine of the museum, not only in their breadth and depth, but in the way that they have come to us and what they can tell us about war and human behaviour. The Museum now holds some 170,000 three dimensional exhibits, ranging from larger pieces such as tanks, aircraft and artillery pieces down to uniform items and children's toys and ephemera. It also hold over 15,000 sets of private papers, letters and diaries, approximately 270,000 printed items ranging from monographs to ration cards, more than 10 million photographs, 11,000 hours of film and 56,000 hours of historical sound recordings. To many people's surprise, the Museum has the second largest collection of twentieth century British art anywhere in the world, an exceptional collection of art and graphic design of 19,000 paintings, drawings and sculptures and 15,000 posters. The nature of the collections is also what makes the IWM unique. By and large, the material in the collection is not the work of a select few great men and women and nor is it based upon the once-private collection of a wealthy individual. It is far more democratic than that. Large parts of it are made up of memories and possessions that ordinary people have given to the Museum so that their experience of war, or that of their family, can be passed on to future generations. So, in physical terms much of the Museum's collection is made up of the intensely personal, such as the diaries or letters, or small trinkets, items which were mass-produced but have held huge personal significance to previous owners. It is through these "ordinary" objects that the Museum delivers its key messages and tells the story of ordinary people in exceptional times, the sacrifices they made and the dilemmas they faced. Their value lies not in their intrinsic beauty or monetary worth, but in their historical value, what they tell us about our past. What marks out the IWM is that it is also a museum of narratives – rarely can an item stand on its own merit. Interpretation and context are crucial if these are not just to be dead relics. What matters about the objects are the stories behind each of them – how it was made, by whom and when, why and how it was used. The onus is upon the historians and curators at the IWM to explore each object's biography, to make what might otherwise seem, at first sight, dull, everyday items – a spoon, a faded photograph, or a letter – come alive in our displays.

As regards causes and consequences of the Second World War, these have been dealt with successfully in temporary exhibitions such as *Windrush* (2008-2009) which looks at the experience of West Indian immigrants to Britain after the war, many of whom had served in the British armed forces. Such issues are excluded from the permanent galleries by the operational/military historical approach – as is the role of the Empire and Commonwealth itself. These give the impression that the civilians who, in the main, made up the armies, and the men and women working in war industries and agriculture, knew no existence other than war, that they were somehow *different* from us.

As regards the causes of the Second World War, the IWM gallery covering the interwar period, with its showcases full of SA, SS and British Union of Fascists uniforms and ephemera is more concerned with the paraphernalia of Fascism and National Socialism than it is with any examination of what brought about the conflict. It barely touches upon the enormous social change created by the First World War and its effect upon the established international order. The 1930s policy of Appeasement of Hitler, most closely identified with British Prime Minister Neville Chamberlain is given only cursory treatment. Likewise, when it comes to the consequences of the Second World War for Britain, these are scarcely touched upon. This means that we lose narrative threads which could include, among other issues, the rebuilding of Blitzed cities, the hardships and dreariness of the 1945-1951 'Austerity' years, immigration from the Empire and Commonwealth and the establishment of a political consensus which would last until the 1979 election of Margaret Thatcher. In the *Conflicts Since 1945* permanent exhibition which follows the *Second World War* galleries, Britain's changed role on the international stage is implied, but not dealt with directly. Rather, there is a staccato presentation of conflicts involving British and Commonwealth forces from 1945 to date. This lack of

THE POWER OF THE OBJECT

narrative string betrays the uniqueness and strength of the Museum. Our subject matter helps to explain why British society is like it is today – but also has a global perspective and significance for world history. As Andrew Marr observed of the importance of past behaviour and the generation which grew up during and after the Second World War: *...these alien people were us. They are us... It was their lives and the choices they made which led to here and now. So although they might stare at us and ask, 'Who are these alien people?' we could reply, 'We are you, what you chose to become.'* (Marr xxxii):

Our new mission also frees us to examine controversial aspects of our subject matter. Museums should be dynamic places of learning – places of change, which are able to deal with controversial and contested issues, as well as puncture some myths. Our role is to deliver history, not heritage – that is history which has been given a good wash to remove the historical 'dirt'. Twenty years ago, the Museum's strategy was to be 'objective', that is to tell didactic, often typological stories about objects. Yet recent experience has shown that visitors prefer us to engage them actively, to acknowledge where a debate is still open. Visitor evaluation showed us, before we began work on the permanent Churchill Museum at the Cabinet War Rooms which opened in 2005, that our audiences knew that he was a controversial figure and wanted to know why. They did not want us to present him simply as a two-dimensional icon. This did not mean that we had to engage in revisionism. Far from it. Our approach in the Churchill Museum was to give different sides to the many arguments about Churchill, and allow visitors to form their own judgements on contested historical issues surrounding him. Was he an idealist or opportunist? Was he the great strategist of popular imagination? Was he, at least in part, responsible for the current situation on the Middle East? These are some of the questions which we dealt with in the gallery in some detail. Crucial to this process was to place him in his proper historical context, so, in an interactive on Churchill and race, we reveal that he often made throwaway remarks that today would be considered racist. At the same time we place him in historical context by placing in the visitor's minds the idea that those attitudes to race were forged in the Victorian era and were typical of the time. The intention was not to excuse, but rather to understand. In an interactive on the British interwar policy of Appeasement of Hitler, we point out that far from being the weak man of legend, Neville Chamberlain ruled the Conservative Party with a rod of iron. Moreover, while Appeasement failed, we will never know if Churchill was right that an Anglo-French Russian defensive alliance would have halted Hitler's territorial demands or would even have been possible. Indeed, Appeasement, now a dirty word, seemed a policy of pragmatism to a British population haunted by the losses incurred in the First World War and desperate to avoid further conflict with Germany.

This principle of presenting history in its context is one we take seriously. When judging historical personalities, we endeavour always to use the words of contemporary witnesses whose judgement we respect. Thus, in an interactive on Churchill's relationships with his military commanders, which includes information on Admiral Lord Louis Mountbatten, 1942-1943 Chief of Combined Operations Headquarters and 1943-1946 Supreme Allied Commander South East Asia Command, we describe how Churchill greatly admired Mountbatten's physical courage, and liked his dashing personality. Unfortunately, this led him to appoint Mountbatten to positions that others knew to be beyond his abilities. To support this, we quote Chief of the Imperial General Staff Field Marshal Sir Alan Brooke, who wrote in his diary: 'Seldom has a Supreme Commander been more deficient in the main attributes of a Supreme Commander than Dickie Mountbatten.' (Danchev. 715)

I have already written that we want to challenge

and engage our visitors. I feel we should also surprise them, to make them rethink often long-held assumptions about our past which are often embedded in nostalgia. The evacuees who left Britain's cities from September 1939 are imagined as grubby little urchins who were welcomed with open arms into comfortable homes in the country, where they played in the countryside for the remainder of the war. Many of the child evacuees in fact came from extremely deprived backgrounds and, when the expected German raids did not materialise, returned home within months. Many of those who took children into their homes could be hostile to their young charges and use them as unpaid child labour. Indeed, a significant proportion of the evacuees comprised not children, but also expectant mothers and people with disabilities. Some two million people from wealthier backgrounds privately evacuated themselves. Another area for nostalgia, the summer of 1940 – the so-called *Spitfire Summer* – is so often portrayed in feature films and documentaries as baking hot. In the public imagination, British and German aircraft battled it out for supremacy in bright blue skies over lush, sun-drenched Kentish countryside. In fact, that summer was, from July onwards, typically British – wet and damp. Were the French during both world wars the *surrender monkeys* of British – and Bart

THE POWER OF THE OBJECT

Simpson's – popular imagination? Hardly. French casualties in the First World War were almost double those of Britain. And during the Second World War, 100,000 French troops were killed in just six weeks of fighting before the June 1940 Armistice, nearly half as many as suffered by Britain during the entire conflict. As well as surprising our visitors with different approaches to what they already know, new ways of looking at our collections through the key messages allow us to explore avenues which have hitherto been locked away from us. We can release nuggets of information which might seem trivial, but which we know will spark discussion among visitors when they have left – *pub facts* if you like. One example of these might be the *Cookie* displayed in the IWM Atrium, the 4,000lb bomb dropped by British bombers over Germany to blow tiles off roofs and so to ensure that the smaller incendiary bombs would drop through and into buildings rather than roll into streets. The *Cookie* was also known as a *Blockbuster* and was the origin for the word we use today for hugely successful films.

In terms of the physical areas for new galleries, we are looking at multi-paced spaces which will implicitly reflect the nature and significance of events. These will use a variety of media and will exploit new technologies. Clearly, the different interpretational approaches through which we amplify and expand upon themes generated by our collections, could amount to potentially huge amounts of information. That being so, we are looking at the concept of creative journeys which would offer visitors choices of narrative threads through the gallery spaces. These journeys would link objects which are physically separated and might be guided by, say, portable digital media, people or print. They might be generated by the visitors themselves or even by other visitors. Of course, for those who prefer a tour of this nature to be determined by the Museum, then that option will be available. The challenge of the creative journeys will be to connect and order physically separated material: how to make displays and key objects function in a variety of contexts and from a number of perspectives. We have already sketched out one such journey, starting at the Lancaster bomber section, one of our iconic objects. From there, the journey might explore any number of associated themes in line with the key messages – from the controversy surrounding the RAF Strategic Bomber Offensive, to how and by whom the bombers were built and the personalisation of mass-produced weaponry through aircraft nose art.

In conclusion, I think that the founders of the Museum would be pleased at how the interpretation of the

Museum's subject matter, not least the Second World War, is changing. The aim of our Director General since October 2008, Diane Lees, is to redevelop the permanent galleries from 2014. In the process, we will be reaffirming a vision of a museum of public ownership and human experience which distinguished the Imperial War Museum at its inception. In 1917, in a letter to the editor of the Daily Telegraph, Sir Martin Conway, the IWM's first Director General wrote of a *divergence from the accepted museum idea*. He pointed out that: *Never before have the people been able to see the work of their own hands as distinct from the work of a few highly specialised exhibitors, and here the humblest war worker will be able to find examples of the work he or she did for the Empire.* (IWM C/F: A4/1)

Over ninety years later, our historical knowledge has widened and new thinking and technology offer us new possibilities to engage and challenge our visitors. We must focus our interpretation in order to ensure that the Museum remains relevant, inspiring and challenging to current and future audiences, whose diversity and tastes are ever-changing. New approaches will inform our entire public programme, not just exhibitions, so that we give the museum back to the visitor, whose ancestors are not just the subject of the museum, but also its benefactors. By doing so, we will keep the founders' vision of a place for public engagement with a shared past very much alive.

Discussion

Question: Do you feel an obligation towards your collections – that we have to show this? You say that you start with a story – but do you also feel an obligation to your collection?

Taylor: Yes we definitely do. In the case of temporary exhibitions we tend to borrow more objects. But the story does come first. In the case of the Holocaust exhibition we had with Bergen-Belsen and a lot of material to do with the refugees who came to Britain in the 1930s or indeed after the Holocaust. But clearly you can't make a Holocaust exhibition out of that, it is just not enough. So we did an awful lot of exchanges so that the material became part of our collections. And I think entering into partnerships becomes more and more crucial. Britain is part of Europe, and we increasingly need to tell the European story. This is a personal point of view, but I think we need partnerships to enable us to tell those stories. As for documents, we have a more open policy than other institutions, you can come and see the Montgomery papers as an undergraduate (under supervision of course) but you get the originals.

Question: You start out with the story...

Taylor: And see what fits...

Question: You mean you write a book, and then make an exhibition?

Taylor: I know exactly what you mean. It is give and take. We start off with a concept document, which we work up with the designers. We mention key objects. So we know we've got, say, five chapters, five spaces, with two or three key objects for each section. And then the thing develops in tandem. Objects, designers and historians working and gradually feeling their way. But I should say that for most of the stories we want to tell, our own collections are sufficient. They are huge. But the WWII collection is not as strong as the WWI, and there is a good reason for that. During WWI a Canadian major was sent out to the front to collect what were called sacred relics. So we got all the personal stories and got the provenance. In WWII most of the museum curators were WWI veterans and saw the new war as more of a sideshow, and so did not undertake contemporary collecting. We now do collect in Iraq and Afghanistan. But it is more difficult. For example, people do not write letters anymore.

Question: I have visited the IWM several times and have thought that the different atmosphere here is that the political consequences of both WWI and WWII were not as devastating for Britain, as on the continent? Many states crumbled, but the British state survived.

Taylor: That is true. WWII created an immense consensus in Britain lasting until Margaret Thatcher. Under Attlee, Britain came as close to socialism as it has ever been. WWII was a massive social experiment in Britain where people from the upper classes met other people. Wealthy landowners suddenly had unwashed children from Liverpool living with them. I think the point you make is a very strong one.

Question: In some continental states the stories told in

museums have been very selective.

Taylor: Well this comes back to the initial question of outside pressure. Luckily we have had very little of that. It is true that some veterans from the war in the Far East felt their story was neglected, particularly those who had been Japanese prisoners. But we could show that in fact we did give them a lot of space in the permanent exhibition, particularly compared to those who had been prisoners in Germany. And they left it at that.

Question: I noticed that you take an Empire-wide perspective in the Churchill exhibition, but this seems to be lacking in the permanent exhibition. It is all seen very much from a British point of view with grandfathers showing grandchildren (i.e.: not from the Empire, despite the name of the museum), and there is not much conflict described.

Taylor: That's a good point and a fair one... But there is a difference between the Commonwealth and the Empire. The former was more independent, whereas India had no choice but to take part.

MUSEUMS AND WORLD WAR II

3

The European Forum of Contemporary Conflict

ANNE GODFROID

Exhibition Curator,

Musée Royal de l'Armée, Bruxelles

In November 1994, the Royal Army Museum (RMM) in Brussels staged an important exhibition: *I was 20 in 1945*. This exhibition was conceived as part of a series of commemorative events to mark the 50th anniversary of the end of the Second World War. The Museum was a key partner, putting its personnel, galleries and collections at the disposal of the organisers and occupying a seat on the Scientific Board, but was not, however, a principal in this mega-budget project. The results proved spectacular, in keeping with previous Euroculture presentations such as *Tout Simenon* or *Tout Tintin*. A striking media campaign was mounted and drew a massive response from the public. The exhibition, with its elaborate design, abundant use of audio-visual resources and important objects from all over the world, was a great success. Over eight months some 850,000 visitors saw the exhibition, that is, one out of every ten Belgians.

This success encouraged the RMM Board in its decision to remodel its Second World War galleries, especially as Belgian politicians, headed by the Prime Minister, had supported the concept. However, the road to the opening of the first two phases of the European Forum of Contemporary Conflict, in 2004 and 2007, proved to be particularly long and winding. Indeed, the changeover from temporary exhibition to permanent museum implied a whole new concept based on new perspectives and involved an impressive number of skills. That is the story I would like to tell here.

The exhibition gallery and its history

The European Forum of Contemporary Conflict is housed in the spectacular Bordiau gallery, an exhibition space some 40 meters wide, 60 meters long and 30 meters high. Built in 1879-1880 by the Belgian architect, Gedeon Bordiau, this elegant gallery unites modern and traditional materials such as metal, glass and stone. It was originally designed to house commercial and industrial fairs, but over time it housed the collections of the Museum of Education and a cast workshop, before being taken over by the RMM, which turned it into the Albert 1 gallery after the death of the *Roi Chevalier* (or the King Knight), and was opened in April 1935.

Painstakingly assembled over a decade, the Second World War collections were also put on display there. Opening on May 10, 1955 to mark the fifteenth anniversary of the invasion of Belgium, the exhibition was completely lacking in visual displays. It was limited to a taxonomic presentation based on a series of objects: a series of mannequins, a series of medals, etc. History was perceived as consisting of military typologies and hierarchies, in exactly the same way as a 19th century natural history museum would display its collections. The exhibition remained untouched until it was hurriedly taken apart in the mid-eighties. The collections, with their 15,000 objects, were then put into improvised storage rooms, awaiting future display. Visitors left and workmen came; armoured vehicles were replaced by building equipment.

Between 1984 and 1987, the *Régie des Bâtiments* (in charge of the management and upkeep of government property) considerably modified the appearance of the Bordiau gallery. Modelled on two contemporary renovation projects – the Musée d'Orsay in Paris and the Art Institute in Chicago – the size of exhibition rooms was increased to 6,000 m², through a system of mezzanines, stairways and walkways. A serious lack of both exhibition and office space was thus remedied, but these solutions also ruled out certain display options, because the new structure could only support one thousand kilograms per square meter. On the upper level, the current exhibition cannot display heavy equipment such as aircraft, tanks or artillery. As these cannot be presented logically as part of the exhibition, they are grouped in distinct areas, where they are out of context, which is regrettable.

The building works also included the renovation

of the two 450 m² rose windows on the north-east and south-west of the gallery. The former, as the more exposed, was completely replaced, while the latter, apart from the cast iron work, was able to be repaired in situ. Daylight once again flooded the hall. Although the windows on the ground floor are covered up, luminosity can still reach up to 6,000 lux on bright summer days. The use of hammered glass, said to block the most damaging of the sun's rays, did not bring much relief. Needless to say, this situation put the objects on display (most of which were textiles) at risk and new work was undertaken. Two options were considered. The first envisaged installing mobile blinds in front of the windows, the second building vaulted alcoves. The second option was finally adopted and carried out in 1998. The alcoves not only reduced the luminosity but also gave the exhibition a certain rhythm.

The preceding explanation will have made it clear that turning a classified building into a permanent exhibition area, respecting both the environment and present day museum norms, is no mean feat. Contrary to creations starting from scratch, in which the story reflects the environment (for instance, the Caen Memorial), in this case we were faced with an environment (albeit a most prestigious one) which dictated the story. Historians and architects working on the project had to consider all these imperatives, regardless of the inherent difficulties. They were conscious of the aesthetic value of the building and so created rest areas, enabling visitors to fully enjoy the incomparable architecture.

The exhibition storyline and content

By the end of the eighties, when the workmen and their machines had left, the time had come for the installation of the First and Second World War collections in the Bordiau gallery. Several museum staff and volunteers worked on the project, in close collaboration with a firm of architects. Then the idea arose of presenting the collections within the context of a story. A visit would take some ninety minutes and interest would be maintained through varied resources. Unfortunately, the project was nipped in the bud. While, behind the scenes, museum staff worked on the project, the Bordiau Gallery hosted numerous temporary events, such as *NATO Uniforms from 1900 to 1990*. Then came the *I was 20 in 1945* exhibition, bringing new hope and expectations. Unfortunately, expectations often have a way of being dashed. The project would need the tenacity of committed supporters, chief among them Patrick Lefèvre (Chief Curator, 1995-2005) to get off the ground.

Begun in 1998, this ambitious museum project (rather pompously entitled *European Forum of Contemporary Conflict*) is meant to eventually cover the period between 1917 and 2001 in some 6,000 m² of exhibition space. Entirely funded by the Ministry of Defence (responsible for the Museum), the refurbishment was planned in successive stages. This phasing of the project was dictated by budgetary constraints. Each stage was budgeted at approximately 1.5 million Euros. Today, only the first two stages have been completed and were opened in 2004 and 2007 respectively so that visitors can now enjoy an exhibition of some 2,000 m².

Before discussing the options selected, I would like to focus on a number of Museum decisions.

The RMM is a government scientific institution, but nevertheless decided not to call on academia (universities or research centres) for help in mapping out the historical storyline. It did not consider that it had to rely on a board of experts. It did not, however, hesitate to call on specialists to elucidate specific details. Generally speaking, the historical story, its outlines and key stages, was put together by museum staff. Texts written by them enabled the scientific committee to validate their approach. The Museum also chose not to call on veterans' associations, (resistance fighters, deportees etc). It nevertheless wished to avoid a complete rupture between history and memory. Through *The Story of Witnesses*, a series of testimonies taken from Belgian television archives or specially recorded, a dialogue between the two sides was established. Through the diversity of their experiences, the men and women interviewed help visitors to gain an understanding of the daily realities of war.

In terms of content, the Museum opted for a broader vision: the story had to become an international one. It wished to avoid a purely Belgian – and therefore limited – perspective. The globe of the world at the entrance to the exhibition is significant in setting the appropriate tone. For the presentation of events occurring between 1917 and 1939, Belgian and international approaches alternate. From September 1st 1939, the story becomes truly international. The 18-day campaign, marking the invasion of Belgium by troops of the Third Reich, does not receive more emphasis than the French or Polish campaigns. This choice offended a number of people, especially military or retired military personnel. In cases like these, the Museum is at pains to point out that a section on occupied Belgium gives a detailed explanation of the occupation of the country and its consequences. It is unfortunate, however, that this small area remains cut off from earlier and later events. The third phase of the European Forum of Contemporary Conflict will remedy this situation. Although the chosen storyline favours an international approach, every now and then it focuses on outstanding Belgian personalities, such as Lieutenant Colonel Frans Burniaux, a pilot with the South African Air Force, Commodore Georges Timmermans, captain of the 202 Landing Flotilla at Juno Beach, or Lieutenant Colonel Hugo van Kuyck, seen as the architect of the Normandy landings for his participation in the Beach Intelligence Service.

The Museum also opted for a storyline with a chronological and themed approach. Every so often, visitors can escape from the main route to admire the architecture of the building, listen to eyewitnesses (*Story of the Witnesses*), or learn more about the period (through a CD-ROM about the interwar period). This dual approach makes it possible to discuss certain topics in surroundings more suited to their subject matter. Telling the story of the gruesome actions performed by the *Einsatzgruppen* in the exhibition area dedicated to the Eastern front would not have enabled us to situate these ghoulish events in the context of the Nazi policy of genocide. Treating this topic in an area dedicated to the National Socialist policy of extermination seemed more pertinent. Unfortunately, the phased development of the project can sometimes lead visitors to think that the Museum, deliberately or not, omits certain themes.

Let's now focus on the museological choices.

Many Second World War museums employ colour to dramatise the story. Brussels acted differently. The choice of colour is purely aesthetic: the characteristic green paint of the metallic structure complements the eggplant shade of the walls and showcases; the cream backdrop of the display cases recalls the colour of the ceiling and makes for an advantageous contrast with the often dark objects in the collections. However, on one occasion, the Museum broke this rule. In presenting the rise of totalitarian regimes, it chose to bring out the colours and symbolism used by these regimes. Red, black and brown were applied to different elements (timeline, text panels, plinths…). The Museum decided to group Fascism, Nazism and Communism in one area to highlight their similarities and differences. One of the characteristics the three systems had in common was the cult of personality of the three dictators. On posters and photos illustrating this theme, busts of the three leaders stand out in striking detail. Their display is the result of a fortuitous consensus. With the preparations well underway, the Museum director welcomed a Russian delegation headed by the Russian military attaché in Brussels. (The project was reviewed and the building yard visited.) In the gallery with the three leaders, the visitors stopped, quite baffled. A long and seemingly heated conversation in Russian then started up; the director even feared some kind of diplomatic incident. Eventually, after what seemed like minutes, the military attaché started to explain. He did not dispute the totalitarian character of the communist regime, but was nevertheless quite put out by its apparent linking together with Nazism and Fascism. He suggested moving Stalin's bust and rotating it 180° so that Stalin, Mussolini and Hitler now faced each other. This suggestion met with the approval of the Museum team, as it provided a way of symbolically suggesting the regimes' ideological antagonisms, which would inevitably lead to war.

Symbolic references have, however, generally been avoided (the incident with the busts is an exception). This dimension, while easily expressed in writing, often escapes visitors. We wonder how many of them feel lost and oppressed, robbed of their freedom and identity, amongst the profusion of showcases presenting different aspects of totalitarian regimes, be they left or right wing. It is difficult to assess to what extent the message intended by historians is communicated. In spite of its name, which suggests a discussion about democratic values - and so has a more symbolic than historical meaning, the European Forum of Contemporary Conflict is first and foremost a museum about history, placing wars and their consequences in an historical perspective.

The location of objects

This large historical fresco contains some 2,500 objects, all the property of the RMM (with the notable exception of the Danish infantry uniforms). Some pieces have been in our collection for many years (thanks to the visionary measures taken by the first Head Curator); others have been or will be acquired in order to complete the story (such as a female Red Army uniform, which we have not been able to locate as yet).

The objects in the collection underpin the story. The exceptional nature of some explains why the circuit halts at seemingly minor events. Although historical accuracy is never compromised, these stops could seem out of proportion with the whole story. In keeping with their geopolitical importance at that time, the emergence of the Latvian, Estonian and Ukrainian states, on the ruins of the Tsarist empire, is extensively illustrated. Thanks to numerous gifts by the respective governments between 1927 and 1935, the Museum possesses uniforms and equipment which, because of their unique character, have to be exhibited. The same logic is applied today, when buying new items for the collection. These new acquisitions are, or will be, included in the storyline. The Enigma coding machine, acquired in 2004 by the Museum some months after its opening, will very shortly become a focal point in an ever-evolving exhibition.

In the same way, the objects have influenced the content and structure of the educational material. The result of close collaboration between the education service and the historians in charge of the exhibition, it presents teachers and their students with the opportunity of learning about the great events of history through the smaller stories connected with the objects.

Besides numerous anonymous uniforms of all ranks, all armies and all nationalities (collected by the *Office de Récupération* immediately after the war, presented by descendants in the years following the war or recently bought), the Museum proudly displays a few outfits belonging to famous foreign officers, such as Marshal Mannerheim from Finland, Admiral Dönitz and Generalfeldmarschall von Kluge from Germany or the future American President, General Eisenhower. The latter, then Supreme Commander of Allied Forces in Europe (1951-1952), personally presented the RMM with one of his outfits, amongst which is the famous "Ike" jacket he made so popular with US Army officers. Although this particular piece was manufactured some time after the Normandy landings, it remains indisputably linked to them and the same goes for the *cricket clicker* distributed to young 101st Airborne recruits, immortalised in the film *The Longest Day*. Apart from the trio of uniforms, weapons and scale models, the European Forum of Contemporary Conflict displays some true gems, literally and figuratively. Because of their value, the necklaces and great crosses presented to King Albert I during the interwar period are displayed in special showcases. But the insignia, medals and decorations presented to humbler soldiers also provide us with a history lesson. The medal awarded to the participants in the North African campaign shows an allegorical battle against the British crocodile fought by armoured German and Italian knights. One of the most impressive pieces in the exhibition, both because of its size and its rarity, is undoubtedly the rear gun turret of a British Whitley medium bomber. This aircraft (no example of which is still airworthy) amongst other feats also took part in the Allied strategic bombings against German interests in occupied countries. Completely restored by the Museum, it is mounted on a structure recalling the aeroplane's tail section and now proudly sits in the centre of the Forum. As an anecdote, we can add that a gunner was installed in the turret, together with his mascot, a small plush cat wearing glasses. The little animal notched up quite a few hours of flight. It belonged to WJ. Henry, a Belgian pilot in the Royal Air Force. It goes without saying that these few examples do not do justice to the richness of the collections displayed. Describing them all would be rather boring. A visit to the exhibition is therefore mandatory!

In order to engage the interest of as many visitors as possible, the exhibition alternates between, on the one hand, traditional exhibition spaces, giving pride of place to authentic and often unique objects (such as uniforms from the Latvian, Ukrainian and Estonian armies dating from the twenties), and dioramas on the other hand (which sometimes use replicas). The dioramas and scenes in the Forum have nothing in common with the occasionally garish presentations of *I was 20 in 1945* (the exhibition which triggered a series of spectacular visual displays), and have been put together with great attention to detail and authenticity. Museum staff travelled extensively throughout Europe (London, Hamburg, Lorient and so on) in order to photograph, measure and take casts of objects. The idea was to reproduce objects and situations as faithfully as possible. But even if these scenes can briefly transport visitors to days gone by, regardless of the care and effort involved, reconstructions can never fully render the wartime atmosphere of fear and helplessness. That is why dioramas are placed alongside other media. Scenes of people fleeing unfold against a backdrop of photographic enlargements giving a most poignant image of the misery and distress felt. The same feelings can also be gathered through the story of eyewitnesses. A few meters away, the evocative ruins of Coventry, using authentic materials, are displayed together with a film about the Blitz.

To sum up, the European Forum of Contemporary Conflict owes its success to a combination of historical rigour, rich collections and dynamic museum practice.

Readers who would like to make a virtual tour of the European Forum of Contemporary Conflict, can consult the website of the Royal Museum of the Armed Forces and Military History:
http://www.klm-mra.be/klm-new/engels/main01.php?id=menu_links/plan
or http://www.klm-mra.be/klm-new/engels/main01.php?id=collecties/virtueel#
They'll find there images which give a sense of the atmosphere of the exhibition and of its most important objects.

Discussion

Question: Did the change in perspective from national to international also involve a change in message? Perhaps from a more technical perspective to an emphasis on Human Rights?

Godfroid: The exhibition is not strictly technical at all, but shows the human side. But Belgium is a small country in the middle of Europe, and too small to talk only about our side of things.

Question: How can the visitor differentiate between the authentic objects and the replicas?

Godfroid: Most of them are authentic, and it is mentioned if it is a replica.

Question: So it is not that if it is behind glass...

Godfroid: No, nothing like that.

Question: (Compliments the exhibition): Why did you call it The Forum... which suggests debate?

Godfroid: The museum director Patrick Lefebre thought debate would come. There are in fact two forums built into the ground floor where debates and conferences were planned. But they did not happen. Nobody uses that title.

MUSEUMS AND WORLD WAR II

4

The Exhibition: Between Book and Film

HANS HENRIK APPEL

Head of Education

Royal Danish Arsenal Museum, Copenhagen

The Royal Danish Arsenal Museum has for many years held a special position among international military and arms museums. In the early part of the 20th century, the director of the museum, Captain JFVV Stöckel, managed to create a hugely impressive exhibition on the evolution of hand weapons in the 160 metres long Armoury Hall of Christian IV's arsenal building dating from 1604.

Stöckel intended his exhibition to be strictly scientific. Every weapon was fitted into its correct place in a long series of objects, carefully arranged according to typology, chronology and origin. 8,000 objects reflected the technological evolution of handweapons. A space of 3,200 square metres reflecting the museological ideals of the 19th and early 20th century. Stöckel's project was more or less completed according to his intentions – and the 160 metre long rows of weapons stretching from one end of the hall to the other are still what visitors encounter at the museum today.

In this exhibition, it is possible for the expert to spot rare pieces or variations in special weapons. For the general public, however, there is not much guidance or information, the texts being limited to brief statements of typology, year of production, nationality, calibre, and accession number.

As much as experts, collectors and professional

museum people find the exhibition awesome, the general public more often than not find themselves lost, the language of exhibition being far from what they have nowadays come to expect from a museum.

At the same time, the museum management has decided to shift the museum's focus from the technological history of weapons to the cultural history of war and its impact on the state, the individual and society. This shift is reflected in the present collecting practice and research policy at the museum. But it is not reflected in the permanent exhibitions.

The challenge for the museum is therefore to transform the display of hand weapons into an exhibition on Danish wars and their impact on society from 1500 to today – or tomorrow. A shift from the display of a collection to the communication of historical complexity. How should this shift be implemented?

All members of the curatorial staff at the museum are trained historians, the museum giving priority to in-depth knowledge of the subject and the collections. Most of the staff have taken courses in museology or communication. But that does not alter the fact that all of them have been reared on academic discourse as style of communication. And this academic discourse is basically a written discourse, taking the form of either a monograph or an article.

The basic characteristics that define the academic discourse can be summed up as follows:
- The definition and testing of abstract concepts usually plays a central part.
- It is a strictly structured chain of argument.
- It is built on critical reflection and documentation.
- Within the defined field of study it strives to give a well-balanced if not complete description of the subject.
- It is essentially a verbal discourse; pictures and objects usually only serve to illustrate the linguistic argument - even if it is an analysis of physical objects.

This is, of course, a generalisation reflecting the Danish-German rather than the British academic tradition, which often gives more emphasis to the narrative. But the essential point is that academic discourse is basically written discourse.

This is often evident when historians make discursive exhibitions instead of simply displaying collections. Many exhibitions are enveloped in text. But perhaps even more important, the exhibitions turn out to be conceived as written arguments in which objects mainly serve as illustrations.

This is an essential point. The status of the object is easily reduced to something secondary in a discursive exhibition, very precisely formulated by the 19th century director of the Smithsonian, George Brown Goode: *An efficient educational museum may be described as a collection of instructive labels, each illustrated by a well-selected specimen.* (MacDonald 2006: 140) The object is conceived as the nail on which to hang the instructive label that carries the real argument. Visitors are not supposed to dwell on the individual object or ask their own questions. The object is there to make the acquisition of the information from the instructive label easier. The selection of objects and their presentation is guided by the underlying chain of arguments, not by the power of the object.

I am not in favour of avoiding instructive labels; in fact, far from it. And I am not arguing against creating discursive exhibitions. But I am warning against the direct translation of written discourse into physical exhibition. Because visitors rarely manage to pick up the line of argument in such exhibitions. They are often left with the frustration of having missed the central point, or with a bad feeling because they found it too tiring to follow the long line of argument – and therefore gave up. The objects somehow become irrelevant – or lose importance. And as a consequence, the exhibition, as a medium, does not fulfil its potential.

In some ways, the exhibition as a medium has more in common with the movie than with the book, although it also differs from the movie in many ways. The exhibition is very much a visual medium. In the movie there is no room for abstract concepts. Instead of using, for instance, the concept *working class* the movie focuses on an individual or a group of individuals. Instead of abstract statements in the text like: *poor sanitary conditions lead to a high rate of mortality among wounded soldiers*, you are shown the interior of a military hospital in the American Civil War. The movie has to be concrete about the setting and the actors. And it has to be selective.

The movie (or, at least, the good movie) creates a flow-experience. Even if you have no preconceptions about, say, the American Civil War, the concreteness of the story makes it accessible and possible to identify with the actors. And with a good plot you can make spectators forget time and place.

The Danish museologist, Bruno Ingemann (2002), has argued that the exhibition as a medium operates within four fields of experience: knowledge, emotions, values and action. The field of knowledge includes the the generation of new knowledge as well as the activation of the visitors' previous knowledge, which is often a prerequisite for the generation of new knowledge. The field of emotion includes the placing of objects in their historical human and physical relations, as well as the exhibition's representation of these relationships. The field of values includes the exhibition's ability to invoke norms, values and a sense of relevance. And the field of action constitutes the visitor's physical interaction with the exhibition (are you standing up reading long passages of text?).

The more abstract the language of the exhibition, the more previous knowledge is necessary to generate new knowledge. The movie, in contrast, is very concrete. Of course, there are many layers of interpretation, but the basic plot is always accessible whether you have any previous knowledge or not. The movie focuses on relationships – and the good movie always has a premise, a statement of value that it tries to put across. And although the audience is seated throughout the movie, the plot evolving around a conflict drives the action of the movie forward.

So the successful movie manages to create a flow-experience, something rarely achieved in exhibitions. But can we somehow treat objects in a more cinematic, visual way and communicate complex historical messages better than we do in academic exhibitions?

My argument is that if we want to create exhibitions on complex historical issues, we have to challenge the academic discourse – and that can be done by confronting it with cinematic storytelling. In 2007-8 The Royal Danish Arsenal Museum carried out such a confrontation. In eight workshops of two days each, scriptwriters from Sentropa Interactions (a subsidiary of a leading Danish film production company) introduced staff members to basic concepts of cinematic storytelling – and then helped staff in their attempt to apply those concepts to the storyboard of the new permanent exhibition.

Briefly, the process of work has been this:

1. Define the theme(s) of each section.

2. Define the premise, that is, the central message or impression you want visitors to remember.

3. List possible actors in the story – and the objects at your disposal.

4. Locate and delimit the conflict best suited to put across the premise.

5. Choose the subject of the story – and define the central characters in the conflict

6. Find a plot-structure that can set the scene of the conflict at the start, and be suitably resolved at the end.

7. Be careful in selecting sub-plots, so that the central conflict is not blurred.

Instead of striving for a complete, objective, encyclopedic description of a war, this method is highly selective. If you want to give a balanced account of each war, the background, the participants, the events and the consequences, you should do it in another medium. The exhibition should be carried by a special atmosphere; by the power of the objects; by the three-dimensional experience of being there. The exhibition should create an absorbing flow-experience for visitors regardless of their knowledge of the subject. And that experience should inspire them to search for more information in other media - be it websites, catalogues, or films.

The idea of working with cinematic storytelling to create a flow-experience sprang from a visit to several museums in London in June 2007. Before I explore how a cinematic approach to themes of Denmark and the Second World War at the Royal Danish Arsenal Museum could turn out, I will give a brief review of the strength and weaknesses of three of the exhibitions we visited.

The Churchill Museum
The Churchill exhibition in the Cabinet War Rooms is an unusually successful exhibition. It is gripping and engaging – it creates a flow experience. But how? First of all, objects are, although integral, not the main car-

riers of the story. But objects and images – movies and stills – sounds and a huge variety of interactive installations make it possible to get close to Churchill, to get all the way round him - even inside his head.

The setting of the exhibition is the Cabinet War Rooms – you are thrown right into World War II as soon as you enter. The story does not start with the birth and childhood of Churchill. It starts with the iconic Churchill as war leader, the Churchill that most people recognise. As you approach the photos hanging on the wall with iconic quotations such as *Never was so much owed*, you hear recordings of Churchill's speeches. It is Churchill as speaker who is introduced. On the screen, you can choose from his rhetorical toolbox: *Realism. Recycling. Memorable phrases. History. Humour.* You can even try to juggle the words yourself and recreate passages of his speeches. You get the taste of the words, and you get a glimpse of the oratorical genius playing with them.

In this way, the voice of the exhibition is introduced. It is Churchill, the man himself. Just about every textual theme is introduced by a quotation from Churchill. For instance, the section on intelligence: *The great thing is to get the true picture. Whatever that is.*

This is explained at the second text-level: *Churchill had always understood that knowing what the enemy was*

THE POWER OF THE OBJECT

planning was vital to winning the war. And at the third level is a more elaborate text on the intelligence service at Bletchley Park that Churchill nicknamed his golden eggs – and it is told that the Germans never realised the British intelligence had broken their code.

The Golden Egg is used as the basis for an interactive installation. Visitors can choose between six physical, golden eggs. When they place one of them on a plate, a question is flashed on a screen: "Did Churchill know that Coventry would be bombed?" A comprehensive text on the intelligence service on a digital screen is then dissolved and leaves about 50 words on the screen forming an answer denying the question.

Instead of long, didactic texts following a logical argument, the exhibition uses Churchill's own words – stimulating the curiosity of the visitor to find additional information for him- or herself.

This is especially well done on interactive computer screens: *We would like to know your opinion. Churchill was a great leader. Do you: Strongly agree, agree, not sure, disagree, strongly disagree?* Before you cast your vote, you can explore documentation structured in the categories: *Using experience, Risk-taking, Ruthlessness and humanity, Self-confidence and communication, Seeing the wider picture.*

As historians, we know that you always start out

with a question when you read a historical document. In this way, the exhibition prompts visitors with questions so they can form their own opinions. At the same time, visitors can leave their mark on the exhibition, as the results of their votes are continuously updated on screen.

About half the exhibition is on Churchill as speaker, leader, and workaholic during World War II. It ends with a short section called *Cold War Statesman* and his death. Then we flash back to the young Churchill, followed by sections on controversial issues, mistakes and lost causes.

But what about the objects? Are they only second fiddle to the quotations and interactives? There are only a few objects in each section. In the section on Churchill as a workaholic a timetable of his average working day is drawn up on a exhibition case containing his hair brush, his appointment diary, his bowler hat, a bottle of champagne, his favourite movie – and one of his chewed cigars. Objects without much text. Objects that would not be very interesting if not for their relationship to Churchill. But by their isolated presence they underline what is now missing. Churchill himself. These simple objects are surrounded by an absent-metaphysical mystery. They give us a sense of presence by underlining the missing element. In

THE POWER OF THE OBJECT

this way, the objects play a decisive, emotional role in making the exhibition come alive. Not only do we hear his voice, see his photograph, play with his words and with the myths, read about his favourite dishes – the objects as relics make Churchill, the absent main character, real.

Not all objects serve this function. Some are there mainly as a setting to make the illustrations and texts three-dimensional. But there are hardly any objects exhibited purely from a technological perspective.

The story works because it is easily accessible. The subject is iconic – and is told with the help of iconic or highly personal characteristics. The use of objects gives the exhibition an emotional dimension. The many innovative ways of storing information and stimulating visitors to look for it make visitors interact with the exhibition. And finally visitors are invited to form an opinion on controversial aspects. In this way, Bruno Ingemann's four fields of experience – knowledge, emotion, values and action – all play their part. But you could also add the plot. The visitor is, right from the start, introduced to the dramatic, iconic peak of Churchill's career. The story continues with his afterlife as cold war statesman and goes on to his death. But it does not stop there. The exhibition proceeds to tell selected stories of Churchill's previous career as flashbacks to examine whether his reputation can withstand closer scrutiny.

In this way, conflict is used throughout the exhibition to drive the story forward. There is no mere background information. There are no superfluous sub-plots, no attempt to write the book.

The Children's War
But it is one thing to tell the story of an individual – and especially an individual of iconic status such as Churchill. Is it possible to tell the story of larger, less illustrious groups? Another exhibition from the Imperial War Museum, *The Children's War* gives an affirmative answer to this question. This exhibition is also very concrete. Children and parents alike can identify with the story of children during Word War II without any prior knowledge.

This exhibition also takes a very personal approach to the story of children in Britain during the war. Two stones in the introductory gallery make the exhibition look more like a place of remembrance for the victims of war than a place of learning: *Gravestone commemorating Violet Webb, aged five, who was killed in an air raid on Doncaster in May 1941, one of the 7,736 children who died as a result of enemy action during the war.*

And next to it: *Headstone for Raymond Steed, aged 14,*

the youngest boy to die on active service during the war. He served with the Merchant Navy as a galley boy and was killed when his ship hit a mine off the coast of North Africa on 26 April 1943. 3,597 boys under the age of 18 died on active service.

You do not, however, get any further information on the lives of Violet Webb or Raymond Steed. They are only there as representatives of thousands of others.

Also in the introductory gallery, photos of individuals show them alternately as children and grown-ups – the story is told as a recollection. It is not the curators who are telling the main story. The texts are mainly quotations from the participants themselves looking back. There are probably hundreds of individuals quoted in the exhibition. But as the quotations are allowed to speak for themselves, they create a single narrative. Many visitors will probably be able to relate the exhibition to the stories of their parents or grandparents.

In the second gallery – foreign evacuees arriving in England – the texts are again highly personal and concrete: *Once we arrived with the boat to Harwich and got out, we saw there was barbed wire on both sides of the gangway. I think they knew the war was approaching. And just outside there was a small shop that sold chocolates with a small placard in front of the window that said Gift Shop.*

And I got scared. Gift - which means poison in German. I thought, Oh my God, they are going to poison us after all! Gift became the very first word I learned in English.

The texts are accompanied by extensive use of contemporary photos – showing children's faces and bodies, often with strong expressions of emotion or striking features such as gas masks. And they are accompanied by objects, powerful objects like a worn teddy-bear or a doll's umbrella. Very personal objects.

They are not just nice stories of how well evacuees were treated. A photo of a group of children being picked up by locals at a station is accompanied by the following quotation: *If you were a child with glasses or with spots you were always left till the end.*

The texts underline the exhibition's atmosphere of being a place of remembrance. They invite elderly visitors to remember and retell their memories. Many museums would have preferred quotations from contemporary letters to be the dominant voice of the exhibition, giving it a more authoritative feel. But choosing memories told long after the events, gives the exhibition a special flow, makes it a narrative.

Of course, there are also quotations from contemporary documents: *The ship carrying your child/children to Canada was torpedoed on Tuesday night, 17 September. I am afraid that your child/children is/are not among those*

THE POWER OF THE OBJECT

reported rescued, and I am informed that there is no chance of there being any further survivors.

This text functions as an object. It is the voice of memories that constitute the main thread of the story.

The use of interactives is rather limited. You can try a game with ration coupons. Or try to recognise silhouettes of German and British planes – as well as estimating the number of planes in a formation. But this exhibition is not so much about action, more about emotion. So objects are more important than interaction. Objects as relics, lost or left behind, giving the impression that they were found during the search for a lost childhood. The exhibition is basically a mosaic of memories. Interactives and recreated interiors cannot tell the story as powerfully as voices, faces and children's possessions.

The final words of the exhibition are, therefore, not the conclusions of museum staff, but the reflections of one of the war children: *All the time I was evacuated I used to tell myself that one day the war would be over and I could go back home. After the war... I made my way back to where I used to live. The whole area had been obliterated during... the Blits and I was quite unable to find the spot where our house once stood. That happened more than 50 years ago ... but somehow I am still waiting to go home.*

The exhibition, then, is very much a journey. Told

by the children who had to leave their homes because of the war. A story of their trials and tribulations – and of their homecoming. The many voices melt together into one – the subject of the story that is trying to carve out a childhood after all.

D-Day
The third and final exhibition from London that I am going to refer to is also from the Imperial War Museum. It is an exhibition on *D-Day*. It also takes an individual perspective, as it sets out to describe the complexity of the operation – and how it unfolded. This is done by going through the entire organisation of the operation, personalising every unit by focusing on individuals.

As mentioned above, one of the main strengths of the movie compared to the academic discourse is that it is so concrete. There are no abstract concepts, only individuals that you can relate to. And this exhibition very much looks like an attempt to adapt the same approach. It is very concrete. Every unit of the operation is represented by a real individual. You see their photos, read their names and their careers – and usually you can see some objects connected to them. The organisation of the operation is personalised – not hidden behind military titles and organisational diagrams.

But it does not work. Because it fails in some of the

other important parts of scripting the exhibition. First of all, there is no subject. In *The Children's War* and the *Churchill* exhibition you went on a journey with a subject. And you reflected on the changes to the subject that had taken place during that journey at the end of the exhibition. But here there is no single subject – just an endless list of actors. They are introduced – and then disappear from the story immediately afterwards. So you never engage in the destiny of the individuals.

Secondly, it never quite succeeds in personalising the stories. The individuals seem to be there as illustrations to the academic, encyclopedical texts. It is not the lived experiences of the individuals which are central.

In the introduction, the very first section is on *Ultra and Deception*. Under the headline, the visitors are faced with a long, didactic text: *German forces used Enigma encrypting machines which they believed made their wireless messages impossible to decipher. From May 1940 British Intelligence staff in a secret establishment at Bletchley Park in Buckinghamshire began to decode these messages, and intelligence reports, code-name ULTRA, were passed to senior Allied Commanders. In 1943 a deception plan, codenamed BODYGUARD, was devised by the invasion planners. It consisted of two parts, Fortitude North encouraged the Germans to believe that a joint British-Russian-American attack might be made in Scandinavia. Fortitude South convinced the Germans that the main invasion would be in the Pas de Calais. Dummy tanks and vehicles, fake radio-traffic emanating from FUSAG, an imaginary US Army Group in Britain, together with false information sent via a double-agent, were used to complete the deception. ULTRA reports helped the Allies to assess whether the deception plan was working.*

You have to read your way through all of this, before you are introduced to the individual: *One of the people involved in the Allied deception plans was a Spanish-born double-agent called Juan Pujol Garcia. He was code-named Garbo by the British Authorities. Based in London, he had offered to work for the German secret service in 1941 and began sending them fictitious reports. He was then recruited by MI5 staff and together they invented a network of agents who were supposedly supplying him with information. He transmitted messages to the Germans, giving false details about the British War effort and preparation for D-Day. His messages leading up to D-Day itself and beyond helped to convince the Germans that the invasion of Normandy was merely a decoy for a major assault further along the coast near Calais. Believing the information from Garbo and other sources, the German reinforced the area they were told would come under attack and held their armoured divisions in reserve.*

THE POWER OF THE OBJECT

No doubt, it is a most interesting story. But it does not work. There is far too much text – and it is written from the omniscient, didactic position of a curator. The attempt to personalise the story by introducing Garcia fails, because we never get close to him. We do not hear the story in his words – we do not hear of his doings or feelings at a concrete level.

The technique of telling about intelligence in the *Churchill* exhibition was completely different. Here, the curators started out with a Churchill quotation to catch the attention of the visitor. And it was followed by a very short text capturing the essential message, before an interactive installation enables the visitor to search for information himself. In fact, there is much more information on intelligence in the *Churchill* exhibition than in the *D-Day* exhibition. But it is presented so that you do not feel you are reading a book while standing on your increasingly tired legs.

The story of Garcia and intelligence is just one of about 50 similar stories. They do not drive the main story forward. In most cases you get a description of the individual's military career before and sometimes after D-Day; and quite often this career-information is given more weight than the person's activities in the D-Day operation.

There are quotations where you can hear the words

of the actors themselves. One such is the ambulance driver, Monica Littleboy. A quotation from her journal finally gets down to the concrete level of lived experience – with all the pain and emotion of the operation: *One was unconscious, the other had a fractured skull and a badly cut face. Both shot-up naval casualties. But never am I to forget the pathetic dased expression on the face of the conscious one. He was very young, only a boy, but the look of bewilderment and suffering was too awful in one so young.*

But whereas the Churchill museum tried to attract the attention of the visitors with quotations, this one is in small print at the end of an introductory text on ambulance drivers and their tasks. Somehow the voice of Monica Littleboy is drowned by the voice of the curators.

The same applies to the objects. They are usually exhibited in exhibition cases with between 5 and 20 objects in each. Objects that might have been able to catch the attention or imagination of the visitor disappear in the crowd. And that is a real pity, because there are many interesting objects.

Eisenhower is introduced as one of the decision-makers. The text presents his entire military career – and tells us he became president of the USA. There is no focus on D-Day in the text. In the exhibition case beneath, there are a number of documents. One of them is a handwritten draft for the speech that Eisenhower would have given if the operation had failed. Some visitors – perhaps most visitors – will never notice, as there is nothing spectacular or eye-catching about it. Just imagine if this draft had been used as the introduction to the story on decision-makers, instead of the long biographical text that you could read in any encyclopedia. The possibility of failure was real – and that was what the decision-makers had to deal with. I cannot think of a better way to introduce the story of the entire operation. Through this object it would be possible to introduce the conflict – the possibility of failure – right in the centre of attention.

The draft itself has no visual power. But other objects are spectacular and draw the attention of the visitor to them. Like the dress and bag that Yvonne Cormeau was carrying when she was shot – you can actually see the blood-stains on the bag. But the bag and dress as well as her story are drowned in a big exhibition case on *Behind Enemy Lines* with many other objects and stories. You never get close to the event or the person. We are told that she sent 400 messages during the war and afterwards was awarded the OBE and a French decoration.

In fact, in this exhibition the objects lose their power. The uniform did not even belong to Monica Littleboy. And it turns out that other exhibits are only similar to those used, not the ones really used. And once you have discovered that, a certain distance to the objects and the individuals is created.

The exhibition is somehow a long list of biographies, or tributes to selected individuals, as it carefully lists their entire careers. The exhibition fails to use the operation as a kind of waterhole, where all the actors of the war come out and meet. There is no conflict, no plot, no subject to the story, no drive – and no flow-experience. It operates entirely within the field of knowledge, emotion, values and action seem to be absent.

Of course, the *Churchill* exhibition had an outstanding subject. *The Children's War* exhibition created one – as the many voices of remembrance blended together into one. In *D-Day* you have some 50 voices speaking at the same time and level – without a focus on D-Day. As a result, it is very difficult to keep them separate and give them attention. The *D-Day* exhibition arguably has the best conflict – the delicate line between success and failure – but it fails to use it to create a plot. It fails to address the exhibition as a visual medium, closer to the movie than the book. There is no journey, no trial, no transformation. Although it tries to use individuals as a storytelling device, it remains very abstract.

The Royal Danish Arsenal Museum

How, then, should the Royal Danish Arsenal Museum present the story of Denmark and World War II? There are four major challenges. Firstly, Denmark's special situation in World War II, as Denmark was not technically at war. Secondly, this special situation has very much become a political issue of late. Thirdly, the museum's visitors rightly expect to see at the museum actually give an impression of Denmark being an active, warring nation. And fourthly, the presentation has to be fitted into a room of only 18 square metres.

To look at the first challenge first, Denmark's policy at the outbreak of World War II was to stay neutral, just as Denmark had succeeded in doing in World War I. In March 1940, however, Denmark was included in German plans for an attack on Norway, and on April 9th German troops invaded Denmark. As the Germans threatened to bombard Copenhagen – and at the same time stressed that they had only come to protect Denmark – the Danish Government decided to keep the Germans to their word. They protested against the violation of Danish neutrality, stopped the military resistance – and stayed in power to avoid either the Germans themselves or the tiny Danish Nazi party taking over government. Thus Denmark was in a peculiar situation of being a neutral state "protected" by German troops right up to August 1943, when German demands for a military curfew following riots throughout the country made the government resign.

So it is difficult to speak of Denmark as a participant in World War II. As a state, Denmark was not at war. But Danish territory was occupied – the Atlantic possessions by the British, and the Danish ambassador in USA handed over Greenland to the Americans. As for Danish people, thousands of Danish seamen sailed for the allies, and a number went into allied service. On the other hand, about 6,000 Danes were recruited for German service on the Eastern Front and thousands of Danes worked for German industry. And during the occupation, a resistance movement started to grow (particularly after 1943) – amounting to several thousands at the end of the war.

As for the second challenge, ever since the war, the debate about the government's decision to stay on rather than put up a fight against the Germans has been intense. Especially in recent years, the Danish Prime Minister, Anders Fogh Rasmussen has condemned the politicians in 1940, comparing Denmark's participation in the war on terror in Iraq and Afghanistan to the situation in 1940, when Denmark according to the Prime

THE POWER OF THE OBJECT

Minister ought to have joined the alliance against the evil forces – even though it is debatable whether such an alliance can be said to have existed in 1940. The interpretation of Danish World War II history has therefore become a political issue of current interest.

Another contentious element is the Danish government's decision in 1941 to pass an anti-communist law - on German demand - and consequently arrest leading Danish communists, making the communists a predominant group in the early phases of the resistance. Finally, the large number of Danes serving in the German army and the fact that Danish industry supplied the Germans have also been controversial subjects.

So whenever the story of Denmark and World War II is told, it generates a lot of controversy anout where the focus should be. Or to return to the vocabulary of filmmaking – who is the subject of the story? Who are the villains – apart from the Germans? The Government? The Danish volunteers in German service? Danish industry? Danish communists? The vast majority of the Danish population, who as late as March 1943 gave the Government a vote of confidence at a general election with a massive turnout?

Moving on to the third challenge, if we look at the objects that people would expect to see in an exhibition at the Royal Danish Arsenal Museum, a destroyed field cannon from the sparse fighting in Haderslev in Southern Jutland on April 9th is an almost iconic object. There are famous photos of it, and with its damaged barrel and bullet-holes in the shield it is, indeed, a dramatic object. Together with tombstones, originally erected where Danish soldiers fell during the fighting, a bullet-pierced helmet and other equipment, the cannon makes the documentation of the fighting quite overwhelming. These objects were handed over to the museum during the summer and autumn of 1940, the cannon accompanied with a specific request on how it should be exhibited to prove to the Danish people, that the Danish army was, in fact, prepared to take up the fight against all the odds and did so at a cost, until the Danish government interfered.

The problem of using a large part of the very limited exhibition space to display these items is, of course, that it will give a completely distorted impression of Danish military action. And that leads us to the fourth and final challenge – the limited exhibition space. The exhibition concept involves three separate elements. First, a chronological presentation of wars in Denmark from 1500 to the present-day; second, a presentation of the museum's central collections and the story behind their origin and life; and third, three thematic exhibitions on the agents, the tools and the landscape of war.

The idea behind the chronological presentation is to measure out 500 years of war, using the 160 metre-long room as a gigantic timeline – with about four wars in each century. This puts the identity-shaping wars of 1657-60, 1864 and 1940-45 into perspective. They take up a disproportionate amount of space in Danish national identity, so the trick is to give all wars the same amount of space and so challenge this identity. But the cost is that it only leaves 18 square metres for each war, including World War II!

The search for an answer
Considering the lively debate on controversial issues and the frequent accusations of the suppression of information whenever the war is discussed, it would be tempting to give a balanced account of all aspects of World War II. But if so, you are quickly dragged into an academic discourse, far removed from objects. To avoid this, I decided to go through the museum's accession register from 1939 to 1950 to find the objects best able to tell the different parts of the story on their own. I discovered, that the records actually reflected some of the main twists and turns of the war.

The first entry after the German occupation on April 9th 1940 was a German submachine gun bought from a Danish lawyer. That set the scene for a story of its own. It was quickly followed by other reflections of the war. As weapons in private possession in June 1940 had to be handed over to the police, people started to hand over their weapons to the museum. A safe haven in the middle of war.

Then came the first glimpse of the war outside Denmark. In the early months of 1940 about 1,000 Danes had volunteered for the Finnish army to fight the communist Soviet Union. As Finland accepted Soviet peace conditions in March, the volunteers hardly saw any service before returning to Denmark, hugely disappointed. Some of them handed over their uniforms to the museum. At least one of them, a Danish lieutenant, volunteered to go to Finland again a year later, as the Germans encouraged the Danes to join in the war against the Soviet Union. This time, he died after a few days' service.

The story of the Danish volunteers in Finland in many ways encapsulates how the character of the war was changing. In winter 1940, Danes volunteered to fight for a fellow small Scandinavian country, attacked by the aggressive, totalitarian Soviet Union. In summer 1941, the Danish Volunteers fought the same war – this time, though, along with the German Nazis. A shift that made both the Soviet Union and the Danish Communists appear in a different light to many.

THE POWER OF THE OBJECT

As I went through the records, I realised that the war years were in fact a boom time for the museum. Confiscated weapons. Weapons handed over by private collectors – probably to save them. A famous collection of Russian uniforms of the exiled Russian general Leukowitch (living in Paris since 1917) was given to the museum in 1942 – and with great difficulty transported from Paris via Switzerland to Copenhagen in 1943. Private memorabilia were handed in by individuals – just as the objects from the fighting on April 9th 1940 can be seen as institutional memorabilia. As expressions of a desire to preserve and communicate an individual perspective on the war – reflecting the ongoing debate about the war. Historic, military collections were also handed over to the museum by the Army, especially after the resignation of the Government in 1943 and the dissolution of the Danish army.

At the end of the war, of course, the number of weapons in the accession register multiplies. The country had to be disarmed. The museum was offered thousands of weapons from the allied forces in the country and the police – as well as from German depots. The resistance brought in trophies such as the German Commander Lindemann's jacket, taken at his arrest. Allied forces brought a Danish monument commemorating a victory against German forces at Isted in 1850 (a gigantic lion!) to Copenhagen, after the Germans in 1864 themselves had taken it as a trophy and brought it to Berlin. It is still outside the museum. Finally, there were also weapons and uniforms confiscated from Germans living in Denmark under the law on the Confiscation of German and Japanese Property which was intended to leave Germans with only a minimum of possessions.

World War II memorabilia continue to be given to the museum. Personal belongings from members of the resistance, from allied servicemen – and from German servicemen. In 1969 for instance, a Danish SS-officer handed in a complete set of uniforms and equipment as well as the chest he had carried with him to the eastern front. His family recently handed over his military orders and personal belongings after his death.

On reflection, it is interesting to note that the many trophies and memorabilia of war have no place in the present exhibition. For example, although the Haderslev cannon was accompanied by the wish of presenting it as a monument over the Danish Army, the curators at the museum had their own project – to show the evolution of weapons. It shows in the information that the curators bothered to register; and it shows in the collection of a German 38 cm Naval Gun that at the end of the war was about to be installed in the German fortification of Jutland. At great pains, the gun was brought to Copenhagen and until recently exhibited outside the museum. To the museum, it was more important to show the biggest cannon than to engage in the discourse on Denmark and World War II.

The files of the museum during the occupation period complement the objects, giving concrete glimpses of life during the war. To name just three examples: in 1943 a request (which was granted!) for tobacco of the highest quality to be given to the Russian General Leukowitch when he arrived with his collection of uniforms. A report on the German soldiers taking control of the museum on August 29th 1943 as the Danish army was dissolved and the government resigned. A German officer had orders to place anti-aircraft guns on top of the roof of the giant Arsenal building which dates from 1604. But as he was being shown round the building, he expressed his interest in history – and decided to spare the building from the risk of becoming a military target. Finally, in 1944, an armed group of 30 members of the resistance raided the museum for guns.

The Royal Danish Arsenal Museum – the solution

As the search through accession records and files at the museum unfolded a mini-cosmos of Denmark in World War II, the obvious step to take was to make the museum the subject of the story: *The World Explodes – The Museum Expands*. The World War seen through the records and files of a military museum.

Briefly, the story is this: the museum has a vision – to become the greatest collection of weapons in the world. As war breaks out, an entirely new field of risks and possibilities opens up. The museum becomes attractive as a place to store weapons, as a safe haven – and there are many more and more exciting weapons in circulation. On the other hand, the museum risks being targeted – by the resistance, the Germans, the allies, the politicians and the public. At the same time, the museum is caught up in the historic struggle. People hand in their different stories and expect the museum to tell them; the museum tries to maintain a purely technological perspective.

In this way, the exhibition becomes a meta-history. The Haderslev cannon, the tombstones and the bullet-pierced helmet are not displayed to illustrate the events of April 9th 1940. They are exhibited with the accession record – and the letter from the captain stating his wishes for how the museum should present it. The "voice" of the exhibiton is constructed by the contemporary documents, the reports from the museum and the letters from the donors.

Of course, there has to be some curatorial text to

THE POWER OF THE OBJECT

set the scene. As well as a brief binding it all together – events in the worldwide war, events in Denmark, and events in the museum. And some factual information has to be added: the Danish officer who volunteered for the two wars in Finland, and was killed in the second. But basically, the objects, their story and the importance attributed to them by their owners carry the story. And it is not just the memorabilia. The exhibition will also include a selection of the thousands of objects from military collections as a more general reflection on events.

There are many advantages to this strategy. It is not prone to be caught up in political debate. It will be very difficult to argue politically against the display of a SS-uniform, as the exhibition is not about the importance of the Danish contribution to World War II but the growth of the museum. In the same way, it will be difficult to complain that the museum does not give enough information about Danish industries cooperating with the Germans, because such cooperation is not reflected in the accessions. The exhibition does not aim to give a complete, well-balanced overview of Denmark in the war.

On its website, the museum can guide the interested visitors to literature which will give them such an overview. But the exhibition itself must focus on its own story. With a clear subject. With the objects as the central element. With a storyline which unfolds but is introduced at the start – and concluded at the end - of each section.

We have attempted to do this in 22 stories on Danish wars since 1500. The stories differ – and they should differ, since they reflect the objects and characteristics of the different wars. The section on World War II is special, as it is the only meta-history of its kind. Some people may argue that it is too insular an approach to focus on the history of the museum in the context of the millions of war victims worldwide. But apart from the obvious difficulties of presenting the story of the entire world war within 18 square metres, the exhibition is about how war has played its part in shaping Denmark, not how it has affected other parts of the world.

A focus group of youngsters (17-19 years of age) were very positive in their reception of a draft for the story for *The World Explodes – The Museum Expands*. They had expected to hear the same old story as in the classroom. This was quite different. They could read the story first-hand in the documents and through these come closer to the objects. It became concrete and relevant. It made the past present in a different way and raised a lot of questions. And that, I think, is what we should strive for when using the exhibition as a medium. Only

THE POWER OF THE OBJECT

then can we exploit the power of the objects – instead of merely using them as illustrations in a book we have written beforehand.

MUSEUMS AND WORLD WAR II

5

The Breendonk Memorial

PATRICK NEFORS

Head of Scientific Activities and Publications,
Musée Royal de l'Armée, Bruxelles

The day of 6 May 2003 was a happy one for the National Memorial of Fort Breendonk, one of Belgium's most famous Second World War sites – if, of course, the word "happy" can ever be appropriate when speaking of a place infamous for the gruesome events that took place there. King Albert II, Patrick Dewael, Prime Minister of Flanders and André Flahaut, national Defence Minister, were all present at the inauguration of the renovated National Memorial.[1] The following day, the newspapers were almost unanimously positive and visitor numbers were up; there was some minor criticism, however, in certain quarters, notably among some former prisoners, though others were full of praise.

This paper will focus on the philosophy of the old museum, as well as that of the renovated one, and try to explain the political contexts in which both were conceived. I must immediately declare an interest here, as one of the principal members of the small team in charge of the renovation project. The pages that follow will try to provide an answer to the questions: Who conceived the museology of the "old" Breendonk, and in what circumstances? How did we go about creating the "new" Breendonk? Were there any external pressures, political or other? Did our predecessors, did we, or did the authorities that financed the renovation – in this case the Belgian Defence Ministry – have an ideo-

THE POWER OF THE OBJECT

logical or other agenda? Why did we display almost no objects?

A short overview of the history of Breendonk is necessary to provide the historical context.

Fort Breendonk, 1914-1945[2]

Breendonk is an old Belgian Army fort, built between 1906 and 1914 as part of the second circle of forts around Antwerp, Belgium's most important port and the city that was intended to serve as a National Redoubt in case of war. The Army and Government would fall back to Antwerp, safely protected by its mighty fortifications, and wait there for the assistance of the countries that had guaranteed the country's independence and neutrality. That was the theory. In reality, German heavy artillery quickly reduced Belgian illusions to rubble as early as October 1914. Fort Breendonk surrendered in ten days. It was damaged, not too heavily, but damaged nevertheless. Today, one can still see the impact of the bombardment; cracks and fissures appeared in the concrete, contributing to a humidity problem – an element we had to take into account during renovation.

Between the wars the fort partly fell into disuse, though towards the end of the Thirties it was chosen to become the General Headquarters of the Belgian Army in case of war. The second German invasion, on 10 May 1940, transformed this relic of the Great War overnight into King Leopold III's buzzing headquarters, from where he directed military operations against the Nazi invader. He had, however, to leave the fort after only seven days, due to the rapidity of the German advance. Subsequently, the fort again stood empty until September 1940, when it became an SS *Auffanglager*. There are very few contemporary records on the birth of the Breendonk camp, but it is clear that the *Sicherheitzpolizei-Sicherheitzdienst*, recently installed in Belgium, wanted a camp for its "own" prisoners, and that the Military Government or *Militärverwaltung*, headed by *Militärbefehlshaber von Falkenhausen* and *Militärverwaltungschef* Eggert Reeder, put the old fort at its disposal for these purposes.

The military authorities would always be the nominal superiors of the SS commander of Breendonk, though in reality their impact was rather limited. They put a stop to the worst excesses in the middle of 1941, when a series of prisoners died of the lethal mix of malnutrition, forced labour and beatings, but in other instances simply looked the other way or winked at atrocities. The forced labour that prisoners were compelled to undertake consisted of "uncovering" the fort. The prisoners had to remove its protective earth layer with no equipment beyond shovels, wheelbarrows, and carts.

THE POWER OF THE OBJECT

In September 1941 Breendonk became a *Durchgangslager*: from then on prisoners would regularly be deported to the big concentration camps in the Reich. Jews made up about half the prisoners in 1940-1941, but very few were left in Breendonk after 1942, when they were transferred to the Dossin Barracks, the Belgian Drancy, from where they would be deported to Auschwitz. From June 1941 onwards, when, in the wake of Operation Barbarossa, the Germans arrested as many Belgian communists as they could lay their hands on, political prisoners would make up the majority of the Breendonk population. As the war ran to its close, more and more Belgian resistance fighters, some famous ones amongst them, would end up in Breendonk.

In order to interrogate them, a torture chamber was specially constructed in the middle of 1942; and towards the end of that year a place of execution was created where, upon the orders of the Military Government, 164 Breendonk prisoners were executed by way of reprisal for resistance attacks and 21 or 25 were hanged for resistance activities punishable by death. In total between 3,500 and 4,000 people passed through Breendonk, two thirds of them deportees. One in two prisoners would not live to see the end of the war, most of them dying far from their homes and loved ones. In Breendonk itself 84 prisoners died as a result of prison conditions (hard labour, violence, lack of food).

The camp was evacuated on the eve of the country's liberation. British tanks, dashing for the important Antwerp Port, rolled past it on 3 September 1944. Breendonk now became a prison again, serving as an internment centre for people suspected of collaboration with the Germans. At first, this happened without official authority, as the fort was in the hands of the local resistance. It was a time during which some excesses took place, and suspects were beaten or humiliated (though it seems that only one died, a case of suicide). After six weeks, the Belgian State finally put a stop to this. In 1945-1946 the fort became an official internment centre, and prison conditions reverted to normality. The internment centre – especially the first, unofficial one – would be called *Breendonk II* by former collaborators. It would become part of their *dark legend* of a severe and deliberately "anti-Flemish" postwar "repression" of the collaboration. It remained a symbol of their neverrelenting rancour against the Belgian state, just as Breendonk "I" would always be seen as a patriotic memorial to Belgian resistance and suffering during the Nazi Occupation.

The memorial before renovation
The National Memorial of the Fort of Breendonk was

created in August 1947 by an Act of the Belgian Parliament. Yet, Breendonk had already formed part of the Belgian patriotic memory of the Second World War before then. The fort was well-known in Belgium because former prisoners started to write their memoirs – the earliest had already been published in the first months after the liberation – and because of press coverage of the 1946 trial of the Belgian SS guards of the camp (who were almost all of Flemish origin). The former prisoners had created the *Association Nationale des Rescapés de Breendonk* and held an annual ceremony – a so-called pilgrimage – in the camp where they had suffered. Until the end of 1946 this had to take place in an internment centre, much to the chagrin of former political prisoners, who deplored the fact that tourists came to the pilgrimage to see the interned collaboration suspects.

When the internment centre was finally abolished, former prisoner and Socialist deputy Gaston Hoyaux introduced a bill designed to turn Breendonk into a National Memorial, for commemorative purposes only. Any reading of Hoyaux's speeches, of the law of August 1947, or of the speeches of the first president and the first curator of the Memorial, picks up a clear message: Breendonk has a definite part to play in conserving the patriotic memory of the war. The law of 1947 stipulates that: *the Memorial must take all useful steps to ensure that the memory of Fort Breendonk and the events that took place there, remain alive in the spirit of the Nation, stimulate its sense of public responsibility and favour the patriotic education of young people.* [3] The people responsible for the Memorial would act in this frame of mind.

During the first year-and-a-half of its existence, a power struggle took place between Communist and anti-Communist members of the Board of Trustees (the latter mainly Liberals and Catholics), with the anti-Communists eventually gaining the upper hand. The outcome of this struggle ensured the victory of the patriotic perspective [4] – liberty-loving Belgians of all regions and classes struggling side-by-side against the Nazi German invader – over the Communist perspective on the war. This, in its turn, would influence the way the story of the Auffanglager and its prisoners would be presented in the Memorial.

Since the patriotic perspective stresses the unity of all Belgians in their struggle against the German Nazi invaders, there was no desire to dwell on the all-too-real differences between different groups of prisoners or the resistance movements they had belonged to. Therefore, the diversity of the camp population would not be brought to the fore: a diversity in terms of race (Jews and gentiles), gender (women were only a small minority), cause of arrest (because of anti-Jewish measures; as a hostage; because of an anti-German or anti-Fascist attitude; or because of resistance activities – which themselves might vary from the amateurish to the professional) or political opinion (ranging from conservative and royalist to Stalinist).

The patriotic perspective deliberately drew a veil over political tensions between left-wing and right-wing resistance movements. Furthermore, it did not draw attention to the fact that Jewish prisoners constituted half of all prisoners in the first year. In general, as is well known, little attention was given to the fate of specifically Jewish prisoners in the first decades after the war, when collective memory was still shaped by the survivors, rather than by the dead. Now, of course, this trend is reversed, and it is the ever-dwindling legion of former political prisoners that has to struggle to have its story heard.

The story of the camp personnel was only to be told in that section of the museum devoted to the post-war trials of the so-called "Breendonk henchmen", the SS men or other camp personnel of Flemish origin, showing through posters of the verdict the just fate suffered by these Nazi collaborators.

The creation of the old museum in the fort and its presentation was largely the work of one former prisoner, the first curator (1948-1949), vice-president and ultimately president of the Board of Trustees from 1979 to 1997, Paul M. G. Lévy, a social scientist and journalist of Jewish origin who married a Christian and converted to Christianity in 1940, and after the war described himself as a "Christian socialist without a party". With the seal of the convert, he was convinced religion had its place in the Memorial. Religion would show its influence mainly in the attention devoted to the memory of Monsignor Gramann, the chief *Wehrmacht* chaplain in Belgium, a man of Austrian origin who had assisted the condemned prisoners in their last hour before execution. The room that had served as the workshop and storeroom of the camp tailors, was transformed into something akin to a chapel, with an altar in honour of Mgr Gramann. Lévy had formed a friendship with Gramann after the war, and Gramann himself had remained very attached to "his" Belgian victims. Yet, whatever human qualities the Monsignor might have had – and nobody ever commented adversely on these – his political profile was more ambiguous. In a letter of 10 July 1941, for instance – when the *Wehrmacht* was crushing the Soviet armies – he expressed the hope that "this victorious war" would soon reach its conclusion...

The story of life in the camp was told in the prisoners' rooms – in fact the same rooms in which the soldiers of 1914 stayed, though of course in very different circumstances and conditions – and partly also in the adjoining museum rooms, which date from 1955. At five key points of the visitor's tour (the entrance gate, one prisoner room, the torture chamber, the place of execution, and the cells for solitary confinement), essential information about life in the camp was given through a primitive audio system: one had to push a red button and the voice of a former prisoner gave some essential information (in French this was the impressive baritone of Paul Lévy himself, but one had the choice between Dutch, French, English and German). The texts were well written. Lévy was a brilliant journalist who was not lacking in literary flair. In other places, visitors had to make do with a small map of the fort, with essential information about those places open to the public.

Guided tours had, of course, always been available, though the quality of the guides could vary. In the past, one could easily find a former prisoner acting as a guide, which would provide a very interesting and often emotional experience, though of course not always a historically accurate account. Some of them were very good witnesses, but naturally they all tended to see Breendonk through the prism of their own experience and background.

Places that the Directors and Board of Trustees considered of no historical interest were closed off and inaccessible to the public. Such areas included the stables, the workplaces and the new latrines, which were built during the Occupation.

Renovation

When, at the end of the Nineties, the Board of Trustees started thinking about renovation, visitor numbers had fallen from the peak of almost 110,000 in 1949 to about 40,000 in 1983, rising again in 1984-85 (the 40th anniversary of Liberation), but never again reaching their post-war peak. The audio-system, innovative when first installed, by then seemed old-fashioned; a number of rooms suffered from humidity; reliable guides were ever harder to find; and the museum rooms looked decidedly musty. Under the forceful and charismatic stewardship of a new president, Roger Coekelbergs (a former Breendonk prisoner and Emeritus Professor of Chemistry at the Royal Military Academy),[5] renovation was decided upon. Coekelbergs found a willing sponsor in the person of the then Defence Minister, André Flahaut, a Walloon Socialist who never ceased to stress the "duty to remember" (*le devoir de mémoire*). (One of the first acts of his successor, the Flemish Catholic Pieter De Crem, by contrast, was to no longer put army buses at the disposal of a Buchenwald visit by school children and former political prisoners).

As a scientist, Coekelbergs understood that the renovation had to be based upon thorough historical research, which, until then, had been severely lacking. The only synthesis of the Fort's history published since the war was a small book by Paul Lévy.[6] It was, as was to be expected, well-written but remained – as Lévy himself acknowledged – essentially the view of a single witness. As major sources in Belgium, Germany and elsewhere lay dormant and unexploited, a new history of the fort was an essential condition if the renovation was to be historically accurate and in tune with the latest research. Coekelbergs entrusted me with writing this new history.

The "presentation" side of things, the museological part of the renovation, was entrusted to the well-known and experienced Paul Vandebotermet, who had masterminded, among other things, the renovation of the Dossin Barracks in Mechelen (which tell the tale of the fate of Belgium's Jews during the Second World War) and the Gulbenkian Museum, and who afterwards also became the exhibition curator of the Belgian Pavilion in Auschwitz. Paul and I were immediately on the same wavelength and devised the script for the "new" Breendonk in close consultation with one another. Together, we made the following choices:

1. To open up to the public as many places as possible; they all had a human interest story to tell.

2. To devote an important place to the hitherto unused photo collection of the German propaganda photographer Otto Kropf,[7] which contains the only known images of the Breendonk *Auffanglager* during the war (they were taken over a couple of days in 1941). Three giant enlargements were produced, two to be placed in the inner courtyards (one showing the daily roll call, and one showing what the structure looked like in 1941) and one behind the fort (showing the prisoners slaving at hard labour under German surveillance), and smaller reproductions were placed elsewhere. These photographs – and especially the one showing the prisoners performing forced labour, digging up and transporting the earth that covered the Fort – allow visitors to visualise the fort and its inhabitants in 1941.

3. To restore the Memorial's confessional neutrality. As a consequence of this, the altar of Mgr Gramann was to disappear, as it was almost unanimously considered, by Catholics as well as others, to impair such neutrality. The room in which it was placed, which served as a tailors' workshop during a part of the war, would be dedicated to the memory of the Jewish tailors' families who had worked there, as well as showing photographs

of the uniforms of the concentration camps to which inmates of Breendonk were deported.

4. To concentrate all commemorative aspects in one room, the so-called Room of the Names, where the names of all known prisoners were written on the wall. The different urns with ashes of deported prisoners that had died in he concentration camps, were replaced by new, uniform ones and transferred from the former tailors' workshop (the Gramann Room) to this Room of the Names. The ashes were transferred by an undertaker, from one set of urns to another, after approval of this decision by the Board of Trustees, on which the local mayor has a seat.

5. To simply show the historical facts about what happened at the Breendonk Auffanglager as truthfully and impartially as possible, without lecturing or patronising the visitor, whom we judged to be sufficiently intelligent to draw his or her own conclusions.

6. On the presentational level, to tell the story in a sober fashion, just as had been the case in the Dossin Barracks, one of Paul's earlier realisations. We thought this the best way of respecting the historical site and its tragic history. This basic option did not preclude the use of modern audio-visual media, but it would be discreetly done. The story of the prisoner's life in Breendonk would be told by audio-guides,[8] photographs (by

Kropf and others) and oral and visual testimonies.[9]

7. To let the storyline be dominant. This is an important principle: you decide first which story to tell and where to tell it. All objects or audio-visual material would be chosen to illustrate and support the storyline, and not the other way round.

8. To tell the story of life in the Auffanglager, of what it meant to be a prisoner in Breendonk, during the tour of the site, and only there. In the past, certain aspects of the prisoner's life were also treated in certain sections of the old Museum, which was rather illogically situated in the middle of the visitor's tour.

9. To tell, in what had been the SS office in 1940-1941 (in the first half of the visitor's tour), the story of the most important members of the German and Belgian camp personnel, not limiting the story to their trial, but retracing their origins and their lives before the camp. This was possible through a study both of the archives of Belgian Military Justice and of the SS files kept in the *Bundesarchiv Berlin-Lichterfelde*. We emphatically did not start from the idea, popular with certain academics of Flemish origin (some of whom are the descendants of collaborators), that a repetition of events such as happened in Breendonk can only be averted through a study of the perpetrator's innermost feelings and motives. Defenders of this, in my view – in so far

as it is sincere – naive idea, most often assume that in comparable circumstances anyone could have behaved in the same manner as the perpetrators.[10]

10. To do away with the contents of the old museum rooms in their entirety. This old museum outlined the history of the fort in 1914, showed the rise of Nazism, told the story of Breendonk in 1940-44 and of the creation of the National Memorial. We wanted to concentrate on the story of the *Auffanglager* and therefore, unlike the old museum, the new museum would not cover the events of 1914 or of May 1940; these would instead be outlined in a introductory film at the start of the visitor's tour. We did not feel the need to devote space to the rise of Nazism, as this subject was well covered by the *Between the Wars* exhibition in the Royal Military Museum.

11. To place the four new museum rooms at the end of the tour and devote them to the following topics.

In the first room to show what kind of people the prisoners were to visitors who, unlike their parents or grandparents, have no knowledge of the war. Since there were more than 3,500 prisoners in total, we did this through a selection of twenty-one representative prisoners; representative that is, in terms of political affiliation or racial or regional origin, as the choice admittedly, and perhaps inevitably, was weighted in favour of the more famous prisoners, such as Maxime Vanpraag, fourth consecutive leader of Zéro, one of Belgium's biggest intelligence networks. A portrait and essential information were provided about each one of these prisoners and the resistance movements or intelligence networks they belonged to. To show some examples of "bystanders" as well, people who lived in the neighbourhood of the camp or were connected to it, such as the old woman who looked out on the camp from her window; the German photographer Otto Kropf; and of course the mayor of Breendonk, a Germanophile brewer, member of the collaborationist VNV party, who in 1940 advertised his beer in the VNV paper with the motto *one people, one state, one beer* (sic)...

In the second room: to show in a condensed and easily accessible way the whole apparatus of German repression in Belgium (prisons, transit camps, torture chambers, places of execution) as well as the ulterior (and sometimes final) destination of prisoners transported out of Breendonk to the major concentration camps. Photographs of camps, prisons, as well as maps of Belgium and Europe locating these, were displayed, and small portraits of the prisoners talked about in the first room were placed next to the camp they ended up in. We also devoted some historical (rather than religious) attention to the figure of Monsignor Gramann, who was a witness to so many executions.

In the third room: to tell the story of the site after Liberation, briefly mentioning, and historically contextualising, the abuses of the period immediately following Liberation. We also devoted some space to issues of "memory" (the Memorial, writers and artists on Breendonk) and retribution (the post-war trials of the Breendonk war criminals).

At the very end of the tour, in the fourth and last museum room, a film, commissioned by the Ministry of Defence, was shown. This film was to convey "the message of Breendonk". Coekelberg shared the desire to show such a film. The problem, however, would be in the execution: though in all other cases we were left to do the job as we saw fit, in this case the Memorial was faced with a direct order by an overzealous collaborator of the Minister who liked to throw his weight around and who, with one of his cronies, dictated the content as well as the style of the film. The result of his intervention was a film that showed men and women waiting for a bus in a bus shelter while the rain poured down outside. These people were of different origin, elderly whites mixed with coloured youngsters. The elderly whites were initially clearly distrustful of the coloured youngsters, but at the end they all became friends, and – rejoice, rejoice! – it suddenly stopped raining.... Alas, few visitors understood the film. Why it had to be shown at Breendonk also eluded comprehension. Some people even thought it was a publicity film sponsored by Belgium's official bus companies. Moreover, the film was costly, running to about 25,000 Euro. It was shown at the opening, but was then discreetly replaced by another film on human rights. It was the only place in which mention was made of the "message" of Breendonk; in all other instances, we simply showed the historical facts as truthfully as possible.

The small objects displayed in the old museum rooms disappeared into the Memorial's storerooms; some, but few, were shown in the new museum (Gramann's crucifix, for instance). We did not want to display objects on the site itself, because we did not want to transform the historical places (the prisoners' rooms and so on) into a museum, particularly as the humidity meant they would require special protection.[11] Above all – and it cannot be repeated often enough – the storyline would determine what objects were to be shown, and not the other way around.

The renovation project was approved by the Scientific Committee of the Memorial as well as by the Board of Trustees. On this Scientific Committee there were eminent academic historians such as Professor

THE POWER OF THE OBJECT

José Gotovitch, who was then Director of the Centre for Historical Research and Documentation of War and Contemporary Society, as well as heads of museums (who happened to be good historians themselves) such as Dr. Patrick Lefèvre of the Royal Museum of the Armed Forces and Military History and Yves Le Maner of La Coupole. (Sadly the present Scientific Committee, apart from myself, no longer comprises members with museum experience).

The Scientific Committee was more supportive than the Board of Trustees, which was then still composed of former prisoners or their (also ageing) descendants. Still, the project was approved. In the case of the first museum room, with its presentation of 21 prisoners, this would have been unthinkable in the past, for reasons already explained (the dominance of the patriotic perspective). There were still remnants of this attitude when Paul and I presented our project to the Board of Trustees and representatives of the association of former prisoners. We were inevitably criticised for certain choices. Always backed by Coekelbergs' firm authority, we were obliged to give in on only one small point: the inclusion of the President of the Association. Since he had been part of the "reserve team" and since his family's story was an interesting one – he had been imprisoned in Breendonk with his father and two brothers – neither Paul nor I had to strain particularly hard to concede.[12]

The coverage of "Breendonk II", by contrast, passed without protest, since the text was short and events were well explained: abuses were anyway undeniable, and demonstrated by historical research; they were short-lived and the Belgian State put an end to them.

Finally, a year after the renovation, in April 2004, a new art room was opened,[13] showing the artworks of two former prisoners, the fine drawings (portraits mainly) of Jacques Ochs and the expressionist watercolours of Wilhelm Pauwels, alias "Wilchar", and placing them on equal footing. In the old memorial, pride of place had been given to Jacques Ochs, a fine draughtsman but also an establishment figure; relegating to second place the – admittedly notoriously difficult – anarcho-communist Wilchar, who, as rumour had it, had fallen out with Levy.

Press coverage of the opening of the renovated Memorial was, as mentioned earlier, almost unanimously favourable. Criticism sometimes came from former prisoners, some of whom were nostalgic for the musty museum rooms crammed with objects. One son-in-law of a former prisoner filed a complaint with the police over the urns, which he did not like. He accused the Memorial of not having taken the necessary care in transferring the ashes. The enquiry is still on-going. The same man threatened to go on hunger strike over the Minister's decision to change the composition of the Board of Trustees in 2003, reducing the number of former political prisoners (though keeping Coekelbergs in place). The threat was not carried out. The main negative reaction from the general public was to the film at the end, which people did not understand, or worse, accused of "inverted racism". As has been mentioned, the Memorial has subsequently replaced the film with a different one.

The public reaction was largely one of great satisfaction with the renovation. Visitor numbers doubled to over 100,000, back to the post-war peak of 1949. I sincerely hope that the whole concept of the renovation continues to be grasped in future by those running the Memorial and that change for change's sake, inspired by a certain need to "mark one's territory", will never become the slogan…

1. There are some photographs of the event on the official website: http://www.breendonk.be/EN/index.html (click on : Memorial, then look for "renovation").
I refer to the official site of the Memorial for all other photographs as well. For the actual situation after renovation: "The Fort today - virtual tour". For the postwar ceremonies: "Memorial - pilgrimage". For historical photographs: "The Fort" and "Trials of War Criminals".

2. For the history of the Fort I refer to my own work: Nefors, 2004 (in Dutch; translated into French: Nefors, 2005). A short overview in German in: Nefors, 2005b. All figures given about prisoner numbers (totals, deaths, executions etc.), are subject to caution, as I clearly state in my book. The Belgian War Victims Service is currently undertaking a review of its figures, as a result of which certain figures might be altered. Intermediate reports are already available, but I, for one, would need to see more proof before adopting them. This will not, however, fundamentally alter the main picture of the camp's history.

3. "Prendre toutes les mesures utiles pour que le souvenir du Fort de Breendonk ainsi que des évènements qui s'y sont déroulés demeure vivant dans l'esprit de la Nation, stimule son esprit civique et favorise l'éducation patriotique de la jeunesse."

4. On the wider context of the issues of patriotic memory and national recovery in the post-war years, see Lagrou, 2000.

5. Coekelbergs was one of seven patriots from the small Walloon town of Mons who were imprisoned for a month in Breendonk in 1941, after having protested against the departure of Belgian collaborators for the Eastern Front. For his biography and Breendonk experience: Nefors,

2004: 294-297 or Nefors, 2005: 282-285. For the memoirs of one of the "Mons Seven", see Jacob, 2005.
6. Lévy, 1971.
7. By this I mean unused in Breendonk. The photographs had previously been published in a book (CEGES, 1997). The photographs had been discovered by the Dutch journalist Otto Spronk, who holds the rights to them, but who graciously put them at the disposal of the Memorial with the words: "they are back where they belong".
8. Text panels with historical information were in general avoided since they would have damaged the original look of the rooms; the museum rooms were a different matter. Groups would as a rule not use audio-guides but hire guides; the pool of guides was extended and more or less managed by the Fort, though their quality remains uneven. Monthly seminars were organised for teachers.
A 25-page brochure was on sale in the shop for those wanting additional information (Nefors, 2003). A year later my book on Breendonk (Nefors, 2004) was available as well.
9. In 2000 and 2001, new interviews with former prisoners had been conducted by the audio-visual service of the Army. In my view little of this material was usable, so we mostly had recourse to older interviews, recorded by Belgian national television or other producers.
10. With regard to this issue I share the view expressed in Conquest, 2001: 76, that: "In any country there are doubtless elements psychologically available for the right moment and the right regime... A morally and intellectually half-educated stratum exists, in varying form, everywhere in the world." Some of the academics to whom I referred seem

to have a particular aversion to any preoccupation with the fate of the victims, which they view as "futile" and "scientifically irrelevant"; one of them seems to think there is no higher crime than to "demonise" the perpetrators (a crime of which I have apparently been guilty). The same man compares concentration camps to "hospitals, barracks, schools" which he views as comparably "total" and "dehumanising" institutions - see http://www.serendib.be/gievandenberghe/artikels/opvangkamp.htm. I have no hesitation in declaring myself in full agreement with Michael Burleigh's statement that "most of the 'victims' were considerably more interesting than the 'perpetrators' upon whose character and psychology so much attention is lavished" (Burleigh, 2001: 305).

11. *Humidity was a major problem. It even provoked the Board's (hotly debated) decision to construct a new floor in the torture chamber.*

12. *The President, François De Coster, clearly did not realise that being the object of historical research is not necessarily an advantage. He was not amused when he discovered that I had published his own admission in a post-war administrative document that he had no idea as to the reason for his arrest, which rather deflated his story about his resistance activities. Nor was he pleased to read my citation of his clumsy and insensitive allegation in a newsletter for former prisoners that "... the large majority of the Jews who were, for racial reasons only, gassed immediately upon their arrival in the Polish extermination camps, thus suffered less than the Belgian political prisoners" (Nefors, 2004: 317 and 319).*

13. *Fortunately, after initial hesitation, the Memorial opted for Paul*

THE POWER OF THE OBJECT

Vandebotermet's proposal for the presentation instead of trying to entrust it to unqualified people.

Discussion

Question: You have been doing what other speakers also have talked about: showing personal stories, but without objects. Do you think that you have been using personal stories in the same way that we use objects: to sustain and authenticate what you say?

Nefors: Yes we use them in the same way. First of all there were not many objects in the first place, really related to life in the camp. There were some playing cards made by prisoners and some other very small objects. But we decided that the most important thing was our storyline, as my colleague from the Imperial War Museum also said. First we decided what story we were going to tell, and how we were going to tell it. The story of life in the camp would be told on the historic site itself. All the other aspects would come at the end. We did not want to transform the historic rooms into a kind of museum. That is why we did not put showcases with objects there. We decided to work through the impact of oral or visual testimony, videos and the emotional force of the photographs.

Question: But aren't the original rooms in fact a parallel to Frans Ferdinand's car. They impress you, because you know probably even before you come what they were used for? You do not actually learn anything from looking at the walls.

Nefors: It is the effect of the atmosphere.

Question: But what creates the atmosphere?

Nefors: The fact that even those who do not know much about it

THE POWER OF THE OBJECT

know that it has been a prison, that it is a sinister place, where hanging and torture took place.

Question: I won't argue with that. But what triggers it? The site is itself the object, a large object, but still an object. What you said about the exhibition interested me – I haven't been to Breendonk, but must go – but in Dachau they had an exhibition on the rise of Nazism, and that completely dilutes [the impact of the site]. I also think you are right about the texts. In our evaluation of the Churchill War Rooms the public unanimously said: we don't want texts here. One other issue was really interesting: the use of prisoners as guides. You are going to get something very slanted – but nonetheless a unique thing. What you get from a personal guide and a professional guide is totally different.

Nefors: There are almost no prisoners left to tell their story, and those that there are, are old, memories failing and also physically too weak to do a tour which lasts two hours. Time is also a factor in the decision not to deal at length with the rise of Nazism. If you listen to everything on the audio-guide it will last two hours and that is the maximum attention span one can expect from visitors.

Question: One should recognise that to the ordinary visitor a former prisoner would have much more credibility than a professional story.

Nefors: It is unique. But they also sometimes will only tell of things they have personally experienced.

Question: But former prisoners can make kids shut up.
Nefors: That is true. They hold the moral high ground.
Question: If you have a former prisoner, he is also an object. And as a curator you have no chance to correct him because the object and the story are identical. I wonder if the stories of the prisoners changed over time?
Nefors: If you have interviewed a number of prisoners you can quickly tell the difference between someone who has often told his story, and someone who is doing it for the first time... People like Paul Levy who have told their story all their life are different.
Question: You are absolutely right. I have an expression "a professional prisoner" whose story is well-rehearsed, and where I can tell what he will say every time he gets up. But isn't that what you want, a well composed story? I was interested to hear about Monsignore Gramann, an Austrian. I could not help but think about a German nurse, Hiltgunt Sassenhaus, who helped Danish KS-prisoners - The Angel - and whether these people are archetypes of "The Good German"- who make what happened more bearable?
Nefors: Maybe. Paul Levy after the war was also very active in the European movement, he may have been happy to have a good German. Of course the sources on [the Monsignore] are limited. Most testimonies on him are favourable on the humanitarian side. But in some of the letters he wrote to his monastery in Vienna - although he might be speaking in some because of censorship - you get the

impression he thought it was a very good thing that the German armies were crushing Bolshevism. The source material is limited, but he resembles the Conservative opposition to Hitler, being a greater German patriot but at the same time being in favour of the poor Belgians who are shot just because they are equally good patriots, with an aversion to Nazism.

Question: I am head of a Camp Museum here in Denmark, and there are so many parallels that I would not know where to begin, the only difference being that because of the different political contexts people were not shot here.

MUSEUMS AND WORLD WAR II

6
Challenges of a Memorial
HENRIK SKOV KRISTENSEN
*Head of the Frøslev Camp Museum,
National Museum of Denmark*

The Frøslev Camp Museum (*Frøslevlejrens Museum*) is entirely linked to its location, the former German internment camp just north of the Danish-German border. And, as I see it, the main attraction of the museum is that it is in an original location and housed in authentic buildings. Arguably, this is the most powerful object in the museum.

The Frøslev Camp is also a national memorial, an integral part of the story of German oppression and Danish resistance 1940-45. This is a constant challenge, as memorials (more so than ordinary museums) play a very significant role in creating and maintaining narratives or perceptions of history – presumably because they very often meld the demands of three aspects of historical culture: cognitive, political, and emotional and commemorative.

I shall try to elaborate on these preliminary remarks, focusing on two challenges, firstly that of an alternative historical and political interpretation of the camp area, and secondly that of approaches to the camp area, which can be characterised as practical, diverse, rational, and financial. It would be unfair to simply accuse the champions of the latter of bad will or being unethical. Yet it seems to me, that this approach (contrary to the challenges of alternative historical and political interpretations) poses a serious threat to the most powerful object in the Museum, the very authenticity of the camp area and buildings.

However, before going into detail, it is necessary to outline briefly the creation of the Frøslev Camp and the events that led to its construction.

The Danish exception
When Denmark and Norway were invaded on 9th April 1940, the Danish government yielded, under protest, to the German ultimatum. In return the Danish government obtained a guarantee that Germany would respect Danish "territorial integrity" and "political independence". As a result, Germany still formally recognised Denmark as an independent state, with which Germany was not at war. Occupied Denmark was ruled by a government supported by all the democratic parties and even headed, until the Autumn of 1942, by a Social Democratic prime minister. Danish constitutional bodies continued to function, albeit with limitations.

For Germany's part, relations with Denmark were handled by the Foreign Office. The Germans had no right to issue decrees in Denmark, and no German administrative body was set up to govern the country. In other words: officially, it was business as usual.

On 29th August 1943, the Danish government ceased

to function. However, top civil servants in the administration effectively (with the support of the leading Danish politicians) took over the Government's role as negotiating partner in relation to the occupying power. Denmark remained under the control of the German Foreign Office until the German capitulation in May 1945, although the German *Wehrmacht* and the German police intervened increasingly. Formally Germany and Denmark were never at war with each other, but many Danes felt that there was a *de facto* state of war, especially after August 1943.

Norway was presented with the very same German ultimatum as Denmark on 9th April 1940, but chose not to accept it, just as the Netherlands and Belgium refused similar offers in May 1940. Unlike Denmark, all three countries chose war, and both Norway and Holland became *Reichkommissariate*, whereas Belgium came under German military rule.

The significance of Denmark's status as a *Sonderfall* (special case) in German-occupied Europe cannot, as I see it, be overestimated. It influenced all aspects of political, economic and cultural life in occupied Denmark (Poulsen 1997, Skov Kristensen 2007, 2008).

Sonderfall Dänemark
At the Frøslev Camp Museum, both my staff and I are

quite frequently asked by both Danish and foreign visitors where the prisoners were executed. Some visitors even ask where the gas chamber was. These visitors look extremely surprised – some even look disappointed – when we explain that no such things existed in the Frøslev Camp. Nor were violence, killings, starvation or disease part of camp life.

In other words, the Frøslev Camp was no ordinary concentration camp. Indeed, the Frøslev camp was the very reflection of Denmark's unique status in German-occupied Europe and the camp embodies the peculiar political position held by Denmark.

In the Autumn of 1943, following the *de facto* resignation of the Danish government, the Germans began to deport Danish citizens to prisons and concentration camps in Germany. Referring to international law and the German promises of April 9th 1940, the Danish authorities protested, emphasising the right of every Danish citizen to stay on Danish soil. But this was all in vain. So in March 1944, the Danish authorities proposed to the German plenipotentiary in Denmark, Dr. Werner Best (an SS-General, yet in Denmark representative of the German Foreign Office) that a camp be established on Danish soil to prevent deportations to Germany and for the repatriation of those already deported. This proposal was accepted by both Best and the Chief of the German Security police in Denmark (which had established itself in Denmark with executive powers in September 1943), Otto Bovensiepen. Only the 500 Jews deported to Theresienstadt and some of the leading figures among the 150 Danish communists deported to Stutthof were not to be repatriated.

Thus the Frøslev Camp was built near the Danish-German border. The German authorities were the contractors and owners of the building, while the Danish state paid for both the construction and the running of the camp, and on 13th August 1944, the first 750 prisoners arrived there.

The Frøslev camp was a so-called *Polizeigefangenenlager*. Similar camps existed in other occupied countries. Some were called *Polizeihäftlingslager* and some *Polizeihaftlager*. In my opinion, there was no substantial difference between these camp categories. A common trait was that they housed the prisoners of the German Security Police, and the prisoners were interned without trial. It was the chief of the German Security Police in Denmark who ran the Frøslev Camp, and the camp commandant and his personnel in the camp headquarters were members of the security police and held SS ranks. However, the internal administration of the camp and the surveillance of the internees was carried out by personnel of the German *Ordnungspolizei*.

THE POWER OF THE OBJECT

What seems to distinguish the Frøslev Camp from other similar camps throughout Europe, however, was the existence of the so-called Danish Administration: the Germans had accepted a Danish proposal that a Danish administration, consisting of staff from the Danish prison service, should be in charge of the provision of food to the prisoners. This administration was housed just outside the camp area and had no executive powers inside the camp. Its main bastion within the camp was the camp kitchen, and it is a well established fact that the Danish Administration, which acted as a deputy of the Danish authorities, made sure that the prisoners were extremely well-fed. Added to this was the fact that brutality, humiliation and killing were not the norm in the Frøslev Camp – this has been confirmed by former prisoners who have called the Frøslev Camp "the strangest concentration camp in the world".

And indeed, structurally and in principle, the Frøslev Camp was some kind of concentration camp, just like Grini and Falstad camps in Norway. All three had chains of command connected to the *Reichssicherheitshauptamt* in Berlin. The difference between Grini and Falstad (where prisoners were killed, starved and humiliated) on the one hand, and Frøslev, on the other hand, seems to have been the different occupying policy adopted by the Germans in the two countries. This difference manifested itself in the running of the camps.

However, Frøslev soon proved not to be all paradise: on 15th September 1944, just one month after the camp had been set up, the Germans violated the very basis of its establishment, when 200 Frøslev prisoners were deported to concentration camps in Germany. More deportations followed, so that a total of 1,600 Frøslev prisoners were deported to Germany. Some 230 of these never returned alive.

Although there was no immediate or general repatriation of deportees to the Frøslev Camp, and although 1,600 were deported from Frøslev, the camp must be considered a "success" from a Danish point of view since 7,000 people were interned in the Frøslev Camp, and it would be fair to assume that all of them would have been deported to Germany if the camp had not existed. Furthermore, the duration of their deportation would have been reduced by their stay in Frøslev – which meant a much better chance of survival. Thus the mortality rate was as high as 27% in regard to the first group deported from Frøslev, but it (generally) dropped considerably the later the deportation took place (Skov Kristensen 2007, 2008).

THE POWER OF THE OBJECT

The Frøslev Camp Museum

In 1969 the Frøslev Camp Museum was opened on the initiative of former prisoners, and the Danish state undertook to run the museum under the aegis of the National Museum of Denmark. The museum was housed in a former prisoner's block and the main watchtower. In 1969 the major part of the Frøslev Camp was still in use as barracks for the Danish Army (under the name the Padborg Camp). When I was appointed the first professional head (in situ) in 1989, the existing permanent exhibition was rich in objects, mainly donated by former prisoners. But the exhibition was also extremely introspective and the political context of the camp was completely absent.

From 1992 onwards, the exhibition was gradually redesigned, and today it presents aspects of camp history from 1944 to 1945, ranging from the camp's political context, German administration and surveillance, to the work of the Danish Administration and, of course, what had been the only theme of the earlier exhibition: the daily life of the prisoners. Furthermore, the exhibition shows the conditions of those Frøslev prisoners who were deported to Germany, along with the final Swedish-Danish evacuation of the Nordic concentration camp prisoners from Germany to Denmark and Sweden, since the Frøslev Camp played a vital role in this operation.

Source materials and the exhibition itself show the fundamental difference between the conditions in the Frøslev Camp and those in German concentration camps. Indeed, there are constant reminders of conditions in German concentration camps in the exhibition, giving visitors a clear impression of both the special conditions in the Frøslev Camp and the special conditions in occupied Denmark, of which the camp was the result.

Naturally, the really strong attraction of the museum is, as mentioned earlier, that it is in its original location and in authentic buildings. No exhibition can or should attempt to compete with that, and therefore, aesthetics have played a minor role in the concept of the exhibition. As for the aim, or message, of the exhibition it is the policy of the museum to display the historical facts as honestly and as factually as possible. And if we succeed in increasing the visitor's knowledge of our topic, or perhaps even encourage the visitor reflection, we are quite happy. The museum does not pursue any ideal in terms of relating explicitly to present problems of human rights, racism or the political debate on these issues (Skov Kristensen 2002).

The Faarhus Camp 1945-1949
To the Danish public at large and to the Resistance

in particular, the Frøslev Camp stands as a powerful symbol of German oppression and Danish resistance – and as such the camp is embedded in the narrative of Danish resistance.

But the camp also plays a crucial role in the narrative of the "losers" and "traitors". Particularly for the German minority population in Northern Schleswig (i.e. Southern Jutland), the very same camp, under the name of the Faarhus Camp, is a powerful symbol of what they consider to be an unjust judicial purge after the war. From May 1945 to Autumn 1949, the Faarhus Camp was used first as an internment camp under the command of the Resistance and subsequently as a state prison camp for so-called "traitors". More than 3,000 individuals belonging to the German minority, who had been left north of the new Danish-German border of 1920, fixed in accordance with a referendum stemming from the Treaty of Versailles, served sentences in the camp. These inmates were predominantly male, between the ages of 18 and 55. The judicial purge in Denmark hit the German minority in Northern Schleswig – which involved about 25,000 to 30,000 people – and was harsh in human, political and cultural terms.

The German minority population in Northern Schleswig had been almost entirely Nazi sympathisers and expressed complete solidarity with the occupying power. This minority thus enthusiastically welcomed German troops on April 9th 1940, expecting the invasion to lead to a border revision, just as had been the case with other German Versailles borders. However, the Danish acceptance of the German ultimatum on 9th April 1940 meant that Germany respected Danish territorial integrity. Consequently, the Danish-German border, as the only German Versailles border, was never revised. This was yet another implication of Denmark's special status, as I see it.

The judicial purge after the war produced strong feelings of injustice among the German minority population against the Danish majority population and the Danish state. It was felt that Denmark had not made sufficient allowance for the conflict of national loyalty in this minority. Very few members of the minority seemed to pay much attention to the fact that not only had they shown solidarity with Germany, but also with a totalitarian and inhumane ideology.

The Faarhus Camp itself became the very symbol of the "martyrdom" of the German minority, and for decades after the war the camp became a state of mind of the minority.

This sense of injustice was heightened by the fact that members of the minority, who were mostly sentenced for doing German military service in the *Waffen*

SS or various uniformed and armed corps on the home front, were largely sentenced by laws which had retrospective power. What the minority seemed to forget, however, was the fact that they were sentenced according to exactly the same legislation as other Danish citizens, for instance "ordinary" Danish SS-volunteers, and that the German minority in Northern Schleswig was not collectively condemned or driven away from their land and property as were other German minorities in Europe. Nevertheless, from the Autumn of 1945 until the 1960s the rehabilitation of these previously convicted minority members became a prime political goal of the regenerated German minority, and even today the wish for rehabilitation crops up now and then – and the German minority still refers to the fact that no state of war existed between Germany and Denmark and therefore their services for Germany were not illegal, according to existing Danish Law.

Furthermore, they point to the fact that the legal Danish government also cooperated with the occupying power. So ever since the opening of the Frøslev Camp Museum in 1969, the German minority in Northern Schleswig has voiced its opinion that the Faarhus Camp should also be reflected within the preserved camp area and the preserved prisoner's blocks.

This idea has met with strong opposition, not least

from former Frøslev prisoners who believe that the Frøslev Camp should remain an unambiguous memorial. This debate has also arisen in other places where German camps were used after the war to imprison the "losers", and where museums or memorials were later set up and dedicated to the victims of the Nazis, for instance in Sachsenhausen, Buchenwald, Dachau and even the Falstad Camp near Trondheim in Norway.

For all these reasons, the Frøslev Camp Museum has now decided to set up a permanent exhibition on the Faarhus Camp from 1945-1949 in one of its buildings. I am not going to elaborate on the considerations behind this decision, nor on the way in which we intend to tackle this delicate task, but it is clear that what is needed for an exhibition on the Faarhus Camp is a political contextualisation of the camp – a contextualisation that visualises both the Nazification of the German minority from 1933-1945 and the solidarity of this minority with the occupying power from 1940-1945. Indeed, it is also necessary to debate the problems involved in the Danish judicial purge and its complexity and dilemmas. But first and foremost, the exhibition will show the striking continuity from the one camp to the other, especially during the early months of the Faarhus Camp, when former Frøslev prisoners ran the Faarhus internment camp (Reitan 2005, Skov

Kristensen 2005a, 2005b, 2008).

Struggling for authenticity – the most powerful object
Despite the future presence of a permanent exhibition of the Faarhus Camp 1945-1949, I feel quite sure that the Frøslev Camp from 1944-1945, and the camp area as such, will remain an unambiguous memorial to German occupation and Danish resistance – although it should be recognised that collective memory and the culture of remembrance are not static phenomena.

As I see it, the real menace to the Frøslev Camp Museum and the camp area, is not the struggle between these two different understandings of the camp's symbolic value. Rather, the future challenge will be that of maintaining the authenticity of the camp area in the face of pressure to use the camp area for historically unrelated purposes.

To clarify this issue, we have to fill in some detail to the Camp's post-war history. When the Faarhus Camp was closed down in 1949, the Danish Army immediately took over the buildings as barracks. The camp was then called the Padborg Camp, as mentioned earlier. From 1968 to 1975 it was used as barracks for the Danish Civil Defence, and would probably have been abandoned and torn down in the 1980s, had not the thought of establishing a museum dedicated to the Frøslev camp 1944-

1945 been put forward by former Frøslev prisoners at a rally in the Frøslev Camp in 1965. And as mentioned earlier, the Danish state undertook to run the museum under the aegis of the National Museum of Denmark in 1969. During the following years the Frøslev Camp Museum attracted some 40,000–50,000 visitors a year.

My appointment as head of the museum in 1989, was connected with the reorganisation of The Frøslev Camp Museum when it amalgamated with the newly established Danish Red Cross Museum. This collaboration ceased in 1998, when the Red Cross Museum was closed.

Since 1969, the National Museum of Denmark has owned the two authentic buildings which house the exhibition – a former prisoner block and the main watch tower. The National Museum, however, has no jurisdiction over the camp area as such and the other buildings in the camp area. This is a matter for a private body, *Den Selvejende Institution Frøslevlejren* (DSIF), which was set up and run by the local authorities in 1984, with the primary aim of restoring the buildings in the camp area as a job creation programme and thus preserving the camp. The Danish state, which was (and still is) the owner of the camp area through the Ministry of the Environment, entrusted the local authorities and DSIF with the right to use the camp area and buildings – except the two buildings belonging to The National Museum of Denmark.

The restored buildings were successively let out – it was the aim of the DSIF, that the running of the camp should be financed through rent income. Over the years a number of organisations and institutions moved into the restored buildings: a nature school, a large educational centre (for both private and public enterprise), a museum dedicated to Danish Territorial Defence, an exhibition on Danish Civil Defence, and an exhibition on Amnesty International.

The latest museum/exhibition to establish itself is a museum dedicated to the Danish participation in UN and NATO peace-keeping missions.

Apart from the Amnesty International exhibition, all these exhibitions/museums are situated in former prisoner blocks – in the prisoners' section of the camp area. In 1944-45 this section was separated by a barbed-wire fence from the German section of the camp area, which housed the German camp administration and the guards' quarters. The education centre was based mainly in the German section, but also used three former prisoners' blocks. Originally, there were nineteen buildings in the German section of the camp, of which seven have been restored. The prisoners' section of the camp originally consisted of thirty buildings:

seventeen prisoners' blocks, four watch towers and nine workshops plus camp kitchen and canteen. Of these buildings eighteen have been restored.

Thirteen years ago the education centre went bankrupt and the most of its buildings – mainly in the former German section of the camp – were let out to a newly-established continuation school, The Frøslev Camp Continuation School (*Frøslevlejrens Efterskole*), with 100 pupils, whereas the rest of the buildings – three former prisoner blocks – were let out to a private company, The Organisation of Danish Export Delivery Businesses (FDE), with some 80 employees.

If one takes a look at the more museum-like activities in the camp, the common trait is that they are financed by their organisations – and run by volunteers from these organisations. No doubt, the large number of visitors to the Frøslev Camp Museum made this attractive.

Ferienaufenthalt in der Vergangenheit

As mentioned, the Frøslev Camp Education Centre (*Frøslevlejrens Kursuscenter*) closed in 1995. In 1994, however, the centre managed to put the Frøslev Camp on the world map and provoke a vehement public debate by launching a rather strange initiative. On 25th April 1994 the regional newspaper *JydskeVestkysten* announced under the headline: *Germans on Holiday in Prison Camp*, that *the Gestapo's former prison camp, the Frøslev Camp, is being offered to Germans as a holiday hotel*.

The article was based on a very tangible source, namely a brochure in German, which the education centre had distributed in Germany. The brochure not only promised German tourists a cultural experience under the headline *Ferienaufhalt in der Vergangenheit – und mit Freiheit und Demokratie als Inhalt* (*Vacation in the past – with freedom and democracy as the content*) it also promised experiences such as: comfortable accommodation in the camp buildings, sauna, fitness and a varied menu in the restaurant of the education centre (which was actually situated in the former camp kitchen of the Frøslev Camp).

The story was immediately reproduced by almost all Danish newspapers and electronic media, and the conclusion in the following public debate was one of almost universal agreement that the initiative was in bad taste and inappropriate. Some papers mocked the initiative, while at the Frøslev Camp Museum we could only deplore the fact that it was impossible for the general public to distinguish between the different organisations housed at the Frøslev Camp. The Frøslev Camp Museum was – and still is – equated with the Frøslev Camp as such, and the public largely sees the camp as a single organisational entity.

For example, a well-known chief editor (who was also a former member of the Danish resistance) commented that "the curator must have written the brochure in a moment of insanity"!

The international news agencies also saw the grotesque nature of the story, and this headline hit newsdesks all over the world: Danes transform German concentration camp into holiday hotel.

Numerous newspapers and TV stations – *Le Monde*, *Wall Street Journal*, *CNN*, *RTL* and *Norwegian Television*, published the bizarre story, quite often garnished with acid comments.

Television stations and journalists, not least from Germany, flocked to Frøslev to report on this odd phenomenon. And foreign reaction ranged from disbelief to indignation. The Frøslev Camp was the top story on German Television 3's satirical weekly, and the comments of the respected German magazine *Der Spiegel* pointed to the Danish mercenary mentality.

No doubt, foreigners' ignorance of the unique situation in occupied Denmark, and hence the conditions in the Frøslev Camp, contributed to the international reaction: The Frøslev Camp was automatically compared to a typical German concentration camp. No wonder the idea of a comfortable vacation was regarded as almost blasphemous. Only copious information about the history of the Camp and long explanations over the phone, seems to have prevented Jean-Paul Gaultier from featuring the Camp and the holiday hotel on his notorious satirical programme *Eurotrash*.

There was another incident which made my blood pressure rise. In 1988 the DSIF restored a building next to one of the buildings of the Frøslev Camp Museum. The idea was that it should house changing exhibitions. It started, as far as I can remember, with an art exhibition, continued with a fashion show and ended in February 1990 with a car accessories fair. The concept of the fair was apparently *cowboy-style*, which meant that the building was decorated as a mixture of saloon and stable. Outside, at the entrance, a (genuine) donkey was "parked". But worst of all, the salesmen at the fair were dressed cowboy-style, as cowboys or Red Indians. This, of course, attracted the attention of visitors to Museum, who could not help seeing these strange figures when occasionally crossing the camp, to and from the fair.

Apparently, as a result of this grotesque show (which lasted a week) it dawned on the DSIF and the local authorities, that they had crossed the line. The building was subsequently let for a more worthwhile and durable purpose, that of a UN Museum.

In 1992 the newly established UN Museum was allowed, by the local authorities, to set up a (full-scale!) UN observation post just outside the camp entrance, the idea being to promote the newly established museum. The Frøslev Camp Museum, however, felt this would be historically misleading – a view which we notified to the local authorities. Our objection was accepted and shortly after the observation post was removed (Skov Kristensen 2001).

On the agenda of the Danish Folketing

It will be clear that the range of activities taking place within the Frøslev Camp area is broad, and the organisational arrangements within the camp so complex as to be impenetrable to those not in the know. At one extreme we have a professional museum, owned and run by the National Museum of Denmark – a museum which is embedded in its location, as it deals with the camp's history. At the other, we had until recently (as I shall elaborate) a private organisation of Danish Export Delivery Businesses (FDE). Between these two, the camp area houses a number of museums or museumlike activities as well as a continuation school. All these activities are in themselves commendable. But they have no direct historical connection with the Frøslev Camp. The variety of institutions no doubt often conveys a somewhat blurred picture to the public of the Frøslev Camp. Yet there is no doubt that the Danish public in general sees the Frøslev Camp as a national memorial to occupied Denmark 1940-1945. The public's reaction to the holiday brochure incident bears testimony to that.

Indeed, the idea of a memorial dedicated to the Frøslev Camp and those deported prisoners who did not survive their stay in Germany, was the very motive for the initiative of the former Frøslev prisoners in 1965 to establish a museum in the camp area. And from the deed of conveyance, it appears explicitly, that it was in this spirit that the Danish state undertook to run the Frøslev Camp Museum. In this deed of conveyance only one future use of the camp area was foreseen: when the state in due time left the camp area (which was barracks for the Danish army at the time), the buildings were to be torn down – except for the Frøslev Camp Museum of course – and the bases of the removed buildings were to be indicated in the terrain. Subsequently, the camp area was to be laid out as a memorial park.

Referring to this very deed of conveyance, two former Frøslev prisoners who had been involved in establishing the Camp Museum, protested energetically against the state of affairs in the camp throughout the 1980s and 1990s. They accused the state of having reneged on clear and legally binding promises to the founders of the museum, and they protested against the state having handed over the right of use of the camp area to the local authorities. They also accused the DSIF and the local authorities of profaning the camp area, especially by letting out former prisoner's blocks to the FDE. They pointed to the fact that this tenancy was a clear breech of the local authorities' own local plan for the camp area.

One may suspect the authorities hoped for a "biological" solution to their problem. But the two old fighters managed to stay alive and even managed to raise the issue in the *Folketing*, the Danish Parliament. This happened in 1999 in the shape of a proposal to "establish a national memorial park in the Frøslev Camp". The main aim of the proposal was that "the memorial park, except for the Frøslev Camp Museum, may only house museums and other cultural activities that can function in accordance with the memorial".

The proposal was not adopted, but was passed to the Parliament's Cultural Affairs Committee, who were to find a solution which had wide political support.

This solution was reached at the beginning of 2001 following long and detailed discussions between The Ministry of Environment (owners of the camp area), The Ministry of Cultural Affairs (owners of the Frøslev

THE POWER OF THE OBJECT

Camp Museum) and the DSIF/local authorities (owners of the right to use the camp area and the major part of the buildings). The solution reflected the original proposal and a sum of 1.5 million DKK (around 200,000 Euros) was allocated by the state to establish the memorial. This would re-establish an element of authenticity in the prisoners' section of the camp area – considered more "sacred" than the one where the German administration and guards were housed. It started with the felling of some 40 trees in the inner camp area, which both reduced the idyllic atmosphere and made the characteristic geometry of the camp visible. Inauthentic paths were removed, and authentic ones re-established. Low, modern lighting was removed from the inner camp and replaced with authentic lampposts. The rather heterogeneous signage was rationalised and replaced with the Ministry of the Environment's standard signage. And, last but not least, four parking lots within the camp area were removed and a large new one established just outside the camp. This reduced car traffic in the camp – however, the problem of traffic and parking within the camp area has not been eliminated – far from it. There seems to be very little sympathy for regulation in this matter.

The central axis of the camp, which was a barbed-wire fence in 1944-45, dividing the prisoners' section of the camp from the German one, was marked on the ground as were the outlines of the buildings removed in the post-war years. And, finally, the establishment of the memorial park meant, that the FDE left the camp area in 2004.

The original camp is now more clearly distinguishable, and the establishing of the memorial park emphasises the camp as it was in 1944-1945. This is of course in the interests of the Frøslev Camp Museum, which has always supported – and still supports – all efforts to increase the authenticity of the camp area (Skov Kristensen 2001).

Limits to development and diversity
When the local authorities set up DSIF as a private body in 1984 and began restoring the buildings and subsequently renting them out, the camp buildings were not torn down as had been foreseen in the deed of conveyance of 1969. No doubt the restoration of the Frøslev Camp and the subsequent activities had been started with the best of motives. However, it is obvious that activities must be limited, if the camp is to be a national memorial. It is obvious, that the camp history 1940-1945 must not be overshadowed by other messages and activities, however praiseworthy they each may be.

Normally, diversity is a positive thing, but in the case of the Frøslev Camp one fears that many different (and confusing) signals will only undermine the authenticity and distinctiveness of the camp area – so that the visitor can no longer relate to the prison camp and sense its history. If that happens, a key asset will be lost: since the cultural landscape, the setting, forms part of the museum – and vice versa.

I am bound to say, that my views are not shared to any large degree by the other institutions in the Frøslev Camp. They do not see any lacking of correlation between museum and cultural landscape. On the contrary, they claim that their presence in the camp contributes to a living memorial, where the common denominator of all the institutions and organisations in the camp is, that they "work for peace, freedom, and democracy". And whereas the Frøslev Camp Museum principally has been, and still is, sceptical of new activities and tenants in the camp, the main tendency is quite the opposite in the case of the other institutions – who have no difficulty, either, in justifying their own presence from a historical point of view (Skov Kristensen 2001).

This manoeuvre may at times seem a bit far fetched. The original focus of the continuation school was history and nature – a natural focus considering the location of the school. However, this focus soon changed into music and theatre – probably in order to attract pupils. As a result, the continuation school has for years tried to obtain permission to establish a so-called multi-purpose building in the camp to house such activities – a building that would differ fundamentally from the other buildings in the camp, which are all restored externally, but modernised internally (except from the two authentic buildings of the Frøslev Camp Museum). The creation of the multi-purpose building requires an exemption from the local authorities local plan, which was agreed – but the Ministry of the Environment and the National Museum of Denmark have both objected. Presently, it looks as if the school will obtain permission to build the facility outside the camp area, some 200 yards from the entrance.

The attitude of the local authorities/DSIF is decisive as to the future development of the Frøslev Camp. The camp area is the property of the Danish state, but the state has handed over the right of use to the local authorities/DSIF – who no doubt feel obliged to support all the existing activities and institutions in the camp. The local authorities depend on the rent paid by these institutions to maintain and preserve the buildings and the area. It would not be fair to ascribe merely financial motives to the local authorities/DSIF, who no doubt feel that they act in the best interests of the camp – first and foremost to preserve it. But the Frøslev Camp Museum will need constantly to remind the local authorities/DSIF of their aim in 1984, when they started to restore the camp area. They agreed on a local plan for the area, in the preamble of which the very intention of the restoration was stated as being "to preserve the camp as an historical memorial of World War II".

MUSEUMS AND WORLD WAR II

7
Jersey War Tunnels

CHRISTOPHER ADDY

Collections Manager,

Jersey War Tunnels

The purpose of this paper is to examine through constructivist museum pedagogy, the learning methods, strategies and provision of a specific museum. This critical appraisal of a museum's educational resources from a cultural perspective has as its intention to reveal how the museum understands the nature, and corroborates the needs, of its particular audience. This case study is therefore structured to answer the questions implicit in such an analysis, as articulated by George Hein in relation to constructivist museums, in his book *Learning in the Museum* (1998).

The constructivist agenda necessitates the consideration of a rounded view of the educational potential of the museum; in the light of its supporting theories of knowledge and learning, education in the constructivist museum demands the active participation of the learner in both the manner in which the mind is employed and in the outcome of the activity. In accepting that individuals make their own unique meanings out of experience, constructivists attempt to facilitate this process in such a way that learning is made accessible physically, socially and intellectually. This study endeavours to undertake a museum audit that uncovers how effectively these considerations have been met, and to draw conclusions about the possibilities for future development.

Jersey War Tunnels, a privately owned profit-making institution, formally subscribes to the Museums Association's 2001 definition of a museum and as such it aspires to meet the core values of the MA *Code of Ethics for Museums*. Its current strategic development plan has as its intention to radically advance the scope of educational provision, in keeping with visitors' expectations, whilst sustaining interest in community history in a climate of declining tourism. It is important to note that the museum's permanent exhibition, *Captive Island* was researched and designed by Event Communications, a London-based exhibition design group, although subsidiary exhibitions and educational initiatives since have been undertaken in-house. It is *Captive Island* and its display context that will be examined here, subject to the constructivist pedagogy.

Constructivist education theory

To clarify constructivist education theory, it is necessary to enlarge upon its precedents and the formation of its theoretical content. Hein states, in *Learning in the Museum*, this as being grounded in the educational theories of Dewey, Piaget and Vygotsky, whilst understanding constructivist thought as the transformation of schemas in which the learner plays an active role, and which involves making sense out of a range of phenomena presented to the mind. Where the emphasis was previously upon a transmission-absorption view of learning, where knowledge is understood as external to the passive learner, constructivism is premised upon how learners construct their own meanings and make sense in their own way of the learning opportunities they experience. This expansive perception of the educational role of the museum is seen as part of the theoretical and epistemological shift from the modern to the post-modern paradigm.

Eileen Hooper-Greenhill, in *The Educational Role of the Museum*, emphasises that the learner is active – learning is therefore contextualised by personal, physical and social factors. The cultural model of communication at the heart of constructivism understands learning to include facts, experiences and emotions, hence requiring individual effort, but also as a social experience. John Falk and Lynn Dierking's model of the characteristics of learning in museums, as clarified in *The Museum Experience*, offers a means of conceptualising the factors at play in the process of learning. Here the individual is seen as subject to all the variables determined to be influential in the three coinciding spheres of experience. Hence, as Hooper-Greenhill expands, in the formulation of a learning environment, constructivists attempt to understand their learners and create interactive environments suitable to the learning situation. A successful learning experience is therefore defined, in demonstrating sensitivity to the developmental position of the individual, as the consequent shifting of perception to incorporate the message.

Physical accessibility

Acknowledging the significance of the physical dimension in the experience of learning, a discussion of the case study in terms of ergonomics is the logical starting point for a constructivist critique. How then is the museum space designed to be physically accessible to the visitor, encouraging interest and enthusiasm for learning?

The Jersey War Tunnels permanent exhibition *Captive Island: the definitive story of the Occupation* is located within an underground tunnel complex built under the command of the German forces, during their occupation of the Channel Islands 1940-1945. As a pre-existing structure of historical repute, exhibition design has had to fall within these architectural constraints; nevertheless, the tunnel network with its transverse galleries lends itself to the chronological sequence of events that unfold within. Resulting from its original function and period, the site does indeed convey a cultural message, although its unique character in temporal parallel with exhibition content, serves to facilitate a sense of awe appropriate to the historic narrative, conducive to its uptake.

With relatively few unobtrusive modifications to the existing space, including the installation of dividing walls that mirror those in existence, freedom of movement is encouraged without restriction, although at peak times spatial limitations at the exhibition entrance are seen to cause restrictions to flow. Although the space is made comprehensible through a sequential linear arrangement, reinforced by map guides and orientation boards, the scale and complexity of the site has also not been entirely overcome. Observation of visitor behaviour occasionally reveals a nominal uncertainty that could potentially detract from the focus of the few. Whilst additional overlapping signage could go some way towards rectifying these issues, there is an understandable appreciation of how this can lead to a proliferation of signs that may detract from the historic environment and potentially confuse orientation. However, visitors can move freely in both an intended or random fashion; what may be a source of uncertainty to one, may offer sense of freedom to another. The visitor's tunnel map gives indication of fire exits, which are clearly marked throughout the space, whereas seating is provided at appropriate intervals and where interactive elements require it.

Another ramification of working with a pre-existing structure is the inability to incorporate basic conveniences; with an average time spent to view the exhibition of approximately one and a half hours, this could be perceived as a weakness. An alternative view would be that out of respect for the many forced labourers who are known to have suffered during its construction, it would be inappropriate to make amendments. The evident proximity of the visitor's centre, with its ticket point, shop, restaurant and lavatories, could be considered as overcoming this possible obstacle, acting as it does as the visitor's first point of contact with the site. It should also be noted that both the exhibition and the visitor's centre are entirely accessible for wheelchair users, and that signage is clear and consistent throughout the entire site..

The structural and graphic consistency of gallery signage offers a readily attainable familiarity that materially complements the architectural context; introductory panels are present on entering each individually themed room, where spatial subdivisions reinforce those within the subject matter. These panels provide an obvious landmark from which the visitor can choose their direction; where the lengthy tunnels act as arterial guides to sequence, individual galleries offer a variety of possible routes independent of chronology. An asymmetrical design layout again complements this sense of freedom and choice by avoiding competition between exhibits, and avoiding the fatigue inspired by endless alternatives, whilst allowing individuals to plot their own course dependent upon their level of interest.

In consideration of Maslow's pyramid of basic needs, a theory of psychology based on observations, the visitor's motivation could be affected by prevailing climatic conditions. This large underground space is evidently impossible to moderate in temperature and humidity; although it is explained that the tunnels are cold and advice is given as to the average length of time necessary, its chilly, often damp and eerie atmosphere could be enough to perturb some visitors. Saying this, one of its great strengths is the opportunity to take in its history; the connecting corridors offer the opportunity to appreciate the architectural dynamic whilst contemplating, for instance, the plight of those who were a part of its construction. Stimulation is inherent in this experience; here the physical dimension feeds directly into the emotional and intellectual to their mutual advantage.

Individual galleries differ in layout and character;

but where each has been thoughtfully considered as manageable entities, it is their abiding sense of continuity that maintains both familiarity and interest. A range of palettes, consistent within individual spaces, endorses the content; again, through observation it is evident that colour stimulates the senses by reflecting and inducing content mood. Particularly in an environment with no natural light, lighting levels are used to great effect in encouraging different psychological states; from subdued to elated, lighting plays upon the senses to sustain curiosity. Audio elements are also incorporated successfully into the display; the simulated sound of rock fall in an unfinished tunnel enhances an appreciation of the dire working conditions endured by the workers, whereas the shocking roar of a dive-bombing Heinkel gives an insight into the experience of those who witnessed the horrific *Luftwaffe* raid on St. Helier in June 1940. It could be argued that the combination of these authenticating attributes may be more of a sensory affront to some visitors than a stimulating complement, but observation and visitor comment seems to indicate otherwise.

Working with what is certainly a profoundly unfamiliar space, efforts have been made to facilitate physical association through installations that support exhibition content and in doing so humanise an alien environment. An example of this is the *Resistance* section, where the existing space has been cleverly redesigned to infer homeliness: wooden flooring, wallpapering both actual and virtual, furniture and lighting of a contextual nature transform a cavernous concrete gallery into something recognisable both in form and atmosphere. Drawing upon the prior knowledge and experience of the visitor, these various facets of the design endeavour to overcome a feeling of unfamiliarity and create a sense of belonging. Spaces are consistently appropriated to enable engagement, be it in larger shared rooms or in the privacy of individual booths. The many smaller spaces provide opportunities for individual experience, places for quiet contemplation and reflection on a scale that is familiar and private. It is through this sensitive use of space that interest is maintained; a sense of alienation is combated through these sensory opportunities to retain territorial control.

Given the inherent strangeness of this set of spaces, these design considerations come together to humanise and harmonise the environment without detracting from its authenticity. The consistent attention to detail and the high quality of the materials used throughout, in conjunction with their novel articulation, go a long way towards holding attention. Aside from the constraints that come about as a result of working with a given structure, the visitor should feel empowered to negotiate the exhibition with an inspired sense of wonder induced by the unique parallel between content and form.

Having discussed how the exhibition space is designed to provide for the physical and sensory needs of visitors, it now necessary to turn to the tools used to engage learners. How then is learning, in keeping with constructivist theory, made both active and social through a diversity of learning methods?

Modalities for active learning

As an extension of the developmental learning theories of Dewey and Piaget, the work of Bruner, Kolb, McCarthy and Gardner moves increasingly towards an holistic understanding of the processes of learning and individual preference. The findings of these theoreticians leads to an acceptance of the fact that learners require opportunities to use their own unique combination of abilities; Gardner's theory of multiple intelligences hence informs the constructivist emphasis on the way in which individuals learn directly through experience. He enumerates seven access points which, when used in museums, demonstrate a commitment to meeting the requirements of more than one learning preference; as we all learn in different ways and are at different stages of development, the constructivist museum endeavours to enable active learning of a qualitatively rich nature that facilitates a broad range of sensory involvement.

Building upon the spatial and sensory considerations discussed previously, *Captive Island* offers a range of learning tools that encourage various forms of interaction. In keeping with Davis and Gardner's *narrational window*, the exhibition commences with a series of questions: What was life in Jersey like under German rule? What dangers did the Islanders face? How did the island change? These questions require active, imaginative participation, setting a conversational tone for the exhibition. Visitors are required to maintain this kind of engagement when met, for instance, with an audio-visual challenge; looking into the eyes of a televised "German soldier", the individual is asked questions such as: *Would you let as German soldier buy you an ice cream? He's got children of his own and he misses them.* These unexpected encounters are novel and inspiring, allowing the viewer to identify with the subject matter on a personal level, independent of age or background. The experiential scope is indeed broad, with many opportunities to arouse curiosity, inspire confidence and communication.

THE POWER OF THE OBJECT

In each gallery the initial, consistent spatial cue takes the form of an introductory panel stating the theme of the room. *To leave or to stay?* addresses the quandary of evacuating without one's belongings or staying behind to face life under German rule. This brief textual passage, repeated in French and German languages, (trilingual audio-guides are now available) offers a direct and concisely informative overview. It is upon this that subsidiary sections are built, in this case by an installation that sets the scene for the family's decision making at the kitchen table. Its caption is used to ask their questions of the viewer; this line of questioning is then developed with graphic boards that inform the context by chunking the necessary references, facts, figures and images and objects from which points can be made. The key question is reiterated in the central space: What are you going to do? The narrative and quandary established, audio-visual interview testimony offers multiple perspectives as a form of conclusion and humanisation of the concepts. The spatial synapse between each stage of the process allows rooms to develop and deepen understanding, with each layer as a form of progression. Of course, the intended route may be ignored in preference for a random pathway, or as choice and interest dictates.

A more concrete approach to learning, in this instance from objects, is facilitated by explanatory labelling: *The "Occupation loaf" was made from high-extraction flour. It was heavier and darker than prewar bread and took a lot of getting used to.* It isn't so much a line of questioning that is used here, as an informal statement easily understood and familiar enough to induce contemplation. Here words are used to add, in the spirit of Margareta Ekarv, a deeper dimension to visual experience, whilst the objects themselves record knowledge and represent experience, acting as behavioural evidence synonymous with, and at the heart of the historical context. The downfall of the examples above is their inaccessibility to the visually impaired; the lack of audio labels is consistent throughout the exhibition, although the combination of tactile elements both with and without audio material is some consolation.

The concept of universal design vaunted by constructivists requires unlimited access for all visitors regardless; elements of *Captive Island* seem to have addressed in part this need through serendipity rather than intention. In the *Whispers and Lies* gallery, the controversial subject of civilian collaboration with the occupying forces is the theme. The installation consists of partly open window and door casements from which the hushed voices of black-marketeers and informants can be heard. This context is supported by graphic panels carrying wording such as *Don't tell anyone* or *Do you trust him?* This combination of audio and tactile elements in conjunction with a play on lighting, wall colour and floor texture enables a complex experiential encounter, but it is one, for the challenged visitor, that has arisen by default.

More specifically hands-on features can be found at intervals; the *Resistance* gallery encourages experimentation with ready-made crystal radio sets, complete with user-friendly instructions. To build upon this experience, visitors can choose whether they wish to take their inquiry further by assembling their own radio from the available components. As a means of layering learning material in the light of developmental level, this is a useful tool – although it has often been subject to missing parts or technical faults. This gallery also offers the opportunity for an interplay with other aspects of the display: desk drawers and floor sections can be opened to reveal, for example, a hidden camera and photographs, the serious consequences of which the visitor may at this stage be well aware of. The element of enjoyment and learning through playfulness and the possibilities for social interaction are quite evident. These are all aspects of the exhibition that can be shared, inspiring discussion to make the most of learning as a social activity, enhancing knowledge recall, irrespective of age.

The questions and quandaries arising from discussion, inspired by all these exhibits, encourage a deeper intellectual and emotional engagement with the material. They are both hands-on and minds-on, pitched in such a way as to be appealing and accessible to a wide range of visitors, but inherently limited by their marginalisation of the visually and aurally impaired. In consideration of Hein's concept of an intrinsically motivating exhibition, *Captive Island* incorporates learning modalities more diverse than the visual and textual, complementing a range of learning preferences from the traditional display of objects labelled in cases, to audio-visual interactives, themed computer games and oral testimony. Learning in the exhibition is reinforced by a supporting events programme that offers extra opportunities for visitors who wish to extend their knowledge beyond that offered in the exhibition; interpretive talks are offered throughout the year.

Considering the need for the chunking of information and stimuli in manageable quantities, scriptwriting has been undertaken to capture and maintain visitors' attention, itself in competition with visual material. Indeed, the constructivist view endorses a minimised reliance on words, which places greater emphasis on the need for accessible, legible and interesting writing that engages a diverse audience. The reading style is direct, pared down and concise to eradicate superfluous material; the vocabulary is natural as a complement to the informal explanatory idiom. Headers immediately elucidate content which is thickened through an integrated juxtaposition of text and image; minimal prose passages are personalised by careful quotation, again strengthened by appropriate narrative images. Caption style varies in accordance with preference, from the conveyance of simple factual data, to a more informal storytelling. For example, an image taken at the time of the 1940 evacuation is captioned: *Huge crowds formed outside the town hall as people rushed to register.* The informality and often colloquial tone renders text more readable, interesting and involving. Its precision and sympathetic alignment with visual material lets the texts become an organic part of the whole. The viewer is given an opportunity to actively formulate their own position through an interpretation of these symbiotic elements.

Vocabulary has been pitched at a middle ground of readership without unnecessary simplification; in the light of statistical analysis of visitor figures, this seems an appropriate solution for such a spectrum of age and educational level. Font size varies in accordance with hierarchical role, diminishing in scale from room title to image caption. No formative or summative evaluation has been undertaken to determine whether it is adequate for the visually impaired – and the atmospheric low lighting may also compound this potential barrier.

In noting the pitch and readability of the text, it is logical to consider the nature of surplus materials and resources that are provided on site. An exhibition guide fulfils its function of supporting the visitor's sequential progress, offering a substantial souvenir of the visit and the historical period. The readable style renders it broadly accessible with little prior knowledge assumed; a vibrant but clean graphic approach maintains a parallel visual storyline as a complement to the aesthetic purity of the exhibition space. Although this guide is not available in foreign language form, nor is there Braille alternative, the exhibition audio-guide renders this less of a necessity.

The most significant contribution to further educational provision is the Reserve Collection store. This dedicated area within the tunnels provides a secure home for the museum's archive and artefact material, whilst providing supervised access for any visitor by appointment. A collections catalogue also offers an excellent means of searching and retrieving object data.

As a part of this, the digitised photographic collection can be viewed in its entirety. The Adlib Information Systems Museum Standard software was chosen to be potentially compatible with that used by the local museums service; frequent communication with and advice from these museum professionals serves to strengthen working relationships and sets the stage for the possibility of future collaborative projects.

A flexible approach to visitor services ensures that focused study sessions, object handling sessions and school visits can be arranged to suit the specific needs of the group. Primary school outreach has proved to be a very successful contribution to the local curriculum, as well as enhancing community relations. Partnership with the island's Education Department has seen the drafting of history resource packs aimed specifically at key stages three and four; a diverse approach to questioning has developed a layered learning tool that encourages not just recall but critical and judgemental participation. The lack of emphasis on the learning potential of objects, particularly as they inherently lend themselves to cross-curricular development, could be addressed in order to introduce associated contexts, themes and meanings.

Having considered the facilitation of enactive, iconic and symbolic opportunities for learning in the museum, it is now important to determine what has been done to ensure that exhibition content is both relevant and meaningful for the visitor. Have research and evaluation been incorporated into exhibition planning, or have those decisions been premised upon assumption?

Conceptual access
On the understanding that learning is conditioned by socio-cultural factors, including background and preconception, exhibition planning following the constructivist model aims to incorporate audience research and evaluation into all stages of the development process. To return to the concept of familiarity, the constructivist position emphasises the learner's need for the potential association with prior knowledge. It is therefore important that visitors can establish a personal connection with displayed material that renders their experience relevant and meaningful.

It has been demonstrated that existing spaces have been appropriated to bring them into the reach of visitors by the introduction of elements that facilitate association and this has been bolstered by grounding content in the experiences of real people. In the *Daily Life* gallery, for example, visitors should have no difficulty identifying with home-made household items and the imaginative preparation of ingredients in

THE POWER OF THE OBJECT

times of scarcity. The ration books and Red Cross letters are the evidence of the daily grind, the everyday plight of the family. A display in *First Contact* draws a comparison between vernacular clothing and the alien garb of the fully equipped, newly-arrived young German infantryman. We see letters written by those who informed upon their neighbours through petty jealousy and greed; the content and nature of the material portrayed is indeed illustrative of the prosaic preoccupations evident in the experiences of civilians. Themes have been developed around the concrete, artefactual evidence of persistent and recognisable human truths using display techniques and captions that entice; in keeping with technological development and contemporary graphic innovation, the intention has been to meet the expectations and maintain the interest of a demanding younger audience.

In the formative stage of planning for the exhibition, small scale focus groups were arranged to test basic parameters. Event Communications' remit was to create an exhibition which was sympathetic to the need for the young to learn about their community history, whilst also acting as a tribute to those who lived through those troubled times. In researching the audience, emphasis was initially upon a mid-teenage sample; their feedback on writing style, deemed to be particularly important in consideration of their target status, found that vocabulary use and pitch was both stimulating and appropriate. The age of those consulted for more general and specialist matters encompassed a range of fifteen to seventy-five, whilst both curator and designer were in their twenties. These were factors considered necessary to achieve a balance of subject-based experience and fresh perception. This informed selection of exhibition team members, interviewees and consultants sought also to preclude a parochial bias, hence satisfying the paramount requirement to remain historically accurate and objective. A pattern of criticism levelled at the exhibition since opening has been the omission of information about the individuals represented in the displays. This could perhaps have been avoided through more in-depth consultation with particular minority representatives, but was avoided for fear of additional demands.

In considering the perceived learning needs of present and future users, a priority was the creation of involving multimedia displays as an enduring model for future practice. As a consequence of the positive reception, visitor statistics, in a prevailing climate of tourism decline, were seen to demonstrate a departure from the local trend. The annual introduction of new facets to the site is perceived as an attempt to stabilise numbers through generating return visits. Since the opening of *Captive Island* in 2001, small-scale quantitative research has been undertaken at regular intervals with the audience categorised demographically for comparative use by month and year. As a profit-making heritage attraction, such performance-based research is seen as essential, although by its nature it provides inherently limited data that generates patterns and not exceptions. More recently, such data has been substantiated by small-scale qualitative evaluation using comment books and exit surveys. These have demonstrated the strengths and weaknesses of the permanent exhibition: for example, feedback stating there is insufficient material displayed about the history of the building itself. Addressing such criticism has historically been seen to require the support of statistical evidence; this consistent reliance upon generalisations begs the question how much is really known about the audience's needs and expectations?

In contrast, the planning of exhibitions for 2004-2005 emphasised an holistic approach premised upon broad accessibility and the empowering of community groups to take ownership of the site. Clearly it is naïve to consider meeting all the needs of diverse interpretive communities, but the way forward was perceived to be through communication even if all wishes cannot be met for practical and economic reasons. With a solid statistical understanding of the visiting audience, tentative front-end surveys, formative and summative data collection have been completed to determine patterns of prior knowledge, learning preferences and developmental levels across the community. The purpose of ongoing evaluation is therefore to adhere to the principles of the triangulation of data-gathering methods in order to overcome the limitations of individual techniques – such as the visitor's natural desire not to offend, when questioned directly about their perception of strengths and weaknesses of a site and its features.

The distinct lack of summative evaluation in the context of *Captive Island* makes it difficult to determine whether the expectations and needs of the audience have been met, and if not how the exhibitions could be improved. The initial objectives of the project were arrived at through a managerial conception of the specific cultural context: Jersey, with its diminishing tourism, competing with cheaper holiday destinations, needing to offer an attraction commensurate with European developments, sympathetic to the learning needs of a younger target audience. Without clearly defined objectives being drawn up prior to instigation, strengths and weaknesses cannot be evaluated in summation, in reference to intended outcomes. Minor criticisms can be dealt with as they arise, but it is too late and expensive to significantly alter what is already in place.

It is clear from this discussion that although *Captive Island* can in general be seen to adhere to many of the constructivist tenets as articulated by George Hein, what is done to acknowledge the complex predisposition of the learner and what they bring to the encounter is marginal. Cumulatively there is little qualitative evidence to demonstrate the likes, dislikes and potential improvements that could be made to the physical, social and intellectual content. It cannot, therefore, be corroborated that the exhibition supports the learning preferences of user groups with their disparate knowledge levels, who hail from diverse cultural backgrounds, leading to the occurrence of successful learning.

Conclusion

Constructivists understand the formation of knowledge as occurring within the mind of the learner; their theory of learning is hence internal and developmental. The constructivist exhibition aims to provide an opportunity for the construction of knowledge by actively engaging the viewer through a diverse range of educational tools. Learning is a physical, social and personal experience unique to the configuration of learner's pre-existing schemas and ideas.

The location of *Captive Island* ostensibly constrains basic physical need provision in terms of visitor orientation, although every effort has been made to establish uniform signage and provide maps. This is a consequence of the nature of the site which must also be accepted, given its sensitive history, in the case of a shortfall in basic facilities. The exhibition is by its nature chronological, to which the space lends itself; sequence is reinforced by structurally consistent forms that place no unnecessary restrictions on alterative routes. Although, in Hein's definition, this format perhaps falls short of the multiple entry points and routes required, the balance between architectural form and exhibition content inspires curiosity and momentum – both states which are conducive to the focus needed for learning.

The use of colour, texture, light and sound enhance the thematic content through atmospheric stimulation. These sensual modalities complement a host of appropriated spaces that are conducive to shared or individual experience; a balance is achieved between the familiar in form and scale, and the intensity of the unobscured original structure. The vocabulary of design elements is consistent, as is the quality of materials and finish; the spaces are harmonious in their aesthetic vibrancy, recognisable enough for visitors to feel at ease and in control, suitably dramatic and novel enough to effectively maintain attention.

A range of tools for engaging disparate learning preferences facilitates active physical, social and intellectual experience. Much creative thought has been expended on developing stimuli for dialogic learning relevant across a range of ages and backgrounds. A challenge is implicit in the recurring questioning. Participation is consistently required be it enactive, iconic or symbolic. Text is easy to read, pitched at a generally accessible level to be broadly interesting; the conversational and explanatory tone encourages imaginative and judgemental thinking. Sadly these cleverly juxtaposed learning media are wasted on visitors with physical or sensory disabilities; it is apparent that no effort has been made directly to respond to their needs beyond wheelchair access.

On site access to collections is available in a space specifically designed to offer flexible learning; investment in technology and archival tools has been informed by local museum professionals. Partnership with schools and government is seen as key to developing support materials and structured sessions relevant to the curriculum; these are indeed collections based on and tailored to the needs of primary and secondary school students.

Object-based learning is encouraged through exhibiting the known; thematic content is grounded through reference to the items and experiences of daily life which corroborate the authenticity of the experience. Such displays are articulated in innovative and enticing configurations, made widely accessible with the use of colloquial text. Targeted specifically at children and young adults, small-scale evaluation was undertaken to endorse assumptions about pitch and holding power. The emphasis is upon active involvement which challenges the individual to formulate their own conclusions.

Captive Island successfully meets many of the pedagogic aims of the constructivist idiom, although it was not the theoretical basis for planning. It is evident that solid visitor research and evaluation was not undertaken at the front-end and formative planning stages, although summative evaluation has been undertaken on a small-scale more recently. This may have resulted in the marginalisation of some of the concerns of stakeholders and the needs of the disparate audience. This is not to say that criticisms haven't been addressed, but the historic emphasis upon a statistical point of reference renders a focus upon the differentiated individual impossible. Little is known of the specific needs and preferences or learning outcomes, therefore it cannot be acknowledged that learning has successfully engaged minds and shifted individual perceptions, because no specific objectives were set as premises for any summative reference. The planning of educational provision at Jersey War Tunnels has since been – and will be in future – increasingly rooted in the holistic constructivist agenda, where these findings will be used to inform a programme based on exhibition designers and museum educators working together and with their audiences to meet their defined needs and expectations.

Discussion

Question: What about the controversy caused by the interpretation of the occupation years [mentions a book]?

Addy: Yes it really did create a great deal of dissension. It was a book with an agenda. But the book did not have much bearing on our display as it was published in 1995, I think. Since then there have been more debates and some very strong publications about the occupation. We have a good research team behind our exhibition. But the quandary remains, as in Hasel Smith's book. There is still a great deal of discussion about what constitutes collaboration. At the time of liberation there was, particularly in Jersey, a call for the prosecution of people who had collaborated or fraternised. This didn't happen and that's probably why people have continued to ruminate and debate. In many cases there is no answer. We have a gallery dedicated to collaboration. We are not trying to shy away from it.

Question: Just like Breendonk you have a site that is an object but which doesn't force itself on you in the same way. Instead you've brought difficult issues into the exhibition. Why did you decide to do that – you could have continued as a fortification museum, with an uncontroversial military exhibition. Was it because fortification history would be too dull, or did the subject of collaboration force itself on the institution because of the debates within the community?

Addy: That is a pretty complicated question. The previous pre-2001 displays were much more focused on the site, looking at how the tunnels had functioned and were built. We still have one gallery which deals with the fortifications, the foreign workers etc. But we wanted not only to deal with the chronology of the occupation, but also with the fundamental issues: just what is an occupation? Our exhibition is a story about human experience, in which the elements of the exhibition allow a wide range of visitors to come into contact with history.

Question: I think what you've done is very interesting. I haven't been there in the 30 years since I was a boy and it used to be about how they had dug up this tunnel, very much about the engineering. I think you would have laid yourself open to criticism if you had not done what you have done. It looks fantastic, very very interesting. It is important that you've raised the question of collaboration – not least for British visitors. There's no problem for the British in being open about it (because they weren't occupied), but there is for people in Denmark, Belgium, the Channel Islands and anywhere else that was occupied.

Question: You've stressed that you've use objects as concrete evidence. And you've produced as evidence that the German forces were very aggressive such things as weapons and handcuffs. But how can you use objects as objective evidence, because it is still the curator who's making the statement, it is his argument that you have to believe.

Addy: There has to be some confidence placed in the role of the curator. And if we can't assume that visitors will the curator's role it's hard to see how museum displays can function.

Question: So how do you use objects?

Addy: To create a context. In our Resistance gallery we have a section about the manufacture of crystal sets. There are also pamphlets... We're drawing on all available reliable sources and the authentic object functions within this context.

Question: So they are there as props?

Addy: I wouldn't say props because that devalues the object as an entity that came about as a consequence of a particular happening. We're trying to create a whole, and the objects are the core of that, they are synonymous with what happened.

8

Showing Rather Than Telling

HEIKI AHONEN

Managing Director,

Museum of Occupations, Tallinn

I am a museum representative. And my topic, is described in the title, *Showing Rather Than Telling*. Conceptually, there is nothing very new in this. It is very difficult to replace pictures with words, especially against a background of generally deepening illiteracy. Ever-increasing multimedia possibilities have also had an impact. Shaping knowledge into a soft, easy-to-digest cocktail is a key element of mass culture.

Democracy guarantees every person the right to pose questions, which imposes an obligation on us to answer questions, no matter how stupid. Actually, democracy is indivisibly connected to mass culture and *vice versa*.

This is the reality we live in and the question is how to maintain a balance between moderating downright stupidity and disseminating academic knowledge. After all, both these activities are necessary, but how do we carry them out simultaneously and in the same space?

A museum is defined as an institution that collects, examines and displays material and documentation that belong to its sphere of interest. It is clear that for the public, to whom museums are directed after all, the exhibition forms the most important and visible part, be it permanent, temporary or travelling. Their differentiation is important primarily based on their different functions and, also in some sense, on the standpoints of the various target groups. It is extremely important to know whether an exhibition will be viewed by experts in the field, those unfamiliar with the subject, or by viewers that are coming into contact with the topic for the first time.

The concept of a modern museum includes the idea that the visitor to a museum (exhibition) should not only be a visitor, but also a <u>user.</u> However, it is quite paradoxical that only recently have parallels been drawn between libraries (which have users) and museums (which have visitors). Ideally, both should be institutions of enlightenment. Using the word *visitor* makes a museum seem second-rate and incidental. The difference is perhaps semantic, but symbolises the opportunities and limitations of the democratic era.

On the other hand, at a library, not everyone is given the opportunity to browse through incunabula or other rarities – only the replicas or copies are accessible. While, increasingly, opportunities are provided at museums objects from the past to be used and handled. (Of course, if they are absolutely unique, copies are used.)

I have sometimes even heard the assertion that only copies should be exhibited in museums, since then they will not suffer damage from fluctuations in humidity or sunlight. Naturally, the production of such copies is only necessary in case of true rarities. Thus, we arrive at the differences and similarities between books and museum exhibits.

An Old Low German book in a museum exhibition is viewed through glass and the accompanying description explains the importance of this object (the majority of elements used in museum exhibitions are just such objects, be they in the form of documents, photos or things).

In a library, only someone who understands Old Low German would want to use this book, and this limits the number of users to a small controllable minority. Essentially, the real *users* comprise a microscopic minority, which of course, does not mean that the needs of the user should be ignored, this would be unwarranted vandalism against the bearers of culture. The issue is still the possible shift of a "substantive visitor" toward active use.

Books can also be used visually – a totally unimportant, mass-produced book that has been banned for ideological reasons and prepared for destruction (for instance, to be cut up) makes for a very interesting visual exhibit, which described in text would certainly not provide the same information as seeing the actual object. This means that books can be used not only as reference materials, but as objects in an exhibition.

From here on, I will use the word "object" in an expanded meaning – an object may be a document, photo or physical item.

I recently re-read the historical utopia of Estonia's ancient past, as written by Lennart Meri, who was later the President of Estonia. In the book, he describes the formation, transformation and metamorphosis of the meaning of nouns, and bases various deductions thereon, which is very intriguing and promotes the development of thought. Whatever the truth of these deductions, reading this is fascinating, and it invites one to inquire further into the topic. Therefore, it is enlightening in any case and popular science in the best sense.

Even in the best case, this story cannot be transformed entirely into a narrative consisting of things, since the core of the topic is comprised of language history and linguistic development that can only in a limited sense be visually expressed as an object. For instance, by captioning a picture of a fir tree with the name of the tree written in all the languages with which one wishes to prove kinship. How this tree becomes a heavenly pillar, an image of a staircase, and this in turn, becomes a connection between the mortal and the immortal, and how this is connected to the use of a certain tree for lighting ritual fires can be better explained through text than through objects.

There are objects that must be described – the cut-up book is understandable as print censorship only if it is accompanied by an explanation; otherwise, one only sees an object that has been damaged or destroyed for some incomprehensible reason. On the other hand, there are objects that are very difficult to describe, and understanding the information they carry without a visual image is almost impossible. At least, in the emotional sense.

In Estonia, during the German occupation of World War II, wooden-soled shoes were one of the few consumer items that were <u>not</u> rationed; they could be bought freely. However, the clumsiness of wooden-soled shoes is only apparent when they are seen. Also, the advantage of a hinged wooden sole, which is semi-flexible, over a rigid one, as well as the difference between leather and canvas uppers, can only be appreciated if they are seen. The accompanying text can be limited to an explanation of the reasons for using wooden soles – a shortage of high-quality materials during the war; the fact that Germany lacked raw materials; upper and lower classes were differentiated based on the items they used, etc.

I am reminded of a suggestion by a Polish activist

to create an exhibition, or even a museum, dedicated to the absurdity of a Communist utopia. As an illustration of his idea, he showed me a photo of Warsaw in 1981, when martial law had been declared. The photo depicted a movie theatre called MIP, which means peace in Polish. At the time, *Apocalypse Now*, Coppola's film about the Vietnam War was running at the theatre, and a Soviet tank, with a tank driver leaning out of the turret, was parked in front. Peace and a tank against a background of an apocalyptic war movie. One must, of course, see the picture to understand and appreciate its background and meaning.

Understanding and perception are very important didactically. Especially in our democratic era, when we are not willing to be reconciled to a single, simple black-and-white truth, but wish to understand the reasons and context for the events that occur. In democracies, the general relevance of events has become equated with subjective relevance. One and the same event can be seen from different perspectives. This does not change what has happened, but enables us to learn considerably more from what has happened, at least theoretically, than just a simple division between light and darkness.

Moreover, isn't learning, interpreting, or at least moving in that direction, the goal of our process of enlightenment? This does not mean that it is necessary to question all existing truths, although questioning is the force that brings us closer to the truth, if this even exists.

As an illustration, imagine a photo of two soldiers. The photo was taken in 1946 of two young men from the same village in Estonia. They served in the Second World War on different sides – one is wearing a *Waffen SS* uniform, the other a Red Army one – and survived. After the war they met again and decided to take the photo – what could possibly better illustrate the situation of an average Estonian male during the consecutive Soviet and German occupations in the early 1940s? Did they have a choice?

However, back to exhibiting. During the last few years, not to say decades, the restaging of history has become popular. I think everyone has had some contact with documentary films about military history which include archival footage, but rely primarily on restaging. Usually, we are dealing with very simple explanations and examples of military logistics, without which there would not be any wars, only armed anarchy.

When, in modern action movies, we see the hero firing sixty rounds from one gun, which all hit their target, we don't even consider the impossibility of this

– this is just light entertainment.

In order to get an idea of war as an organised activity that wastes the world's resources in the most awful way, it would be useful to know how many rounds fired from a gun actually hit the target – one in a hundred, in a thousand, in ten thousand? The expenditure of materials is noteworthy. One bullet is not heavy – nine grams, like the words of a popular Russian song. One hundred bullets weigh almost a kilo, a thousand ten kilos... How many can a soldier carry? A graphic illustration is always useful in such cases. One bullet versus a backpack filled with bullets demonstrates how realistic carrying such a large amount is.

I once read a monograph about the so-called Great Northern War (1700-1721) between Sweden and Russia, which examined the logistic aspects of the war. Among other things, it seems that for each soldier fighting on the front, 200 horses were needed to transport supplies and for other transport and battle activities. However, this meant that animal feed and horse handlers were infinitely more important than a single soldier.

Based on the US Lend-Lease Agreement, in addition to foodstuffs and military supplies, the Soviet Union placed orders for 50,000 tons of barbed wire per year during World War II. The question is, how much was needed at the front and how much was needed for

Siberian prison camps? All kinds of logistics can be visualised and this is necessary for the interpretation of events.

It is easy to get carried away with visualisation. Observant viewers can often notice exaggerations in exhibitions, or detect misunderstandings based on overstated visualisations. In a way, exaggerations are unavoidable. We would like to show as much of the entire truth as possible in all its ghastliness. Mistakes are caused by arrogance, but often also by a lack of knowledge and experience. (I am not referring here to a <u>wish</u> to falsify historical events, which is another topic altogether.)

Some random examples of ignorance: at a famous Nazi German and later Soviet concentration camp in Germany (now a museum), I was shown the central exhibit in the crematorium complex, which was of course the infamous ovens. In front of the oven doors, there were small rails on which a stretcher-like base with a metal cover moved. The corpses were placed on them, and when the base was quickly pushed toward the door, the corpse holder stopped in front of the door, and the corpse "flew into" the oven.

Try for a moment to set aside the horror that thinking about the use of this tool evokes. It is clear, that the burning of corpses requires sufficient heat and certain burning conditions. I was interested whether the ovens and the constructions in front of them were originals or reconstructions. The guide assured me that there were 100% original. I pulled the flat carriage back along the track and tried to close the oven door. The door got stuck behind the carriage – the track was too short and the carriage could not be pulled back far enough for the door to close. It was clear that this was a reconstruction. The assertion that this is 100% original was apparently meant to strengthen the emotional experience, but it was also fodder for the revanchists and Holocaust deniers. The situation does not change historical truth, but does create an opportunity for needless speculation.

There was a concentration camp in northern Norway during the German occupation of the Second World War, which has been made into a museum and research center. The former camp was administered by the SS and guarded by *Allgemeine SS* troops. In the museum's exhibition, I noticed that various artifacts of the German Air Force or *Luftwaffe* were prominently displayed.

All the German Army's domestic supplies were labelled according to the respective service, thus the SS, *Wehrmacht*, *Luftwaffe*, and *Kriegsmarine* had similar tableware, but they were labelled differently, with the names and symbols of the corresponding service.

I was curious as to whether there had been an airforce unit nearby whose personnel was involved in the activities of the camp. I received a negative answer. They had just used the artifacts of the Third Reich that were easily available for the exhibition.

I was also surprised by an Iron Cross that I noticed, which was presented for military service and dated from World War I. Of course, theoretically, it was possible that a World War I veteran worked at the camp, but in reality? Again, I received an unsatisfactory answer – I was told that the German Iron Crosses from the First and Second World Wars were almost identical. This is unwarranted ignorance, since the Iron Cross from World War II does have the same external shape as the one from World War I, but it has different dates and a swastika instead of a crown as the national symbol.

One can say, of course, that this is small detail, but small details are important in any exhibition. And if the false presentation of small details results in misunderstandings – for instance, that the concentration camp was guarded and administered by *Luftwaffe* veterans of World War One, then we are dealing with distorting historical facts.

Again, these mistakes do not make the existence of the concentration and death camps, and the horrors that took place in them, non-existent, but they give a biased, if not incorrect impression of them.

A separate category of museum exhibits comprises handcrafted items and objects. They include both personal items and commemorative articles. I define personal items as items that it is difficult to do without – spoons, footwear, all kinds of little bags and containers. The range of commemorative articles is endless, from woven or embroidered items, to textiles, drawings and miniature sculptures.

Often made from cheap materials and of very varying artistic value, these items are valuable only in a certain context. At the German museum mentioned, for instance, there were metal dice that were possibly used by Dutch prisoners to raffle off additional portions of food that could not be shared out. This is partially a personal item but also a kind of souvenir, since raffles could have been organised differently without making the dice. And then again, this particular item has specific value as a symbol of brotherhood and solidarity.

The materials used to produce items in captivity tell us what was available – in other words, what materials were used in the workshops of the given camps. The resourcefulness of prisoners is endless – they try to make something useful or commemorative from any available snippet of wire. If they have no metal, it is replaced by some other material. I have seen wooden needles and vests made from handkerchiefs, not to mention footwear made from tires, and all kinds of improvised articles of clothing.

In summary – a picture is better than text in any case. In museums, especially ones that deal with recent history in all its complexity and mythology, as little primary text as possible should be used.

A moving picture is better than a static one. Memories on-screen, so-called oral history, are not always objective, but very illustrative, and can result in a high-quality presentation. Audio-visual technology provides many opportunities, as does all technology, but we should avoid overuse. A museum must be people-friendly – user-friendly. Specialists sometimes have a problem with this user-friendliness – they tend to explain processes too technically and in too much detail.

Keeping more exacting visitors in mind, preference should be given to the implementation of a multi-level information flow. Audio-visuals are essential for this. Text and pictures can be combined – to create new types of solutions for user-visitors who wish to access new levels of information – becoming an interactive exhibition. The truth is that the information needs of most visitor-users are quite limited, but one should not forget the more <u>exacting</u> minority. So, it must be possible for those with a deeper interest to satisfy their curiosity, although more resources might be need to be expended on these more exacting visitors, i.e. for the minority, than for the majority.

I have spoken about the importance of objects, and of their authenticity. Naturally, when planning exhibits, every museum must start from the basis that objects are illustrations, illustrations intended to support a narrative. A narrative is the core of a museum, and if we can convincingly, and more or less objectively, support this with illustrative material, the purpose of the museum has been accomplished.

In conclusion, let's state that for an exhibition to achieve broad, deep understanding on the part of the visitor-user, it is essential to visualise and express stories through things. The display must be justified, meaningful, and as objective as possible. Ideally, the exhibition should include a range of communication levels – for visitor-users that are more and less familiar with the topic.

It is said that one of the basic tenets of Buddhism is an understanding of two types of truth – the divine and the human. The divine is all encompassing, unequivocal and absolute, and therefore unattainable for humans. Human truth is subjective, consisting of many aspects and therefore contradictory. Let God grant us the sense to act rationally and in an enlightened manner within the framework of this knowledge.

Discussion

Question: You said that films are better than pictures. But when you go to the expense of having videos, you also have to ensure that the content isn't rubbish. In Lyons they had a film of the *Maquis* showing an 80 year-old man shooting a sten-gun, women bringing food to the *maquisards* etc., obviously filmed after the war, but presented as authentic. There is a problem with film because it's a narrative medium in itself and must be seen from end to end. An object can be seen in a flash. Perhaps films should be used like objects in museums.?

Ahonen: Probably I did not stress enough that there has to be a balance. One picture may better than a film. You have to follow your intuition. Sometimes it's impossible to tell a story in pictures, it has to be written down. You can't concentrate in a room where everything is flashing. But similarly, a museum shouldn't be as quiet as a church. Today a museum is a place of learning, not a place of commemoration. The difficulty is when you combine a noisy, interactive museum, with a memorial which should be quiet and respectful. It is possible to do it. In the US Holocaust and Memorial Museum the memorial is separate from the museum.

Question: I think you suggested that you should use as little text as possible in a museum. How is that? If you ask the visitors do they say it's OK.

Ahonen: The first text should be aimed at the least interested visitor, and then you can carry on if you are interested. It's common knowledge that the people who really read texts don't need them, they're only looking for the mistakes. The people who should read the long texts don't read them. They're too lazy, or they don't care. So we have to provide a short text but let those who want have a longer one. Perhaps a short text can also encourage the wish to know more.

9

Exhibiting Secrecy

OLIVER BENJAMIN HEMMERLE

Visiting Professor

Masaryk University, Brno

Exhibiting World War II is easy: a few recruitment posters, some weapons, maps, medals and uniforms, letters from the frontline or a POW camp, a ration book, a newspaper with the victory headline, sketches from official war artists, some exotic memorabilia from Imperial Japan – and in the background sound bites of good old Winston or of Hitler in the typical hysteria as imitated by Chaplin, plus martial music and popular 1940s tunes.

OK, to be fair: it takes more to make a good exhibition on WWII. But the objects are not the real challenge. Maybe there are too many objects in the museum store, so the choice of the right items related to a historically sound narrative (without their determining it) separates the good curator from the bad. Secrecy, as a dimension of war, could be added by an Enigma machine, which the audience usually likes to see, having read Robert Harris and seen more or less authentic movies. But what are the *real* secret objects, which genuinely illustrate the secret dimension of war (and peace)? And how can such objects be linked to a historically sound narrative without ending up as Spymania, James Bond style?

To answer these questions this article will first analyse the development of intelligence-related collections and exhibitions and then discuss the items in such collections and their relevance for the story these objects could, should and sometimes pretend to, tell. For comparison purposes this article will not be limited to WWII related items, but will include the Cold War as well. The use of the words "secrecy" and "secret objects" in this article is linked very much to, but not limited to, intelligence work. They apply also to clandestine work in a broader sense, embracing the activity of resistance movements and of undercover activities of all kind.

The place of secrecy in the museum
In the beginning were the military collections of the kings and dukes, developing into museums related to wars during the 19th century (the *Musée de l'Armée* in Paris, and military museums in many German states). This continued well into the Interwar period, when bigger war museums caught up with the new scale of war (such as the Imperial War Museum in London). In most cases, secrecy was not yet an issue as such. Nevertheless, it entered those collections related to communication issues. The family tree of secrecy in the museum also includes police museums, which emerged from internal collections starting in the 19th century (for example the police collections in Paris and Berlin) and which stored the spy equipment seized in counter-

espionage police raids. Postal museums also included references to secrecy, since intercepting mail in the *Cabinet noir* or *Black Chamber* was always at the heart of the intelligence business. But the real ancestors of secrecy in the museum were the internal collections of intelligence agencies, which emerged during the 20th century and which stored items related to the work of the agency as well as objects obtained from the enemy one way or another. These "museums" within the agencies served as collections for training or demonstration purposes for the staff and visiting dignitaries. Sometimes intelligence or spy objects were shown as a form of propaganda show, like the grounded U2 spy plane of Francis Gary Powers in the Moscow of Khrushchev. Secrecy as a topic for special and permanent exhibitions in mainstream museums emerged only in the 1990s.

To characterise the place of secrecy in exhibitions and museums today, I propose nine categories. Some museums/exhibitions belong to several categories.

1. **Internal collections of intelligence agencies**. To educate the spies and (counter-intelligence officers of the future was and is the foremost purpose of internal collections, which over time develop into a form of museum not open to the general public. To celebrate the history of its own service and honour the sacrifice of those lost in action, i.e. to create a nar-

rative of its own secret organisation, is another aim of such restricted-access exhibitions. The former KGB had this kind of internal museum in the Lubyanka. (The Felix Dsershinsky statue was removed in 1991; a memorial for the victims of Stalinism was created in 1991; but the museum is still intact). Similarly, the CIA has a memorial for fallen agents at its HQ in Langley, Virginia. The only major intelligence service to open up such a collection to the general public is the NSA, the US eavesdropping agency: the museum building is near its HQ at Fort Meade, Maryland. Other services sometimes present part of their collection to the general public for propaganda purposes or to increase the public's awareness of counter-intelligence work: the German *Verfassungsschutzämter* (offices for the protection of the constitution) displayed from time to time during the Cold War parts of captured Eastern spy "survival kits". Nowadays such exhibitions tackle political extremism and economic espionage. The Communist East Germans opened a sort of open-air museum in 1956, when the Berlin spy tunnel (betrayed by the Soviet mole George Blake) was "discovered". Items of Western subversion (*diversion* was the Eastern term) were constantly presented to an international media audience – another form of short-run special exhibition (More recently that tunnel has been recreated in the Allied Museum in Berlin). A still existant open-air museum for propaganda purposes is the USS Pueblo, which was taken by force by the North Koreans and is still exhibited in Pyongyang to foster anti-Americanism. And it is worth mentioning the Israeli intelligence memorial at Tel Aviv, which combines in a unique way – as it is open to the general public – a monument to those who lost their lives in the secret war and a small museum.

2. **Intelligence in traditional armed forces or war museums.** Intelligence-related items entered traditional military museums after WWI. The stuffed "spy" pigeon in the *Musée Royal de l'Armée et d'Histoire Militaire* in Brussels is just one example. Secret notepads, postcards with a stamp concealing important information and discovered by a vigilant counter-intelligence are the "human touch" objects among the *Grosse Bertha* monstrosities from WWI. After WWII, special army units devoted to intelligence created their own museums (the Military Intelligence Museum now in Chicksands, Bedfordshire; the Museum of Australian Military Intelligence in Canungra, Queensland). The Royal Signals Museum in Blandford, Dorset, shows items used to secure communication against enemies. WWI stories like that of Lawrence of Arabia also include secrecy, as was shown in a special exhibi-

tion at the Imperial War Museum in 2005-6 and is still on show in the Tank Museum in Bovington, Dorset. Naval museums do not refer explicitly to intelligence in most cases, even though reconnaissance is a main purpose of modern navies. Submarine museums as in Gosport, Hampshire, are very much concerned with intelligence, although this tends not to be emphasised, because the convoy system of WWII and the nuclear capability of submarines are at the centre of most presentations. With the end of the Cold War, some former Soviet submarines entered Western ports peacefully for museum and tourism purposes, as at the German harbours of Burgstaaken, Hamburg or Peenemünde. The Israeli Air Force museum near Beer Sheva owns aeroplanes, which were really a major intelligence success, the Israeli secret service "convincing" Arab pilots to fly and land some state-of-the-art MIG fighters in Israel – to then be examined in great detail by the Israelis, Americans and other Westerners. Another example of intelligence in traditional army museums is the presentation of a *BRIXMIS* display in the National Army Museum in Chelsea, London. These legalised spy missions took place during the whole Cold War period on both sides of the Iron Curtain, as the four Allies had agreed on such reciprocal missions in Germany. The Russian Air Force Museum in the region around

Moscow shows the remains of Gary Powers' U2; a 2003 special exhibition of the Russian Armed Forces Museum commemorated *SMERSH*, the anti-spy shock troops used during and immediately after WWII. Terrorism entering military museums from the 1970s is also linked to exhibits related to intelligence as a major source for any counterterrorist activity. The Turkish have plenty of it in their galleries devoted to the fight against Kurdish separatism (PKK) in the Istanbul-based Askeri Müse. The British have it as well, since Northern Ireland was a terrorist hotspot for several decades. Last, but not least, the Imperial War Museum (IWM) was the first major war museum to devote a complete permanent exhibition to the Secret War in the 1990s. Starting with the arrest of the spies of the Kaiser during WWI, continuing with the challenges and exploits of WWII and leading on to the counterterrorism against the IRA (the IWM being itself a target of Northern Irish terrorism) and the SAS actions at home and abroad. The line between intelligence agencies, police, military and special forces is not very clear in such presentations – thereby reflecting reality.

3. **Intelligence in resistance museums of WWII.** Most of the resistance work against Nazi occupation and suppression had to be performed clandestinely. Many resistance movements supplied intelligence

to the British secret services (MI6, SOE etc.) or to the American OSS, the forerunner of the CIA. The Allied intelligence services provided support through weapons deliveries by airdrops. This story is sometimes included in regular war museums, but in many cases it is presented in museums devoted solely to the resistance effort during WWII. Examples are the *Musée de l'Ordre de la Libération* in Paris, the *Centre d'Histoire de la Résistance et de la Déportation* in Lyon, the *Musée National de la Résistance* in Brussels, the *Múseum SNP* in Banská Bystrica (Slovakia) and the *Museum Powstania Warssawskiego* in Warsaw. Resistance exhibitions in communist states were mostly devoted to communist organisations only, the non-communist Polish *Armia Krajowa* (Home Army) entering museums in its own right after the collapse of the Communist regime. In the *Gedenkstätte Deutscher Widerstand* in (former West) Berlin, documenting the anti-Nazi movements in Germany from 1933, it took a long and agonising debate before Soviet-sponsored German POW-resistance groups like the *Nationalkomitee Freies Deutschland* were allowed into the permanent exhibition. The relation between the tiny German resistance groups and Allied intelligence is largely a *rendezvous manqué*, meaning that the relative lack of such liaison efforts is reflected in the exhibition. The substantial intelligence work provided by French resistance for the Normandy landing in June 1944 is documented in the D-Day museum in Southsea, Hampshire. The Saints-Cyril-and-Methodius-Church in Prague harbours a museum dedicated to *Operation Anthropoid*, the killing of SS-mass-murderer Heydrich by Czech resistance and British intelligence. During and immediately after the war there were small exhibitions in the unoccupied or liberated territories highlighting the role of the resistance in the Allied war effort (for example in Paris and Brussels very soon after the liberation). More recently a SOE museum opened at Beaulieu in Hampshire on the historical spot, where this British-sponsored organisation had trained Allied personnel to engage in clandestine work in Nazi-occupied Europe. Concentration camp sites sometimes show intelligence links in their exhibitions, for example in the KS Flossenbürg, where the Nazi spymaster Canaris was killed after he fell from grace. Many Holocaust museums, for example in Jerusalem and Washington, dedicate some space to the as yet unclear fate of Raoul Wallenberg, which seems to have some intelligence background. Secrecy of another kind was presented in some German museums after the Nazi ban on freemasonry for Nazi propaganda purposes. The looted property of masonic lodges in Germany and – later on – in Europe was presented for example in the *Sächsische Logenmuseum* in Chemnitz to "expose" the "secrets" of the freemasons. After the end of Nazi rule many of these objects stolen by the Nazis ended up in Soviet stores. Some of the objects of non-German origin were returned recently to their rightful owners, the lodges. Secrecy in this case was a mixture of the self-styled rituals of the lodges and their "exposure" by the invented conspiracy theories of Nazism. (Museums representing the official story of freemasonry can be found at Bayreuth, Paris and London.)

4. **Museums at places once used for intelligence or clandestine purposes**. Places with a link to intelligence work are not accessible while in use and often soon forgotten when they have served their purpose, Bletchley Park being the perfect example of such a location. On this spot, with the breaking of the Enigma code, undoubtedly the major intelligence success of WWII materialised. After the war, the location was used for other purposes, the wartime importance of the place still being guarded by the Official Secrets Act and therefore unknown to the general public. Television documentaries and semi-fictional books like *Enigma* by Robert Harris raised public awareness and the place was rediscovered by veterans, interested laymen and professional historians alike. Bletchley Park is also a perfect example of the problems facing an

interested part of the public during the transformation of such a site into a museum. It starts with the actual commercial use of the site, which is not related to its historical role. Property rights have to be gained from the Ministry of Defence and/or by private parties, which is usually a lengthy and costly process. The site at that stage may differ very much from its condition at the time of the secret work. The recreation has to start with a mixture of refurbishment and restoration. Financial and legal problems lie ahead. The volunteer historical site developers have to gain the support of private collectors and public collections to fill the newly-acquired spaces, which in many ways may not be the ideal places to house museum exhibitions. In the case of Bletchley Park, the creation of a permanent memorial site seems to be still under review after more than a decade – including a possible failure. Even longer is the development story of the former site of the *Reichssicherheitshauptamt* in Berlin. On this spot most of the Holocaust was planned, but the building also housed important sections of the SS intelligence service SD (*Sicherheitsdienst*). The debate on how to use this site and how to remember the crimes organised and planned there started in the 1970s, when the location was part of West Berlin adjacent to the Wall. It became clear that this site had to be developed by the state.

THE POWER OF THE OBJECT

For a time, a non-permanent open-air exhibition was created to interpret the ruins (mostly only cellars) to an interested public. Several decades and architectural competitions later, the non-permanent exhibition remains the only permanent thing on the site, with a partly-built museum joining the ruins on the site and another building project on the way. Another failure in Berlin was the development of the *Teufelsberg*, the former US eavesdropping headquarters, as a private spy museum (see 8 below). The remains of an Eastern eavesdropping hotspot on the famous Brocken mountain on the Eastern side of the former Iron Curtain remains a sideshow to the tourism attracted by the mountain, which has been accessible again since late 1989. The Glienicker Brücke between Berlin and Potsdam is still in use, but also forms an open-air memorial for the exchange of imprisoned spies during the Cold War. In this context the graves of people like Markus Wolf in Berlin, Kim Philby in Moscow or Richard Sorge in Tokyo should also be mentioned. Capital cities as living, open-air museums of intelligence-related buildings and sites can be explored through spy-focused guidebooks in The Hague/Amsterdam, London and Washington D.C.; spy tours are organised occasionally in Berlin and Vienna; as well as a *Mystery Tour of the Nathan Hale Homestead* in Connecticut and a

Soldiers and Spies in Revolutionary New York tour. Terror memorial sites, such as for the Oklahoma bombing or – under development – for 9/11 demonstrate the lack of intelligence or of appropriate analysis. Secret Cold War bunkers are increasingly being opened to the general public, like the British one in Kelvedon Hatch, Essex, or the German one in Ahrtal. The Cu-Chi-Tunnels in Vietnam are already a tourist attraction. Colditz Castle with its exhibition on the various escape attempts during WWI somehow complements the museums dealing with the story of SOE and resistance.

5. **Museums and memorial sites related to the Cold War and to Eastern bloc intelligence agencies and political police**. Of course these museums would easily qualify for 4 above, but the sheer number and variety of such museums justifies their being dealt with separately. The openness of these places was a result of the peaceful revolutions in the Eastern Bloc in 1989, when the people claimed the HQs of the state security, which in most cases held the offices of the foreign intelligence service as well. Afterwards, these locations were sometimes transformed into memorial sites. This in many cases stopped the complete destruction of important documents as the last action of the old regime, which consequently provided the necessary inventory for a museum/archive in the future.

THE POWER OF THE OBJECT

The largest number of such museums and memorial sites is undoubtedly on (former East) German soil. The opposition movement in the former Communist part of Germany successfully established both memorial sites and open archives; even so this took a lot of effort, including a hunger strike. These are today both privately and state-run. *Runde Ecke*, the former Leipzig HQ of the *Stasi* (East German state security agency – *Ministerium für Staatssicherheit*) houses a museum run by former opposition groups and an archive under the control of the BStU (federal agency for former archives of the *Stasi*; more commonly referred to as *Gauck-* or *Birthler-Behörde* (office), according to the names of the heads of this agency). In East Berlin the former ministry of state security *Normannenstrasse* building is also run by former anti-communist opposition groups, whereas the official BStU has opened a museum near the Brandenburg gate. Other museums include the former *Stasi* bunker (for use in wartime) in Machern near Leipzig. As the *Stasi* was a mixture of political police and internal/external intelligence service, it ran prisons as well, where real or alleged spies were the inmates. Several prisons are now transformed at least partly into memorial sites, like the *Roter Ochse* in Halle. In a part of the (still functioning) prison a museum is devoted to the *Gestapo* (Nazi secret police), post-1945 Soviet intelligence and *Stasi* past of the site. The former *Stasi* prison in Berlin-Hohenschönhausen is probably the most controversial memorial site in Germany today. It is under the direction of Hubertus Knabe, who has written largely about the *Stasi* and is also a vocal opponent of the transformed Communist party. The depiction of an alleged torture scene caused particular controversy, as the sources are highly debatable. There is an ongoing cultural war between Knabe and the (sometimes extreme right-wing) associations of victims of Communism on the one hand and the organisations of former *Stasi* officers on the other. Other prisons in the former Soviet bloc have an intelligence relationship, too, such as the former KGB prison in the East German city of Potsdam or the GDR execution place in Leipzig – the last person executed in East Germany in 1981 was a captured *Stasi* defector. Parts of other museums featuring Stalinist-type Communist regimes like the Hungarian House of Terror Museum in Budapest, the Museum of the Occupation of Latvia 1940-1991 in Riga or the Checkpoint Charlie Museum in Berlin also address intelligence issues and some are equally contested. Mentioning the names of former secret police and intelligence officers in such memorial sites, exhibitions and museums sometimes results in court action – with an as yet uncertain outcome in

Germany (currently the courts tend to decide in favour of naming names). An open-air exhibition at Wenceslas square in Prague in late 2008 not only mentioned names, but showed large pictures of former leading Czechoslovak state security officials, many of them still alive. The political importance of such museums in the former Eastern bloc territory is still high, for example an exhibition on the *Stasi* was recently visited by German Chancellor Angela Merkel to keep the memory of the resistance against dictatorship alive. The Polish Institute and Sikorski Museum in London documents the work of the Polish exile government during WWII and during the Communist rule (including intelligence work as a form of resistance).

6. **Intelligence in police, postal, technology, science museums**. Police and postal museums have already been mentioned as one of the roots in the genealogy of intelligence museums. Police museums mainly display items related to counter-intelligence. The *Museum Policie* in Prague still contains some of the former communist propaganda exhibits about real or invented espionage on Czechoslovak territory. The small exhibition in the FBI Hoover-Building in Washington D.C. is related to counter-intelligence by the very nature of the agency; the same is true for the anti-drug-related intelligence efforts presented in the

DEA museum in Arlington, Virginia. Postal museums generally include some items related to censorship and thereby to more or less clandestine surveillance. The German postal museums in Berlin and Frankfurt showed special exhibitions related to *Stasi* involvement in the East German postal system and about (not so) secret communication. Parts of the postal exhibition ended up in the Berlin museum of the *Gauck-/Birthler-Behörde*, this German federal agency being the owner of most exhibits "inherited" from the former East German *Stasi* (see 5). Unsolved terror attacks have entered the National Postal Museum in Washington with an exhibit on the post-9/11 anthrax letters. Customs museums such as in Hamburg or Jerusalem usually contain some exhibits about intelligence (proliferation). Technical museums are more inclined to show methods of secret communication, for example the German *Heins-Nixdorf-Museumsforum* in Paderborn. A special exhibition at the *Museum Industriekultur* in Nuremberg in 2007-8 was devoted to all aspects of spy technology. The *Sächsische Psychatriemuseum* in Leipzig deals with alleged abuses of psychiatry by the *Stasi*.

7. Intelligence in "normal" museums (regional connections, special exhibitions). Intelligence aspects enter mainstream museums if there is a regional or local connection – usually to a famous spy. An example is Margaretha Seller, who discovered the world of the Dutch colonies, of exotic/erotic dancing and – tragically – of WWI intelligence under the name of Mata Hari. Her life was cut short by a firing squad in Vincennes near Paris in 1917. She was a native of Leeuwarden in the Netherlands, so the city honours (only in recent times!) her (in)famous life not only with a monument, but also by a section in the regional *Fries Museum*. Probably the first mainstream national museum to devote a special exhibition to intelligence issues was the Swedish *Nordiska Museet* (Nordic Museum) in 1999-2000. It covered espionage in, for and against Sweden from 1600 until the present and was certainly influenced by the permanent *Secret War* exhibition at the IWM, which really became the model for most intelligence-related exhibitions around the world. It exhibited the endangered neutrality of Sweden as a result of Nazi and Soviet espionage and the history of the *Säpo* (Swedish secret police). Other national historical museums like the German *Haus der Geschichte der Bundesrepublik Deutschland* in the former capital, Bonn, also include some items related to intelligence as part of general history (for example the East German spy, Günter Guillaume, who worked in the federal chancellery of Willy Brandt). Special exhibitions about the 1970s German left-wing extremist terror in Berlin and Gras included some exhibits related to intelligence gained (or missed) by the state, too.

8. **Intelligence museums with a commercial purpose**. There have been several failed attempts to create intelligence museums for commercial purposes, the Berlin-Teufelsberg project has already been mentioned. The International Spy Museum in Washington D.C. is the only commercial project so far, which has passed the planning stage and has been open for some time. Its location – a few blocks from the White House and near Ford's Theatre, where Lincoln was assassinated – in the tourist centre of the US capital provides the potential to attract a sufficient number of visitors. But not only are sufficient visitor numbers needed. Also required are several long-time private collectors (usually with links to the intelligence community), the goodwill of one or several intelligence agencies (or at least of some veterans) and – last but not least – investors prepared to pay for the initial costs. Commercial projects can only survive, if they combines the museum aspect with elements of the entertainment industry. Some (anti-)Communist museums are privately owned like the Checkpoint Charlie Museum in Berlin or the Museum of Communism in Prague. Internal and external intelligence always features in such museums; the line between the political motivation of the museum own-

ers and commercial interests is in some cases thin. A pure tourist attraction is the 1984 show (including KGB interrogation) in a Vilnius bunker. The possible transformation of the former East German prison *Hoheneck* into a tourist recreation site failed due to the protests of former inmates. The Peenemünde site of Nazi rocket production, once a key target of Allied intelligence efforts, was transformed into a mixture of a memorial site, museum and tourist attraction. It is an *Eigenbetrieb* (enterprise run and owned by the local authority). The twin aims of remembering Nazi victims (forced labour in rocket-production and the victims killed by the rockets) and earning money for the impoverished region make for a difficult balance and ensured controversy from the beginning.

9. **Fictional intelligence in the museum**. Aspects of popular culture items feature prominently in many intelligence exhibitions. In the *Secret War* exhibition at the Imperial War Museum, such objects form the entry to the parts presenting *the real thing*. Objects of popular culture will be discussed in more detail below, but it should be noted that the same Museum devoted a special exhibition to the fictional James Bond in 2008. Such fictional themes may even attract more visitors than the real thing – and may attract to the museum audiences not reached by historical exhibitions. The

role model might be Star Wars, entering science museums in the 1990s and confronting science fiction science with real science. The line between cultural mission and commercial enterprise in traditional historical museums may be thinner; nevertheless such exhibitions are perfectly legitimate for any cinema or literature museum, presentation a famous actor, director or – as in the case of Ian Fleming – an important spy fiction author.

The objects to exhibit secrecy
An exhibited object ceases to be a secret object. The (past) secrecy of the object can only be demonstrated by explaining the once-secret character of the object. The headline for all exhibitions of once-secret objects is the title of the British early post-WWII film about the secret war effort, *School for Danger*, better known as *Now It Can Be Told*. Not quite, however, as the most important aspects of the secret aspects of WWII – like the breaking of the Enigma code – were disclosed only in the 1970s. And even details like *The Man Who Never Was* only being disclosed in the mid-1950s, a decade after *Now It Can Be Told*. The "human intelligence factor" – spying itself and analysis – is hardly reflected in any specific objects (The exhibition of archival paperwork related to such events does not hold much visitor

appeal.) So instead of *Now It Can Be Told* the available objects are really much more *The Story So Far (Released)*. For WWII, the period of protection and partial disclosure is probably over, but the issue of only partial availability (due to the Official Secrets Act etc.) is still a factor that has to be taken into curatorial account. Setting aside the availability problem, a much more practical issue arises, which splits into two parts: What actually is a secret object? What object is appropriate to demonstrate (former) secrecy in a museum?

The first question is answered relatively easily in a formal sense: a secret object is an object which was kept secret by its user. The user could be the spy with his Minox camera as the concealed object; the user could be the state protecting (or at least trying to protect) by guards and legal measures the filing box with the names of its agents. Both secret objects pose problems for museum purposes. The Minox camera, highly symbolic for espionage, gets its special meaning only from its context. The camera itself is a technical or design museum object, the secrecy element is derived from its story, which has to be explained to the visitor – and under ideally be linked to the spy case by another object. An image showing the spy with the camera (for example in a police reconstruction) or a picture of the police press conference after the seizure of the camera might be such an object. As far as the filing boxes and all those documents stamped *(NATO) Cosmic Top Secret* are concerned, no reminder is needed that paper documents – while in some cases essential parts of an exhibition – tend not to be eye-catchers from the visitor's point of view. The main requirement in the search for suitable objects has to be the *immediacy* of secrecy and the need for objects which transcend paperwork.

1. **Objects of intelligence administration**. These are the files, reports and anything produced as output of the intelligence field work to be stored and analysed at the HQ of the intelligence agency. These objects are in most cases more suited to an archive rather than to display in an exhibition. Files as samples of the bureaucracy of intelligence work, or those relating to well-known spy cases, may be an exception to that rule. In the *Secret War* exhibition at the Imperial War Museum, an interactive multimedia element was introduced in which modified files of the intelligence agencies were made available to visitors, who could explore the (fictional, but factional) "secret careers" of the heads of MI5 and MI6. Similar virtual file presentations are used to tell the story of certain intelligence operations.

2. **Means of secret documentation**. The Minox camera has already been discussed as the most iconic

technical object relating to intelligence work. This is supplemented by other photographic equipment, ranging from the film development kit for home use by the agent on foreign soil, to the much more sophisticated optical equipment of spy planes and satellites, including optical aids for analysis. Technical objects linked to computers might change this, but the intelligence link is in most cases not obvious without further explanation.

3. **Means of secret communication and objects reflecting secret interception and censorship**. As a symbol of secrecy second only to the Minox comes the Enigma. Less sophisticated technology provides objects related to the production and reading of Microdots, or the older secret ink messages. Radio transmitters used in resistance work are a common feature of many exhibitions. Secret messages smuggled out of prisons, concentration camps or POW camps also belong to this category. Or the pigeons once used to carry secret messages in the Franco-Prussian/German War of 1870-71 and during the two World Wars. The breaking of the Enigma code is more difficult to visualise: a DIY-replica of the Enigma by Polish intelligence or a recreation of the *Colossus* computer as at Bletchley Park might do. Large collections of postcards and letters intercepted and stored by the East-German *Stasi* are a very drastic example of state-sponsored censor-

ship and surveillance. Instruments to open and reseal letters fill Communist intelligence/secret police exhibitions as well. Intercepted and confiscated items provide a rich source for exhibitions (for example a *Charta 77* exhibition in Bratislava in 2009), as these objects document the work of opposition movements, which might be otherwise lost, since the main actors were imprisoned or went into exile without any archive being preserved.

4. **Objects of concealment**. In the pre-Internet age combs with holes in them, or boxes with false bottoms of all kinds were used to transport secret messages. The ingenuity of concealment seems endless, as are the relevant objects. But it is the accurate knowledge of the historical background of the object, which counts.

5. **Forged objects**. Intelligence services produce forged documents of all sorts. These, and the technical equipment used for such purposes, are objects to exhibit. This is especially true for exhibitions related to resistance movements – these items provide a glimpse into clandestinity. (Paper) money, bills and stamps were forged on a large scale during WWII (*Operation Bernhard*), and are now exhibited at Sachsenhausen concentration camp. Black propaganda leaflets also belong to this category.

6. **Weapons**. "Wet job" is the concealed name for

killing by intelligence agencies. All sorts of conventional weapons were used for such bloody purposes. Unconventional weapons comprise letter bombs, as used by Israeli intelligence to punish SS mass murderers protected by their new Arab masters and thereby evading justice (as in the case of Alois Brunner). Or umbrellas capable of injecting poison, which were employed by Eastern secret services to silence the exiled voices of *Radio Free Europe* in Munich. More recent official or private Russian killing devices, such as the Polonium introduced into the drink or meal of defecting spies in London, might overstretch the safety requirements of conservators, since even the coffin had to be specially secured against radiation. Again the *Secret War* exhibition shows a wide range of conventional and unconventional weapons. Planes like the U2, or the already mentioned "redirected" MIG fighters, belong to the weapons category as much as submarines and unmanned aerial vehicles (UAV) used for intelligence purposes.

7. **Other objects used as equipment for intelligence work**. Weapons are an important, but usually not the decisive, element in the typical spy kit. Concealed maps, or clothing adapted to the enemy host nation's style are as important as weapons. The SOE during WWII went as far as to print a sort of catalogue with items available to agents entering Nazi-occupied

territory. The East German *Stasi* tried to collect olfactory samples of political adversaries, which are now in some of the BStU exhibitions. Such exhibits still have a political meaning: when the police, before a recent NATO meeting in Germany, tried to collect olfactory samples from possible violent anti-NATO protesters, the BStU-head Marianne Birthler received media coverage of her views on the samples in the museum and archive's collections.

8. **Objects used for tradition-building and corporate identity within intelligence agencies.** Some objects produced by intelligence agencies were and are used to "educate" and raise the awareness of the general public (the WWI posters *Feind hört mit* or *Keep mum, she's not so dumb*). The Eastern bloc secret police and intelligence services had quite a culture of producing PR items relating to their secret work, ranging from medals to handkerchiefs. Their Western counterparts only more recently discovered the propaganda value of a corporate identity carried on merchandise. The US agencies have set up stores selling such stuff for some time now, while the German *Bundesnachrichtendienst* only recently started selling such items at the building site of its new Berlin office. This merchandise will show its museum-worthiness as time goes by and such items become rarer, whereas the Eastern – sometimes

very tasteless – *Stasi* and *KGB* products already have a collectors' market and are exhibited in several museums. In some cases, for commercial reasons, fake post-1989 objects have entered exhibitions (such as insignia in the exhibition at the *Roter Ochse* prison in Halle).

9. **Items of popular culture related to intelligence.** Many exhibitions related to "real" intelligence make use of fictional intelligence objects like James Bond puppets and toy cars to introduce the real thing. Again the *Secret War* exhibition acts as a role model: after a showcase with Bond merchandise from the 1960s onwards, the visitor is led into a small film theatre for a "briefing". There the contrast between the fictional objects and the real objects in the rest of the exhibition is highlighted: *As you walk these rooms, you will see for yourself, that fact is more incredible and exciting than fiction.*

In museums related to Eastern Bloc intelligence and the secret police, objects of popular culture are usually derived from state propaganda: a (Soviet spy) Dr.-Richard-Sorge-button for members of the East German communist youth organisation, Soviet Union postage stamp sets celebrating the achievements of famous spies, high-quality handicraft miniature books about *Kundschafter des Friedens* (explorers of peace, the communist synonym for "good"= own spies). In the West there are children's board games about espionage, nowadays supplemented and sometimes replaced by film-like computer games about spies. Usually these objects are not presented for their intrinsic value, but to facilitate the visitor's entry to the "real" world called "secret" by comparing fiction and fact. In the museum of the British film studio which produced the Bond films, the "golden colt", an iconic exhibit, was stolen recently.

10. **Artwork related to intelligence**. Artworks, as shown in the 2009 exhibition *Embedded Art* at the Berlin Academy of Arts, belong to this category. Official war artists in the West rarely address intelligence issues, whereas official artists in the former Eastern bloc produced many more or less artistic works about Dr. Sorge and other (mostly dead) spies. *Conspiracy Dwellings* was the name of a 2008 *Symposium on Surveillance in Contemporary Art* at South Hill Park, Berkshire.

11. **Places related to the work of intelligence agencies**. Location as an object has already been discussed. Sometimes the location is "transported" into the exhibition: in a Swedish exhibition a piece of a bugged concrete wall from the Swedish embassy in Moscow (1986) was shown.

12. **Modern technologies as a supplement to real items or for visualisation**. The use of modern technology has already been discussed. Another example are the puppets used in a Swedish exhibition to illus-

trate with audio some of the VIPs of Swedish history (the Soviet spy Stig Wennerström, the wartime postal censor Astrid Lindgren).

13. **Possible exhibits regarded as inappropriate**. Soviet intelligence gathered up the burned remains of Hitler in 1945. Some parts were dispersed on German soil, others ended up in the KGB archive in Moscow. Apparently most of the material was destroyed under KGB director Yuri Andropov; later on, the rest – which is said to be now in a state archive – was not shown at exhibitions on relevant WWII topics. The remains (probably only the head) of the executed Mata Hari ended up in the collection of a Parisian anatomy department, but they have been unseen for several decades and are therefore considered as lost.

Secrecy meets the public

During the last 20 years the world of WWII and Cold War intelligence has entered museums in full force: permanent exhibitions (*The Secret War* in London), special exhibitions (in Stockholm, Frankfurt, Berlin), special museums (International Spy Museum, Bletchley Park, two *Stasi* Museums in Berlin). Sensationalism – a current feature in the process of museum commercialisation and in the big "special exhibitions" business – remains a constant threat. Especially for museums presenting secrecy. So far the general outcome is no worse than in other fields of applied museology. The process was aided by the disbanding of the Eastern Bloc intelligence agencies – providers of countless now historic objects (both in the East and in the West) – and by the simultaneous development of intelligence studies as an accepted academic field of research. *The Secret War* exhibition was really a bonanza, a worthy role model. The *War on Terror* has yet fully to enter the world of museums; Guantanamo Bay may become later in the 21st century an appropriate site at which to represent intelligence gathering and the democratic debate about the purpose, means, ends and limitations of intelligence and secrecy.

For the time being, the benchmark is lower. Even if many things "remain sketchy", at least the visitor should leave any intelligence/secrecy exhibition with the clear idea that James Bond is not the real thing. To induce historical or political interest, in the context of an exhibition whose theme is perceived to be sensational, is the curator's challenge in this "wilderness of mirrors" [1] of funding, visitor numbers, historical accuracy and curatorial professionalism.

1. *Former CIA Deputy Director J. J. Angleton with reference to T. S. Eliot.*

10

Objects and the Power of their Stories

MARCEL WOUTERS

Director, Marcelwoutersontwerpers BV

Eindhoven

People want to save all sorts of things. In the first place themselves, their cars, their bicycles, their suitcases and the members of their family. So, people want to keep and throw away. People often start having regrets after throwing something away, although there are exceptions. And gradually you start missing the one who has been thrown out of your life. You start collecting things. A photo, a hairpin that has been left behind, two boots that were never picked up. Notes that you read carelessly at the time are now read word by word. You save, you save and you save. If you are lucky, or actually if you are not, it becomes a full day's work. You go so far in saving things, that you start copying what has been thrown away, you start creating. The moment you start wondering if it should be saved, it is already too late. Just as it is in love. At that moment you have already thrown it away. There is nothing left to be saved.[1]

We often attach a personal, emotional value to objects. In the case of historical objects this value can be collective, which makes it worthwhile exhibiting the object in a museum. And then it appears that a lot of people want to admire these objects from the past. Not so much because they want to learn about the past, but especially because old things emanate a historical sensation. Museums are considered among the most reliable sources when it comes to providing historical information. Think of museums, and often the image of a monumental building springs to mind. In this building we expect to find rooms filled with historic objects or large halls displaying art. Traditionally, the museum's main focus has been *the object* or *the collection*. And exhibition design just a supportive shell around this collection. Apart from textual information, directly linked to the objects on display, there is no information about the subject of the exhibition. The design reflects a scientific approach or an aesthetic fashion. Its ambition does not reach beyond the cosmetic.

At a certain moment the mere exhibiting of objects was no longer enough and we, the exhibition designers, made our appearance. We started bringing together objects to fit in with a specific theme, and we started looking for anecdotes and stories to make the objects link into the public's perception. Soon the theme of the exhibition itself became the focal point and we used objects to illustrate the story. For instance, we gave our perspective on history, on nature, or on technology, and we tried to get that across to the visitor in as lively a way as possible. Not only did we provide a visually attractive environment, we also gave the visitor stimulating information and detail about the objects. And when the presentation was still not appealing enough, the introduction of electronic and audio-visual media provided new ways of communicating.

However, in the recent decades the focus in museums has shifted from the objects themselves to the way they are presented, how they are perceived by the public, and how the public experiences the museum and its objects. In the past, the objects were important, in most museums these days the central focus is on reflection and interpretation. Let's look at two examples of exhibitions about the Second World War...

National Monument Camp Vught

The National Monument is located near the former SS concentration camp in Vught. The *Stealing One's Freedom* gallery overlooks a canal with barbed wire, while the strict, rigid gallery on Nazi ideology looks out onto a stern, concrete, grey model of the camp outside. The history of the site is told as respectfully as possible on the basis of personal stories from the people involved. By telling the stories of individuals that speak most clearly to visitors, they gain a better understanding of the big picture of the war and of the Nazi regime.

It was a particularly tough job. On the one hand, attention needed to be drawn to the existence of perpetrators, victims and observers and how their roles took shape. How did those people think and act? Youngsters, often on school outings, are the target audience. On the other hand, the museum should also be accessible to people who are somehow emotionally involved. And, of course, to people who wish to commemorate the Second World War.

Social exhibition
The final area of the exhibition resembles a relaxed pub – except you can't buy any drinks. What purpose does this room serve? It is a social exhibition. An exhibition that leads to a deep, thought provoking experience. Visitors are invited to discuss the elements on display. The visitors' own way of experiencing the exhibition, partly formed by their individual backgrounds, plays an important part here.

Recreated newspapers, with moving images instead of photos, are on the tables next to real ones. Scenes from a pub, in which people hold ordinary conversations, are projected on a nine-metre long wall. While walking through this area of the exhibition you might overhear some people give their opinion on democracy. You can also witness the reaction of the other visitors when a rather unusual person enters the pub. In the background, a colour television set shows newscasts. A man and a woman are sitting at a table. The man says: "If you really love me, you would …" A clear example of emotional blackmail. Visitors might question the purpose of this mixture of conversations and newspaper reports. They might engage in a discussion, or it might urge them to think about it. The exhibition does not end in this area, it just leaves visitors with a clear message: always keep thinking and judging for yourself, even if it deviates from collective opinion or the law.

Authenticity

In an interview, I was asked which exhibitions had impressed me most. It turned out to be an unexpectedly difficult question. After I went through all the presentations I am familiar with in my mind, I drew the conclusion that they were those exhibitions that carried the force and the mysticism of authenticity. "Here, at the spot where I am standing now, is where it happened." Or, "This is the original that he himself held in his hands, imagine the effect it must have had." In spite of all our professional efforts, the efficient transfer of information is not able to match authenticity.

When people speak about more authenticity they are usually referring to material authenticity. The object is still "original", nothing has been changed about it. However, objects always change; the original material can fall into decay, discolour or change. The actual identity of the object contrasts sharply with the actual identity.

Do objects actually have a fixed, authentic meaning? I cannot give an unequivocal answer to this, because an object can have different authentic meanings. I would like to shed more light on one of those...

Conceptual authenticity
The idea behind this is that when the intention of the maker is clear, the technical execution can basically be carried out by other people as well. This may be a good excuse for the construction of copies. However, the technical execution often also forms part of the conceptual authenticity, since the idea of the maker was always limited by the available means. Is a boat in which every board is replaced still the same boat? And if not a single board of that boat is replaced and every original board has rotten away, is it still the same boat? Is it not just a wreck? The materials of our relics from the past are rarely authentic.

An example of this can be found in the National Monument Kamp Vught. It is a site that has so much authentic power that visitors walk through the exhibition room and crematorium respectfully and in silence. One of the barracks has been reconstructed on the site. The result is considered completely representative of the original. Apart from a few parts the barracks is entirely new and that's why some visitors have difficulty with it. However, surviving prisoners experience this barracks as exactly right: "That smell of fresh wood, yes that's exactly how it was!"

The National Monument Kamp Vught project shows our approach to the development of exhibitions. It demonstrates how we deal with a difficult theme and a vary varied target audience. It reflects how we use an honest and respectful approach in our exhibitions that makes visitors to think. The exhibitions are highly regarded by both school groups and former prisoners. One woman, who had loaned objects to the exhibition, said at the opening: "You can keep my objects; they have found a proper home".

Hideout Museum Markt 12 Aalten

With this museum we wanted to avoid giving simple answers to a very complex period in history.

Drawing attention to facts about the German occupation, or the remaining artefacts – like ration tickets – is not the only aim of this museum. Its main purpose is to show that World War II had an immense social and emotional influence on people. The Markt 12 Museum shows how people in the Netherlands and Germany experienced the war and how they, in their personal life, reacted to the occupation.

The story of the war needs to be told so that visitors can understand why people made certain choices. Markt 12, just a commonplace address in the eastern part of Holland, tells that story.

A family, comprising father, mother and a few children, once lived here. Here, some people hid in the attic and the entire neighbourhood found shelter in the basement against bomb raids, while at the same time the local German commander confiscated the large living room for his office. All this information is captured in the interior of Markt 12. It is not immediately clear that you're in an exhibition. Every room has its own theme and a matching interior in the style of the occupation years. However, when visitors look a little closer they will learn that there is a lot to discover and their view of all aspects of the war will grow broader. The chairs are decorated with pictures of certain individuals. When you sit down on one of them you'll get to hear their story. On the radio you'll hear the Queen giving a speech. Hung in the hallway are the coats of a wide range of people. These coats tell the stories of their owners: a collaborator, a profiteer, an NSB member, someone from the resistance and someone who adapted to the German occupiers. This museum does not exhibit, on the contrary, it hides. What else do you expect from a museum that has hideouts as its main theme?

To make the presentation of objects in a museum more authentic, data about the original context of the objects are needed, which are hardly ever available. In the Museum Markt 12 the objects are not only shown as much as possible within their environment, we even use theatrical images in an historical recreation and animate the theme for visitors. The difficulty of this is that the public interprets the presentation as if it were real.

Instead of visible storage – the scientific exhibition of as many objects as possible – we have changed to "historico-cultural arrangement": the reconstruction of context with all kinds of related objects. Museums often attempt to exhibit an object in such a way that its authentic meaning becomes clear. In the United States, a distinction is made between a period room and a period setting. The *period room* is an "authentic" reconstruction that can comprise objects from various sources and even replicas. In a *period setting*, greater attention is paid to general stylistic features, to an authentic arrangement of elements and the sociological aspects of living.[2]

Storing away exhibitions

Until recently I thought that, if we used objects from

the store and returned these at the end of the exhibition, nothing had happened. Now I realise that the vision and the temporary context in which we place objects can strongly influence visitors' perception of the past and the future. Since we place the objects in a room in a certain order, and this way tell a story, we change the interpretation of the objects in the course of time, and we produce a permanent added value to the identity of the objects. Once experiences have been gained they can never be undone. Their reality and the way in which they have moved us are things we carry with us forever.

However, the truth knows many versions. Knowledge is time-bound, context dependent and situated in the subjectivity of the connoisseur. On top of that, every visitor has their own background and perception. Furthermore, in museums we have only stored masterpieces – only the exceptional things and events have been preserved. It did not seem worthwhile to preserve everyday life, which disappeared into obscurity. Every museum constantly distinguishes between what is worth showing and what is not. The mere fact that some parts of the collection are never selected means that a proper portrait of the era is not given.

Settings in museums that relate to the past tell us perhaps more about our situation now than in the past.

In future, would it not be more logical to store objects in their context, for instance by saving a virtual mirror image of the exhibition? This way, a museum would systematically build up an intellectual collection next to a material collection. All the documents of a museum should be collected, both images and records of the collection, such as the exhibition texts. The intellectual collection should be a rich source which is just as scientifically sound as the physical collection. What's more, nowadays the physical and the intellectual collection cannot exist without one another.

The manifestation of an object
Everyone agrees about one thing: the collection is the heart of a museum. The objects are crucial. Presentation and interpretation relies increasingly on the type of media employed. An exhibition has become an environment that contains much more than just a collection of objects. All kinds of "artificial" elements have more or less become a part of a museum experience. Anyone who tries to create a virtual museum experience on a website should not only focus on the objects, but also on the other factors of the museum visit.

The authentic objects in the meantime have acquired numerous interpretations, a variety of educational information, and contexts from various periods.

THE POWER OF THE OBJECT

Perceiving an object has become a relative rather than an absolute matter.

Visual means can only tell a limited part of the story. So choices will always have to be made in presentations. The exhibition designer can show one part of the historical life of the object, but in doing so ignores other parts. Storage used to be undertaken in the name of humanity, the nation or the art community, while presentation was aimed at the general public. The two museum functions that used to complement each other – preserving and showing to the public at large – can now be partially separated from one another. The objects themselves have retained their respect and are exhibited in a responsible manner. There, we can simply enjoy beautiful images and the power of authenticity. The contexts have become autonomous and I refer to them as avatars. These are the various manifestations of the object in its secondary virtual life. They will become increasingly numerous and will lead their own life without the physical presence of an object. They become the virtual part of the museum, which is accessible from any place in the world, and which offers a platform for opinion and education. They will lead a life of their own in our collective memory, the global brain that includes all contexts originating from different times that say something about those times.

Time will tell when an object needs to be present in order to create a historical sensation and a museum experience. The time machine we used to dream of will become different from what we thought and our space will become partly virtual. Time and space are no longer unequivocal.

The perfect design solution does not exist. New possibilities, however, have come to light. We will always be searching for more, on the border where the museum's approach meets the visitor's. We will meet future techniques and are aware of what we want from the visitor. We will go on to show objects by the power of their stories.

"I must have been about the age of five. Before going to sleep, my father always read me a bedtime story. On one evening, my parents had visitors. A cousin took my father's place to tell me a bedtime story. Soon I ran from my bedroom to my parents, shouting: "She hasn't really told it, she only read it out loud!"

1 *From a column by Arnon Grunberg*
2 *Sanne van Galen, University Utrecht: "Verhaal of voorwerp?"*

THE POWER OF THE OBJECT

National Monument Kamp Vught
Lunettenlaan 600
5263 NT Vught
Netherlands.
T+31 736566764
www.nmkampvught.nl

Hideout Museum Markt 12
7121 CS Aalten
Netherlands.
T+31 543471797
www.markt12.nl

MUSEUMS AND WORLD WAR II

11

The Dilemma of Exhibiting Heroism

CLEMENS MAIER-WOLTHAUSEN

Director, History-Memory.eu

Berlin

Neither the Statutes of the International Council of Museums (http://icom.museum/statutes.html#3) nor the Latin or Greek roots of the word *museum* refer to it as a place of remembrance – rather as a place of scholarly study or as a repository. (Kopf, 2001: 387) Like art museums, history museums were meant to be storehouses of things forming part of a nation's or a group's heritage. However, the great catastrophe of the 20th century triggered some changes. War museums, those exhibitions of antique and modern weaponry that had their roots in feudal armouries, encountered a new trend – the trend towards the combination of museum and memorial. The museums became memorials and the buildings became monuments. And every so often the focal point of these new entities was and is the Second World war and the Nazi genocide.

Numerous examples of this new type of museum have been created in recent decades, with the United States Holocaust Museum in Washington and the Jüdisches Museum in Berlin being but two of the most famous examples. Other places have incorporated monuments or memorial halls into their exhibits. A fine and recent example of the latter is the Canadian War Museum. The process of creation of the Berlin Memorial to the Murdered Jews of Europe resulted in a similar space. Only here the process was reversed.

It was initially planned as purely a monument but a small exhibition has been added – not even officially called a museum although in fact it is one. So what are we dealing with exactly?

Paul Williams has in his recent book *Memorial Museums, The Global Rush to Commemorate Atrocities* tried to disentangle the terms monument, memorial, museum and memorial museum. According to him, one of the most important distinguishing features of museums is that they – unlike monuments which can communicate their own significance visually – must construct history (by means of textual strategies) as scientific rather than commemorative. He therefore suggests applying the term *memorial museum* to a "museum dedicated to a historic event commemorating mass suffering of any kind." (Williams, 2007: 8) Although he is focusing on specific museums – created as a reaction to Genocide and mass killings or torture inflicted on a people or a group as a result of dictatorial rule – his observations can easily be applied to many war museums worldwide. Telling "the truth", commemorating the fallen, the comrades and preserving their stories and memories is a common feature of many war museums.

But as Williamson correctly adds: a memorial museum is an inherent contradiction since a memorial is usually seen, if not as apolitical, at least as a safe refuge from history. A history museum, on the other hand, is today regarded as a place concerned almost entirely with contextualisation, interpretation and critique. A memorial museum, however, features the coexistence of remembrance and critical interpretation. And there lies the problem.

The public often endows museums with a very special kind of authority. It expects them to maintain scholarly standards, have a dedication to facts, to present state-of-the-art research and scientific reflection. Today's temporary exhibitions in particular do fulfil this task and often present the findings of current research. Museums are, in the eyes of many visitors, authoritative agencies. This general assumption is based on the expectations of visitors who attribute this authority to the museum. They are not aware that museum exhibitions are the outcome of a long process of selection and simplification, less complete and narrower in focus than any book on the subject. Yet they are much less subject to critical scrutiny than a book would be. (Hein, 2000: 31) However, the museum space in reality represents not only an arena for art, culture, history and science, but also a sphere of influence for political, economic, social and pedagogical deliberations. (Glasmeier, 1992: 7 cited in Kurilo, 2007: 13) Museums are, of course, also places of cultural communication since they are agents in the process of creating memories.

And some war museums even play, as Andrew Whitmarsh has pointed out, "a significant role in commemoration". Their displays confer legitimacy on specific interpretations of history, and attribute significance to particular events. (Whitmarsh, 2001: 1) In these cases, the nature of the museum lends its scientific authority to the memorial feature, which in turn pays back by adding significance to the exhibition. Some memorial museums even herald this feature, or function, in their name: the United States Holocaust Memorial Museum (USHMM). Its mission statement very clearly describes its national and commemorative character: "The United States Holocaust Memorial Museum is America's national institution for the documentation, study and interpretation of Holocaust history, and serves as this country's memorial to the millions of people murdered during the Holocaust." (USHHM, Mission statement, web page, 2008) Memorial museums like the USHMM are intense producers of cultural memory. They often have, as we have seen, an explicit political objective. Sometimes this objective is openly stated as in the mission statement of the Norwegian Museum of Resistance (*Norges Hjemmefrontmuseum*) which states that the museum's objective and aim is to "contribute to giving a true and authentic picture of the years of occupation through the objects, pictures, print-material etc. that the museum collects, preserves and displays." And it aims "to give today's youth and the generations to come a vivid impression of the tragedy that occupation and foreign rule is for a people, and thereby to contribute to the strengthening of the national unity and the defence of our national freedom." (Cited in Færøy, 1997: 106) The museum is located in *Akershus festning*, Oslo's medieval fortress that housed the German army's headquarters during the occupation. In front of it lies *retterstedet*, the place where the German execution squads murdered Norwegian resistance fighters. A small memorial inside the museum not only pays homage to the martyrs, the museum also has – whether by accident or a conscious choice of its founders – a close connection to the national shrine where the annual wreath-laying ceremony takes place.

The messages of the memorial and the museum reinforce each other. Together with its political mission, the place communicates a strong message – not a wrong one, but rather an important one. Problems arise if the memorial, the exhibition and the message fossilise one interpretation and one interpretation alone – mutually reinforcing and perpetuating each other over time. The message and the interpretation, which each of which deserve renewed contextualisation and revision, are buried in an avalanche of reinforcing factors. The mission statement shows the two mutually supporting claims: a true picture is given and a political conclusion is drawn.

Memorial museums still often prove to be immune to a contextualisation of both the story and the exhibition. The example of the so-called *Wehrmacht-exhibition* in Germany, the exhibition of the *Enola Gay* at the Smithsonian in Washington, or the veterans' protest about the description of the strategic bombing of Germany in the Canadian War Museum, all bring sharply into focus the problems and the dividing lines between two different concepts of the role of the museum. On the brink of losing the generation of eyewitnesses and survivors, the debates are becoming ever harsher. Changes to cherished narratives can never, or only reluctantly, be accepted.

Challenging narratives

The Canadian War Museum is not explicitly a memorial museum but has strong memorial features. Its Memorial Hall contains the headstone of the Unknown Soldier from the First World War, which is directly illuminated by the sun each Remembrance Day, November

11, at 11am. In Spring 2007, Canadian veterans became aware of a sign in the newly-built museum which dealt with the allied strategic bombing of Germany. The creators of the new exhibition, which was opened in 2005, stated that the bombing had caused massive destruction and the loss of civilian lives, and that both its moral legitimacy and its efficiency were debatable. The text read: *The value and morality of the strategic bomber offensive against Germany remains bitterly contested. Bomber Command's aim was to crush civilian morale and force Germany to surrender by destroying its cities and industrial installations. Although Bomber Command and American attacks left 600,000 Germans dead and more than five million homeless, the raids resulted in only small reductions of German war production until late in the war.*

The veterans and their main association, the Royal Canadian Legion, were outraged and called for a boycott of the museum that had already attracted hundreds of thousands of visitors. The veterans' opposition was fierce – they feared that the text would dishonour their comrades in the bomb squadrons. (Hansen 2007) One comment called it an "obscene summation." (Worthington 2006) Alongside the press campaign launched by leading veterans, they brought the issue to the attention of the Senate subcommittee on veterans' affairs. Representatives from the Royal Canadian Legion, the Air Force Association and the Aircrew Association asked the senators to help them get the text rewritten. They claimed that the text was a blemish on the reputation of those who should be honoured for their service in defeating Nazi Germany. For them, the museum was not there to provide a space for discussion or criticism, rather just to preserve and to collect. The museum's curators had to give in and they changed the text. It is now no longer refers to the number of victims and the film footage and images do not show the destruction and victims, just aerial views taken from the planes. (Medicus 2007)

Another example of this kind of conflict is that of the failed *Enola Gay* exhibition – the plane that dropped the first atomic bomb. It shows the influence which, in the 1990s, veterans (in this case The American Legion) could exert on the curatorial staff of the Smithsonian Institution – the National Air and Space Museum. The initial, approved curatorial plan was to show the entire plane as a representation of the start of the nuclear age and the conflict of the nuclear powers. The death and destruction the two bombs caused on Hiroshima and Nagasaki were to be mentioned. The American Legion and other veteran associations went on the rampage. What they wanted on the 50th anniversary of their victory was a show of glory. They and their families believed that they had deserved a moment and a place of nostalgic remembrance and not the contextualisation of an historic event by young historians that had not lived through it. If the *Enola Gay* was to be included, they wanted the curators to present the dropping of the atomic bomb as an unavoidable evil, which in the end saved thousands of lives. To create an exhibit that marked the end of "their" war as the beginning of a new one, the cold war, and that also mentioned Japanese victims, was seen as being out of place. (Harwit, 1997: 139-144, Sollberg, 1996: 72) This "clash of memory and history" was resolved by a political compromise. (Hein, 2000: 145) Only the fuselage of the B29 bomber, modified to carry special cargo, was shown.

After this "worst tragedy" for the public presentation of history in the USA for a generation, the Secretary of the Smithsonian proposed avoiding "controversial exhibitions and that its exhibitions cannot combine commemoration and celebration with scholarship." (Kohn, 1995: 1036-1037)

The challenge of long-cherished convictions, interpretations and narratives developed after a war are always hard to change. In the country of the aggressor, this became obvious in the case of the exhibition *Vernichtungskrieg. Verbrechen der Wehrmacht 1941-1944* by the Hamburg Institute for Social Research. Until then,

THE POWER OF THE OBJECT

no previous exhibition in the history of modern Germany had so profoundly altered the fabric of people's memory of the last war. Even though it was refuted and massively criticised, the message had stuck. The view of the German soldier and the army leadership was never to be the same again. And yet the unhealthy and shocking alliance of local politicians who tried to ban the exhibition from their constituencies, right-wing extremist protesters and some conservative newspaper editors and historians, forced the Hamburg Institute to withdraw the exhibition and revise it. The accusations of improper and unwarranted use of primary sources proved to be mostly incorrect. The exhibition and its creators were largely exonerated by a commission of historians. (Heer 2006) The problem was that the exhibition challenged the notion that the German army was not to blame for the Nazi genocide and was only carrying out orders. It showed for the first time the systematic involvement of army units in the atrocities in the East and the Balkans and the fervour with which officers and the rank-and-file interpreted racist orders. It is impossible to communicate here the full intensity of the political debate, which lasted for years. The number of articles, editorials and comments is endless. In addition, historiography was affected and new work on the theme initiated, which has greatly benefited our understanding of the role of the army. (Hartmann, Hürter, Jureit 2005) The new exhibit toned that reality down and was welcomed as a compromise that could once more be integrated into the German national story. This compromise was called scientifically sound. (Seifert 2001)

The question dealt with here is whether exhibitions, and especially memorial museums, should be seen as keepers of tradition or as facilitators – or even provocateurs – of discussion. There are many indications that an exhibition might not be the ideal medium to provoke a discussion, simply because the audience may not respond. The above examples show the difficulties and the harsh reactions that curators may face when challenging old narratives.

Let us now turn to the Museum of Danish Resistance in Copenhagen as an example of a small memorial museum in a country seemingly free of conflicts or internal political strife.

Frihedsmuseet

The *Frihedsmuseet* is a memorial museum as well – and a real memorial. The architecture, right down to the iron nails in the door which are emblazoned with the victory sign, bears all the features of a memorial. The monument by Knut Nellemose in the courtyard and the symbolic urn with a commemorative text in the main hall are all signs of its memorial character. In 1963, for example, the Foreign Secretary of the Soviet Union and the Chancellor of Austria laid wreaths at the Nellemose monument. This commemorative element was already at the heart of the predecessor to the *Frihedsmuseet*: the first exhibition on the resistance movement, opened in the summer of 1945.

There was a tribute to those who gave their lives in the struggle for freedom, in the form of an arrangement of banners, flags and lights in the Hall of Commemorations (*mindehall*) before the start of the exhibition. Even today, an act of public commemoration takes place each year inside its walls. On the eve of 4 May, the museum grounds are lit with torches and the opening hours are extended. A crowd gathers around 7.30pm and at 8.45pm a recording is played over the loudspeaker system. It is the Danish service of the BBC – the message with which in 1945 the Danes heard about the surrender of the German forces in North Western Europe. This audio "document" is always part of the permanent exhibition, but on the anniversary of its original broadcast it becomes a fetish.

Frihedsmuseet is not an original historical site; it has been created solely to tell the story of the veterans. To be more precise, to tell the story of the group of veterans that founded it. These came mainly from the national conservative resistance movement, although they showed considerable willingness to incorporate all other wings of the resistance movement as well.

The veterans who collected the money to build it, and the objects to fill it, never wanted the museum to present multi-causal explanations or the complexity of wartime history. Neither was it meant to show the experiences of the majority of the population, or even discuss the question of how many people were engaged in the different actions described in its showcases. What they wanted was to tell their story before it was forgotten, to document their struggle and maybe to communicate the message they had learned during the occupation.

This lesson, in the eyes of the circle of veterans instrumental in the establishment of the *Frihedsmuseet* was the same as for Norway: a small country needs a strong army and strong allies. (Maier, 2007: 162) Not that they were alone in this view, either then or now. This probably represented the majority view. However, with this aim came trade-offs in professionalism and transparency. And in the 1990s these founding fathers became suspicious of changes.

Objects as relics

Objects were the focal points of change and of the discontent of the veterans with that change in the 1990s. The *Frihedsmuseet* was built to house the original permanent exhibition. It developed from a quickly created "show" into a museum institution under the auspices of the National Museum. However, the wish to be truthful, which was certainly always present, was sometimes mixed with a certain degree of arrogance on the part of the veterans, trading professionalism for assumed truth by virtue of their participation in the struggle.

The first exhibition was planned to show the Danes – bystanders and sympathisers – what the resistance had done throughout the years of German territorial and information control. All resistance groups were to be represented through stories and objects. But how could one represent a struggle that was comparatively less violent than in other countries if not through that symbol of a readiness and willingness to fight – the gun? Guns were everywhere in the exhibition. The galleries were lined with rifles and almost every display had a show of small firearms. However, it was not the technology of weapons that was at the heart of the exhibit – it was what they stood for. Technology was mentioned only once, in the display on the secret weapon factories of the organised resistance. The simplicity of the home-made sten gun and of their replication was important to understand. However, mere technicalities were relatively unimportant, it was the passion of the Danes that was central: David against Goliath. Here, the peaceful Danes forced by circumstances to engage in a struggle using all their wits; there, one of the mightiest war machines of all time. This was also the key concept behind the display of the other guns: guns dropped by parachute, smuggled by boat, stolen from the enemy or self-produced. The most potent of these objects – an icon – is an armoured vehicle: a standard truck, secretly clad with metal plates and painted with the Danish flag to be used as tank in a final battle with the Germans, stands as the first military object encountered, right outside the museum. It was used in action only once, after the liberation, when a group of partisans tried to arrest some Danish collaborators who were hiding on a farm. The important point, however, is probably not how often it saw action but that the Danish resistance was determined to use it if necessary. It is a reflection of courage and determination rather than a witness to military action. (Kjeldbæk, 2000: 120-123) It is the proof that "Objects can be restored as emblems loaded with emotional and historic weight almost certainly greater than that enjoyed in their initial incarnation." (Williamson, 2007: 28) *Frihedsmuseet* was full of such objects.

THE POWER OF THE OBJECT

Objects like these bore evidence to the struggle and subsequently the narrative and the argument of the veterans. But objects could also be a challenge to the prevailing narrative. Since that narrative concentrated on the armed resistance and its role in the liberation of the country, some aspects of the war were neglected, or better forgotten. During the revision of *Frihedsmuseet*, it became clear that the rows of images and showcases were no longer adequate and failed to give context to, and link events in Denmark to, events on other battlefields. New, younger visitors needed an introduction and a background to the war. And more recent research had clearly shown how much the resistance in Denmark had been connected to German defeats on other fronts and allied successes. In a sense, visitors needed a museum about the war and not just about the Danish resistance. (Mørk Hansen, 1988: 94) But this notion was bound to cause problems for the veterans. There seems to have been a clear anxiety on the part of the veterans that such an extension of the museum's scope might result in scant regard for their deeds and the resistance. The former director, Jørgen Barfod, admonished Esben Kjeldbæk in 1991 not to forget that the topic of the *Frihedsmuseet* was the resistance.[1]

Guns used in the actions and events presented had their rightful place in the exhibition, but others were not needed, according to the new curators. They wanted to keep some of the weapons to show how far the resistance was prepared to go. But the emphasis on guns had to be changed.[2] Of course, this was a delicate matter since the guns and militaria were seen as reflecting the veterans' courage – and that of the population – for whom they symbolised a Denmark which fought alongside the allies against the German enemy. The same applied to the flags donated by the resistance groups; and the medals of foreign associations and dignitaries acknowledging the Danish people's contribution. These did not mean much to the overwhelming majority of the current visitors – they had to go. Instead, objects reflecting daily life during the occupation, and a timeline referencing other arenas of war and their influence on Denmark was introduced. The *Frihedsmuseet's* opening exhibition did not need to include everyday objects – every visitor had lived through it or was visiting with parents who had. The exhibition's focus was on what the average Dane had not yet seen, or could not have known, during the occupation: the clandestine war. Today's exhibition needs to include them if the aim is to present a picture of wartime Denmark.

Along with this, the new exhibition – by incorporating the historical context of the war – also contextualised the resistance. This was criticised by Svenn

Seehusen, one of the founding veterans, who thought it would devalue the resistance. (Kristensen, Nørskov Madsen Bar 2000: 9) In a letter to the director of the National Museum he asked whether curators should decide on the image of *Frihedsmuseet* and the liberation struggle, or whether the veterans – those who went through it and founded the museum – should have the last word.[3] He claimed that the current curators had made the description of Nazism and the World War II their main objective and had forgotten the museum's real job.

Ten years later, however, the disputed objects were used in an even greater contextualisation of the war time history. In 2005, the staff of the *Frihedsmuseet* opened a temporary exhibition about the occupation in the National Museum in the centre of Copenhagen. As part of the programme for the 60th anniversary of the liberation, it was to be the most up-to-date presentation of knowledge about the Second World War. This time, the creators also made a point of embedding the history on display with both memories and historiography. The exhibition greeted the visitor with a small three-sided pyramid. A submachine gun was mounted on each side. The guns symbolised three different approaches to, or discourses on, the history of the war. One was the patriotic approach, the view of the 1950s, when the national narrative of a country united in resistance against the German enemy was still intact. The gun on display here was a homemade gun used by the conservative, bourgeois resistance group *Holger Danske*. It reflects the traditional view of the war as a heroic resistance struggle against an powerful enemy.

The next was the so-called revisionist approach, reflecting the view of the 1970s. The gun was a homemade model from *BOPA*, originally a communist resistance group. The gun reflected – according to the caption – the overrated military importance of the resistance that was being explored by the historian Aage Trommer and others.

The last gun on the third side of the pyramid was a Swedish model and referred to a shipment of guns that was secretly bought in Sweden and but later allegedly distributed almost exclusively to groups of former Army officers. This favouring of the conservative wing of the resistance caused a scandal later. This gun represented the "new-moralistic" approach of the 1990s. This was the time the "uneven distribution of weapons" came to light and caused intense debate alongside other so-called scandals. The caption read: *Homemade sten gun produced by "Ringen". A murder weapon made by self-appointed groups and perhaps used for killing inform-*

ers. These "liquidations" often took place without the guilt of the victims having been proven." (*Nationalmuseet*, exhibition *Spærretid*, "Ny-moralistisk", 2005) Obviously this referred to the debate taking place after 2000 about the morality of these informer killings. Here the tables were turned. The most revered object in the inaugural exhibition became a tool for the contextualisation of the narrative – but only in a temporary exhibition.

Memorial museums have two main functions: they are places of learning and places of remembrance. On the one hand, they possess a great pedagogical relevance for the mediation of information on the Second World War. On the other, they are a place of remembrance – even if not authentic. (Kurilo 2007: 13) Their objects give authenticity to their location. They are emblems, but through commemorative practices they sometimes acquire a quasi-religious status. And, the more they do so, the harder it is to change, exchange or recontextualise them.

A catch 22?

The question implicitly dealt with here is the one that curators of history museums all over the world often face: should their history museum be a *temple* or a *forum*? Is there a need, or is it desirable, to transform museums from *shrines* and *statements of truth* into *arenas of discourse?* (Duncan, 1971: 17) The above examples from Canada, the United States and Denmark started as memorial museums and, I suggest, might need to develop further into conventional military history museums. Such a change could allow for a more intensive contextualisation and a more critical interpretation of the many histories of war. However, this could only happen if their memorial aspect decreases in significance. This does not mean being disrespectful or forgetting sacrifices, but rather dismissing the event as having a major influence on one's own self-awareness today – even if for a long time it was a significant influence.

It is questionable whether a museum can ever be an arena of discussion to a significant extent, as it is an authoritative presentation of an accepted narrative. It is doubtful that museums in general are able to illustrate changes in the meaning of objects. These changes occur over time but a museum is usually slow to react to them. Besides, the memories of the martyrs will not change and the connection to the dead and those "who gave their lives" acts as a protection against putting the event into any kind of perspective. It is hard for any counter-narrative to impact this solemn character. The change that might be needed has to be done carefully and with respect and it need not necessarily be a total revision – although the *Wehrmachts-exhibition* is a model for the healthy revision of a master narrative. Maybe what we are talking about is a greater openness to, and awareness of, the pitfalls of including commemorative elements in exhibitions, the pitfalls of exhibiting heroism.

Thirteen years ago, the curators of the Smithsonian were stopped brusquely when for the first time they tried to create an exhibition that was to be more than a museum about military objects and heroism. What this and the other examples exposed was the "gap between public or collective memory shaped by personal experience and exposure to interpretation over a period of 50 years, and changing historical scholarship." (Crane, 1997: 62) Henderson and Kaeppler observe: "The transformation of the museum from the reliquary to forum has forced curators to reassess their role as cultural custodians. Increasingly, curators must ask if museums retain the responsibility of validating and confirming tradition. Who has the authority to interpret history to the public – indeed, who 'owns' history? Is an exhibition always the best venue to present diverse interpretations of complex historical issues, such as the *Enola Gay*? How does an exhibit best present an interpretation that re-evaluates the sacred narrative of a culture in which the public feels a wide ownership?" (Henderson, Kaeppler, 1997: 2)

The question here is whether a museum about war and military history can possibly escape the dichotomy between being a space of learning and being a place of nostalgia. The answer to this question is one that has to be formulated anew by curators for each and every exhibition. The *Frihedsmuseet* has found one way, which caused, as we have seen, some criticism but also garnered some praise. Others have found different answers or no answers at all yet.

1. Barfod, Jørgen H., *Personal Communication with Kjeldbæk, Esben*, 11 February 1991, FM Arkiv box Nyopstillingen 1995.
2. Kjeldbæk, Esben. *Idéoplæg til ændring af den faste udstilling på Frihedsmuseet*. 25 January 1991, Frihedsmuseets Bibliotek, 37a.
3. Seehusen, Sven, PM: *Museet for Danmarks Frihedskamp 1940 til 1945*, 4 February 1996, FM Arkiv, box: Nyopstilling 1995.

Discussion

Question: You seemed to want us to separate the memorial and the historical function at the *Frihedsmuseet*? But we at the *Frihedsmuseet* don't feel under pressure from veterans.

Maier-Wolthausen: I definitely do not want you to separate those functions. What concerns me is merely an awareness of this on your part. An awareness that there are inherent dilemmas and perhaps a dichotomy. You should just be conscious that the objects could acquire a quasi-religious quality. Maybe it could even be a deliberate decision to use it and to play with it. In Germany all museums concerned with the Holocaust do that in one way or another.

Question: It is true that there is a difference between the cognitive and the commemorative aspect. But I think you can balance and pay attention to both without losing your scientific credibility.

Maier-Wolthausen: I am not even sure that an exhibition can be a forum or provoke a discourse. Most of the time an exhibition might not be the right place. But having the memorial aspect in mind might give you better options for the cognitive aspects of your exhibition. But I am not really arguing for a change, you might consciously decide to use the commemorative aspect. And the Jewish Museum in Berlin used Libeskind's architecture for its presentation, even though now when they want to show 2000 years of Jewish history they find it is not easy if the guests start by going to the Holocaust tower and then go into the exhibition because then they see all the history as a preclude to the ovens of Auschwitz. If you decide to make use of the commemorative aspect you must also be aware that you may be creating a problem.

Question: A museum might be pressured into a role where it has to fulfil the demands of, or back up, veterans whose stories they are not quite certain about. Eventually there must be a break here?

Maier-Wolthausen: Yes. I think the two first presentations were particularly interesting, representing museums in Eastern Europe. As a German, of course, I am very strongly connected to a narrative that has the Holocaust as a point of reference, something that is less true of Denmark and something that has a totally different context in Eastern Europe. But my observations are general ones. They can be applied to many, many museums. We discussed the tendency to apologise for everything. Manchester has now apologised for the slave trade because slave ships went through the port 300 years ago. That is also part of it. I think a lot of the questions we're discussing are connected to the dual features of the museum and the memorial. You just have to be aware of this.

12

Post-Communist Museums: Terrorspaces and Traumascapes

LENE OTTO

Associate Professor of European Ethnology,

University of Copenhagen

In newer post-socialist museums in Eastern Europe there has been a growing emphasis on commemorating violent events and honouring the memory of victims of genocides and massacres. How to remember violent events from the end of WWII until the fall of the Soviet Union is a disputed and contested subject, not least in cultural history museums. Here I investigate how the violent heritage of communism is handled, collected and exhibited in some museums founded after 1989 in Hungary, Lithuania and Romania. Several of these museums are memorial museums, meaning that they are buildings in which atrocities took place. The transformation of a place into a memorial or a "memoryscape" requires a blend of design and objects to mediate and thereby transform what is exhibited into a vision of past events. Following the material turn's emphasis on the importance of studying the material processes through which culture is constructed, I analyse museums as arenas for the formation of collective memories of experiences with political violence. In this process of producing memory two strategies are widely used: making a comparison between Nazi and Communist injustice and violence, and opening up to a now-global horizon of holocaust remembrance by drawing on some contemporary icons of memory culture. Both strategies facilitate a national identity as a community of suffering.

My approach is influenced by the New Museology, putting techniques of representation in focus. The museum representations, that is the different ways of narrating, visualising and exhibiting trauma and violence, are analysed in the framework of the politics of memory and the culture of memory. By examining the staging of the past in terms of violence, terror, and even genocide, I will discuss what effects politically, and as regards identity, these representations have. It is not my purpose to find out if the museum representations are true or in agreement with historical facts, but rather how the staging of violence in museums interacts with, constitutes and changes reality.

In his book *The Politics of Atrocity and Reconciliation*, Michael Humphrey explores the way violence is used to unmake the social world and how it is remade through suffering in the form of testimony and witness in the forums of truth commissions and trials. This process also "involves the moral engagement of others by making the victim's suffering visible". (Humphery, 2002) In accordance with this, I will add to his insights by considering a broader forum for remaking the social world, namely museums and sites of memory. Museums are catalysts for a cultural process of remembering and revisiting the past and they play an important role in "the allocation of responsibility and the politics of blame". (Antse & Lambek 1996:xxi)

Much research has already confirmed that struggles over public memory involving historical trauma, genocide and human rights violations abound in the world today. The American scholar Andreas Huyssen, who is also interested in history and its representations, has documented what he calls "the trauma discourse" in contemporary uses of the past. He notes that we, since the 80s, seem to consider the whole history of the twentieth century under the sign of trauma: "The privileging of trauma formed a thick discursive network with those other master-signifiers of the 1990s, the abject and the uncanny, all of which have to do with repression, spectres, and a present repetitively haunted by the past." (Huyssen 2003:8). The discourse of traumatic memory may have encouraged the spread of ideas about "healing" and "grief work" on a collective level, including people who never actually directly experienced violence. To better understand this, we need more studies of how this discourse is produced and how it works in local settings, not forgetting that any local memory practice is also part of a much larger global memory culture. Cultural historians must study what different media actually do: how the public memory of terror is given permanent shape in different settings. Why the materiality of the museum is so persuasive and moving. How museums manage the balance between aestheticising traumatic memory and offering a simple place of reflection to their visitors.

My argument is that when we study the cultural meaning of trauma, we need to include the mediated negotiations of collective memory in local as well as in larger global communities. These negotiations are based on a "will to truth" which is enlarged and generalised on a cultural level, transferring the trauma, as it were, from the involved individuals and communities to entire social and political cultures, thus creating communities of suffering. The creation of memorials and public spaces of commemoration, such as museums, is one way of dealing with historical trauma. Museums are spaces of memory and they play a key part in marking out the contours of an historic event. Of course, museum exhibitions are but one medium for the construction, negotiation, and preservation of memory. They are used as a kind of public sphere of authentic memory that will counter any attempts at the politics of forgetting or silencing. On the other hand, one might say that they do politics themselves – engaging in what has been termed "politics of trauma". They are cultural history museums and they use history and the material presence of the past in what is understood as a cultural reconstruction from social trauma.

I have investigated how violent events in Europe in the period WWII-1989, e.g. the violent heritage of Nazism and Communism, is commemorated in cultural history museums. Because museums in Eastern Europe played an obviously propagandistic role under socialism people are very much aware of their activities now. Injustice and violence are hot issues, especially in some new museums in Eastern Europe. Several of these are memorial museums, meaning that they are buildings in which former atrocities took place. I focus on the material representation of violence, or one could call it material memory; the use of material relics and the construction of metaphors and narrative structures for the telling of the past. This is in accordance with the now classic work by the French historian Pierre Nora, who analysed how historical events have been produced in concrete form. In *Les Lieux de Memoire*, Nora argues that these representations – the sites of memory – are inauthentic substitutes for living traditions – the social milieu of memory. The social environment in which the event would be part of everyday memory has disappeared.

I see another tendency in these years. The development of new museums which are both sites of memory and a social milieu of memory. They are not substitutes but rather they are part of everyday memory practices. They promote an active engagement with the past. I have found that in Eastern Europe the new museums after 1989 serve a liberating as well as a therapeutic function by drawing out memories rather than repelling them. Many post-communist museums seek to play an active role in the discursive production of memory and in the healing of trauma which means that "traumatic memory" is used as an interpretive framework.

The mania for moral museums
This new role of museums has been thoroughly considered in Paul Williams' book, *Memorial Museums* about the global rush to commemorate atrocities. Williams sees memorial museums as playing an important role in the shaping of public historical consciousness, but he also questions the way we tend to accept the premise that tragedies are better remembered than forgotten, and that "remembering as a community activity is a rich and meaningful act." (Williams 2007:165) Williams asks in his book what it is "that makes us today want to create, support, and live with permanent, concrete markers of violence?" (Williams 2007) He proclaims that morality is a topic that hangs over all memorial museums, whether representing disasters associated

with fascism, communism, imperialism or industrialism (Williams 2007:160). Other researchers have also identified the emergence of these new "museums of conscience", which deal with subjects such as genocide, slavery, apartheid, civil rights and crimes against humanity. (Kirshenblatt-Gimblett 2002:59)

Along these lines, moral museums will be my heading for the new museums in the world which are part of a larger effort to confront a shameful past and which are dedicated to awareness-raising and motivating moral commitment. These museums become not only sites of memory but also sites of redress and instruments of identity politics. A moral museum is no longer a mere storehouse for exhibits and collections, but also a centre for research, and an organiser of activities, such as hearings and commemorative ceremonies. They have become catalysts for national recognition and spaces for witness, debate, reflection, healing – and are as such closely related to processes of national, cultural revival and commemoration. These museums have a historic mission, they know that they are making history, and especially that exhibiting atrocities is an act of conscience – of making right historical injustice and misinterpretations. (Kirshenblatt-Gimblett 2002:57)

Independently of the terms we use, it is a fact that

museums which document trauma and conflict have proliferated across the globe in the past decade. In Eastern Europe new museums are founded to create public forums for witnessing the legacies of communist atrocities and they are transformed to socially appropriate places to explore personal feelings of sadness and bereavement. At the centre is the victim, the one who embodies the violence of the past in their memory and suffering. The victim is seen as providing a source of authentic experiential truth about traumatic events in the past. In the "normal" process of political transition, the recovery of victims as individual subjects and citizens has become a major issue. (Humphrey 2002:144) But one can ask if this process is inverted in Eastern Europe, so that the former citizens remain victims when their history is written as a history of suffering. Both Huyssen and Williams point to the problem, that when memory is exclusively understood in terms of pain, suffering and loss, human agency is denied. They also agree that the approach to history as trauma does not help much to understand the political layers of memory discourse in our time. And as noted by Williams: "The expansion of those who consider themselves affected possibly adds to the viability of memorial museums worldwide, as they come to serve a global, cosmopolitan culture sympathetic to loss."

(Williams 2007:165)

What we see is an invocation of museums to promote a moral stance in society; a moral stance based on the recognition of human suffering. This preoccupation with traumatic experiences has as a consequence that museums tend to downplay historical exhibits, since their primary aim is to make people aware of atrocities in the recent past. Here Holocaust discourse functions like an international prism that helps focus the local discourse about the victims in both its legal and its commemorative aspects. (Huyssen 2003:98)

The materialisation of memory

The new democracies in Eastern and Central Europe have in many instances been built on externalising the communist past, presenting it as an alien phenomenon imposed by a foreign force (the Soviets) against the nation's will. The fact that the communist (and before that Nazi) regimes in those countries were for many years supported by certain internal resources as well, is gradually erased from the national memory.[1] This cultivation of an image of one's own people as victims of violence and the rejection of responsibility has often been criticised, but what we also see now is that past events are judged ever more harshly in historical and legal terms. Using the word *genocide* has become an accepted way of talking about and exhibiting repression in post-communist museums, to characterise a broad spectrum of repressive actions such as political repression, sovietification, deportations and collectivisation.[2] According to Andreas Huyssen (2000:24) the Holocaust often function as metaphor for other traumatic histories and memories, and the global circulation of the Holocaust as a trope certifies its use as a prism through which we may remember other instances of genocide.[3] In his article *The Competition of Victims*, analysing memory politics in Ukraine, Wilfried Jilge has also pointed to the tendency in post-socialist countries to construct "national Holocausts" and thus award their nations victim status, positioning themselves as morally superior. (2006:51) This, of course, is in conflict with the view that the role of the victim in the West undeniably belongs to the Jewish people.

Nevertheless, the memory of the Holocaust has come to play an important role in post-communist discourse, in the scholarly memory debate as well as in exhibition design in museums. One might even talk about Holocaust victims' objects as *icons* heavily influenced by the example of the Auschwitz-Birkenau Memorial Museum, known for its display of camp objects and items found at the site after being plundered from the victims of mass extermination on their arrival: suitcases with nametags still attached, shoes, hairbrushes, mirrors, glasses, toothbrushes, jewellery and clothes. In many new museums the forms of historical and political reflection flourishing are those which represent "their" suffering purely as the result of ill will from "others". In the museum context, local representations of trauma and violence, both shape and reflect more global discourses, as the sense of trauma is invoked not only by narration, but also by the use of objects. The materiality and physicality of memory is an essential feature of museums. In the course of history, museums have become familiar public spaces in which the material relics of identity are collected and exhibited. Museums have the opportunity to produce artefactual symbols, that is to endow otherwise ordinary objects with sacred qualities and through the exhibition of these objects to remember and to forget. When scholars study history museums, they usually treat the site as a collage of texts, to be read as representations of the ideology of official history. But we ought also to consider the museum as a kind of theatre where guides and visitors alike *perform* memories of the past.

The museum world takes it for granted that the past is stored in relics from the past and that objects therefore have an effect. However, there is no clear theoretical understanding of how the past in museums may be present in an ontological way. One approach to an understanding is offered by the hypothesis that the relics of the past create "presence" so that the past is present, in the present, for the individual to experience. (Runia 2006, Gumbrecht 2004) According to Runia, it is this possibility of interaction with "the real past" which museums and memorials encourage, and which attracts people. He argues that people are longing for reality, defined as tangible, present history and that they are not satisfied with meaning, defined as representation, interpretations and narratives. Humans are driven by a hunger for reality, a *passion du reel*, that manifests itself in "...the enthusiasm for remembrance, in the desire for monuments, in the fascination for memory. My thesis is that what is pursued in the Vietnam Veterans Memorial, in having a diamond made 'from the carbon of your loved one as a memorial to their [sic] unique life', in the reading of names of the anniversary of the attack on the World Trade Centre, in the craze for reunions, and in the host of comparable phenomena, is not *meaning*, but what for lack of a better word I will call *presence*." (2006:5) In harmony with this, Feldman argues that the relationship between museum objects and the audience is not primarily intellectual. Instead, he describes museums as arenas for social contact and the museum object as a kind of metonymic contact point: "Contact points in the museum can take many shapes, but they involve and are engaged not just through an analytical gaze, but through the full range of bodily senses. In the contemporary world where museums play an every increasing role in global politics, having a sense for contact, therefore, will increasingly constitute the basic act of ethnography and history." (Feldman 2006:266)

Both Runia and Feldman focus on the metonymic quality of objects, and they agree that the metonymic object, because it retains something of the past can thus stand for the whole. Especially intimate objects that have been part of or very close to the body while the person was still alive – like shoes, clothes and glasses – are able to make a traumatic history present. The shoe is the archetype of a metonymic object. Feldman provides the explanation that visitors have to fit the flesh to the shoes in their own imaginative acts. "This initial desire to reclaim the contact between skin and shoe is a key aspect of what would transform Holocaust shoes into such powerful metonymic contact points." (Feldman 2006:260) He refers to the well-known shoes piled in the Auschwitz museum, which are reliquary metonyms, which stand for the physical, sensory experiences of the bodies that are no more. After first having exhibited a pair of children's shoes found in the ruins of a concentration camp in a historical museum in Israel, "children's shoes have become metonymic contact points within a standardised set of global museum routines." (Feldman 2006:261)

It may not be a standard routine, but such objects are certainly widely used in exhibitions of trauma, suffering and loss, because piles of objects like shoes or letters, or just names, contribute to a homology of absent bodies. The deprivation represented by bodily objects gains its power from their corporal nature. But use of the same objects in moral museums and exhibitions of suffering around the world make them into a kind of dominant cultural narrative or into icons of evils.

In spite of calling them icons, it is not my intention to reduce them to symbols or signifiers which can be read or interpreted; precisely because the objects themselves are survived relics, which are *Fremdkörper* in the present, they can do more than that, they can make the past present. Presence cannot be aroused deliberately by using them as metaphors in a narrative, for presence can only arise spontaneously via objects which have been physically involved in the past. It is therefore the authentic stuff, which is made from or which has been physically associated with human hands and bodies that can be said to present the past, rather than to re-present it.

To sum up, my point is, that the use of artefacts

in museums of communism is highly reminiscent of holocaust display tactics; thus telling us what happened in Eastern Europe was genocide, rather than the murder of political enemies. In most exhibitions material reference to earlier examples of memorial exhibitions are used explicitly or implicitly. The Holocaust has been used as a universal trope for historical trauma. This narrative is, so to say, materialised in the museum, artefacts like barbed wire, shoes and a cattle wagon provide a material connection to the Holocaust. Fragments from the past seem to have a special value in the exhibitions, emphasising an inherent metonymic relationship. So, objects are not only the medium, they are also the message because they have a metonymic effect. Not just the symbolic significance but also its true authenticity seems to be of major importance. Objects become relics in both the historic and religious senses of the word. This point will be exemplified and elaborated when I discuss three moral museums, which all engage with history at the level of material practice rather than merely at the level of metaphorical association. This means that visitors can have a practical as well as visual experience of the past.

Trauma in museums of communism

The museums I have chosen are cases in point for how

the memory of communism is currently unfolding in Eastern Europe. I will discuss the different ways museums remember – narrate and materialise – communist atrocities. When visiting, I have observed that these museums are intensely social, dynamic places with a flow of people coming not only to behold, but also to bear witness, mourn, and search for meaning. The three museums I have selected all deal with the discourse of trauma, as concerns genocide, violence, terror and suffering. This is apparent in their names: The Genocide Museum in Vilnius, Lithuania; The Terror House Museum in Budapest; The Memorial of the Victims of Communism in Sighet, Romania.

It is not my intention to assess whether the museum representations are true or in agreement with historical facts. Rather I will discuss their use of some tangible relics of violence and trauma – the performative and material aspects of memory. I will pay special attention to the symbols, artefacts, rites and sites in which memory is embodied and objectified.

The Genocide Museum in Vilnius, Lithuania,
The Museum of Genocide Victims was set up on 14 October 1992 in a building which served as a headquarters for the *Gestapo* and *KGB*. The museum was reorganised in 1997 and responsibility for running it was taken

over by the Genocide and Resistance Research Centre of Lithuania. In the exhibition, Soviet rule is characterised as a "physical and spiritual genocide against the Lithuanian people". The use of the verbally inflated concept of *genocide* is provoking for some groups because it tends to trivialise it by using it to describe every kind of repression and victimhood. The question is whether the term genocide should be used to describe these atrocities, or whether it should be preserved for recognition of the estimated 240,000 Lithuanian Jews that were exterminated during the war. This extermination by the Nazis with the assistance of Lithuanians amounted to 90%-95% of the Jewish population. For example, a spokesman of the nearby Jewish Museum would prefer that the museum commemorate *victimisation*, *exploitation* and Soviet ill-treatment, rather than use the term *genocide* and all that it implies. (Wight & Lennon 2007:527) The meta story in the museum is about the persecution of the Lithuanian nation and visitors are not invited to engage in political reflections.

The museum in Vilnius wants to disseminate and inculcate a national spirit. One particular museum object strongly appeals to national sentiment. It is a figure of a mythological national hero, Vytis. It is not only a symbolic figure. It is a half-destroyed relic, which was used by the Russian soldiers a target to shoot at, and thus it is a materialisation of the attempted extermination of the nation. The figure embodies, so to speak, genocide, and its wretched status speaks directly to national feelings. This is even more the case when former deportees and resistance fighters act as exhibition guides.

The dungeon, which is almost untouched, is regarded as the most important part of the museum. It was designed as a prison in 1940 after the Soviet occupation of Lithuania. It is almost untouched since the KGB left the building in 1991, apart from a few cells, where there are exhibitions. One cell contains only bags of shredded papers – secret files – that the KGB tried to destroy. In another, there are pictures of all managers and employees of the KGB. The climax in the basement exhibition is The Execution Chamber, where there has been an archaeological excavation. In holes in the bare soil are objects that have been dug up, like a cross, a wedding ring, a piece of barbed wire and buttons. There is also a pile of shoes and some glasses. It is not clear whether they have been excavated or placed here afterwards. Barbed wire is also a holocaust icon which tells us that deportation and imprisonment is genocide.

The choice of these precise objects may well be a conscious, or maybe unconscious, reference to the Auschwitz museum exhibition, with its piles of shoes.

The museums' memory strategy is to externalise communism as an alien phenomenon. Communism is presented as an alien episode in the nation's history, the result of external force and aggression. Hence anti-communist and partisan movements and actions play a central role in the new national narratives recounted in museums. This occupation paradigm (also widely used in Estonia, Latvia and most recently in Tbilisi, Ukraine) underscores the foreign roots of communism and thus positions the nation in old Europe. So the hardship of deportees and the resistance movement is inevitably an important theme. Again it is the clothes, shoes, prayer books, embroidery, drawings and letters of the deportees that are exhibited. There is something special about objects which hands have touched: embroidery, drawings and books that are aged with handling, and small objects that are cut or shaped by hard-working hands. The more worn and marked by use they are, the greater the aura they have and the more attention they seem to attract. These things have a metonymic relationship to the past which they reflect. They are fragments, not just from the past, but of the people who made, shaped, handled and kept these things.

The return of the deportees in the late 1950s is materialised in the form of a piece of railway track, a suitcase and a photograph in the background of a cattle wagon. Again we see the use of a global iconic memory language, where train cars and barbed wire, like shoes and glasses, are rooted in Holocaust remembrance. These materialised references are saying, on a more unconscious level, that genocide was also committed in Lithuania just as (though not to the same extent as) in the Holocaust.

The Terror House Museum in Budapest
On Andrassy Street in Budapest, in the large building once used by the Hungarian Nazis – the Arrow Cross movement – and then taken over by the Communist State Security Police, now stands a Museum to the Terrors of Nazism and Stalinism. The *Terrorhása* (House of Terror), as its name suggests, is a museum of horrors. On the building, a black sunshade with the stencilled letters T E R R O R, projects a threatening silhouette onto the pavement. The entrance is spectacular with the arrow cross and the hammer and sickle symbolising the two terror regimes in Hungary.

The exhibition is on three levels around an atrium courtyard, in which a Soviet tank is placed. On the walls around it are mounted hundreds of small black and white portraits. The only text is the word *Victims*.

Everyday life under communism is presented as enforced socialisation, fear and uniformity. It is emphasised that it was a forced socialisation of the Hungarian people, with values totally alien to them. Documents and news clips invoke the feeling of the Soviet regime's pervasive presence in daily life.

The official narrative is that communism and fascism are equally gruesome, but a successful balance is not achieved here. Far more space is given to the terror of the communist regime than to the fascist one. The memory of Arrow Cross is represented by just three rooms. The rest of the very large building is devoted to the crimes of communism. The subliminal messages in the physicality of the museum space make it quite clear that in the eyes of the museum's curators communism not only lasted longer but did far more harm than its neo-Nazi predecessor. Rather than evaluate the distinctions between the regimes represented by these symbols, Hungary – in the words of Prime Minister Orbán at the opening of the Budapest House of Terror on February 24, 2002 – has simply "slammed the door on the sick twentieth century".

Since its foundation, the museum has been vigorously debated and criticised, but also praised. In the museum world it has been given recognition, as it was nominated for the Museum of the Year in 2004. The judges' report on the museum reads: *The House of Terror in Budapest arouses strong feelings in its visitors, as it housed the headquarters of the Hungarian Nazi Arrow Cross Party before the Second World War and later the political secret police of the Communist regime. Each room has its own environment, with theatrical effects mixed with original pieces, the philosophy being closer to a contemporary art installation than a conventional museum display with showcases and text panels. The uncompromising portrayal of recent history has generated strong political debate in Hungary as many people who are still alive have experiences of the House of Terror, both as interrogators and those who were brought to the building for questioning. It was felt by the EMF Committee that the presentations in the museum were founded on sound research and succeed in keeping alive the memory of a series of terrible political and social experiences in Hungary without sensationalising them.* (http://www.europeanmuseumforum.org)

In contrast to this praise is a powerful and sustained critique of the legitimacy of making a parallel between the Nazis' short, but effective eradication of 600,000 Hungarian Jews, and 44 years of political repression of the Hungarian population. Are comparisons possible or appropriate? The criticism is that the museum portrays Hungary too much as the victim of foreign occupiers and does not sufficiently recognise the contribution Hungarians themselves made to the regimes in question. The museum emphasises the forced socialisation of the Hungarian population with values that were totally alien to them. What is overlooked is that the victims of Stalinism were often former collaborators with National Socialism.

This critique is often countered by the museum's director, Mária Schmidt, a well known right-wing historian who served as adviser to the prime minister during the Orban government. She has deliberately built up the museum as a place where the Hungarian nation can seek legal redress. She even wants the museum to serve as a place of pilgrimage. In an interview in the newspaper *Diplomata* on 20 October 2005, she explains what drives her:[4] "We would like to touch our visitors' hearts. We would like our museum to become a national place of commemoration where we can bow together to the victims of those terrible dictatorships".

Visitors can only leave the exhibitions by lift, which inches downwards while a plasma screen comes to life, showing a former guard describing in gruesome detail how the victims were systematically tortured before meeting their ultimate fate. This is, by the way, a device also used by the Holocaust museum in Washington DC. As it stops, the doors open and visitors walk into the torture chambers. Leaving the museum you have to pass through a crypt lined with victims' names. The opposite wall is *The Perpetrators' Wall*: here are portraits of all who supported the two terror regimes, i.e. were employees of the two controlled legislative, administrative and executive bodies. As in the entrance hall, the text is short and punchy, it reads: *Victimisers*. Quite a few of the named victimisers are still alive.

The exhibition has become a platform for the discussion of Hungary's fate but under the guidance of an fundamentalist, romanticised, and ethnically problematical rewriting of the city's and country's past. A past where the Hungarian nation has been the victim of terror and violence. Before the elections in April 2005 when the right-wing Viktor Orbán had to resign, the socialists announced that the House of Terror would be renamed House of Remembrance and Reconciliation if they won. This however, has not yet happened.

The Memorial of the Victims of Communism in Sighet, Romania

Whereas Hungary pursued a course of gradual liberalisation, in the 1980s Romania took exactly the opposite course. Romania did not experience a velvet – but rather a very violent – revolution. Political and economic power was concentrated in the hands of Ceausescu and his family, around whom a personality cult developed. After the revolution The Sighet Memorial was established to remember the atrocities committed by the communist regime. Since 1997, the yellow, former prison has been a museum and International Study Centre, offering seminars and research focused on the importance of remembering and of memory as a tool of justice. The memorial museum has been rated by the Council of Europe as among the top three places of European remembrance (alongside the Auschwitz Memorial and the French Memorial to Peace). The museum also houses an annual summer school for young people (led by the French historian Stéphane Courtois and funded by, among others, the Konrad Ardenauer Foundation) as well as meetings and the annual Day of Remembrance to the Victims of Communism and to the Resistance in which former prisoners participate. The meetings are concerned with subjects such as post-imprisonment trauma.

The building has a ground floor and two upper floors. So far, most of the former prison cells have been presented thematically and chronologically. Each cell presents a different theme. Some contain the original bed and mug; others display texts and photographs of famous prisoners. The two punishment cells have also been left untouched, suggestively named *Black*. *Women in Prison* is one of the most emotional rooms of the museum. Alongside more than 4,200 names of women who passed through the communist prisons, are the stories of some of the women who formed the anti-communist resistance in the mountains, as well as women imprisoned merely because they were the wives, sisters, mothers, or daughters of men regarded as "enemies of the people". Another room dedicated to poetry is highly emotional. Poems were sent by morse code (knocks on cell walls) and later written down by memory. There is a direct appeal to the audience: *We hope that this room will be understood as a profound homage to the poets who suffered, those who became poets through their suffering, and to the people capable of producing this amazing plant capable of growing in darkness: poetry in prison*".

In the courtyard stands a statue, *The Convoy of Martyrs*, which is a prime feature of the museum. It consists of 18 people walking towards a wall which blocks their vision, just as communism "had limited the lives of millions of people". In the courtyard guests can visit a Hall of Remembrance and Prayer, which is an underground chapel or place of remembrance, where one can turn on lights, pray and pay your respects to the memory of the victims. On the wall along the long, winding entrance to the chapel, the names of thousands of victims are engraved. It is not heroes or martyrs that are memorialised but victims – ordinary people. The names are meant to both document state terror and provide a site for mourning, both personal and familial, as well as social and national.

The prison building is in itself a script, a victim narrative, and the official name has also become *The Memorial of the Victims of Communism and of the Resistance*. The victim's perspective is also obvious when Yalta is made a *lieux de memoire* or a symbol of oppression and betrayal. You can read: "1945 was the year of Romania's confinement for at least two decades into the Soviet empire." It is a kind of negative symbolic capital that calls for solidarity from other European countries. The photo gallery used as a means of remembrance in the Terror House Museum in Budapest, was regarded by the Romanian news portal as being particularly effective: "Because words can be forgotten, you bury them somewhere in the back drawer of the memory, but the faces of those who suffered imprint themselves forever. The corridor of portraits of the victims of communism is impressive. You can't pass through that place indifferently". (Boga 2007)

The basic story is that Communist Romania from the beginning was a lie and the rest of the exhibition will demonstrate this. Romanians have been indoctrinated and manipulated with the result that "the traces of this violation of national consciousness persist even today in the mentality of many members of the public". (The Exhibition Guide: 12)

Post-socialist memory: Truth, Terror, Trauma and Testimonies

In these discourses of trauma we find at least four key words: truth, terror, trauma and testimonies. T-words, which are linked to different narratives of communism and materialised by tangible relics of violence.

It is a common experience of Eastern European societies that their history and past during communism was falsified, rewritten, or even destroyed, in order to construct an ideologically homogenised history. (Niedermüller 1998:172) So, one foundation of the new memory discourse is that this misinterpretation of historical truth must be corrected. *Historical truth* and *historical reality* are represented as entities, which are the political antithesis of communism. The assumption is that the truth will heal both individual souls and the collective spirit and become the moral basis of the new society to come. In this way, memory becomes a moral duty, a means of effecting an internal transformation in the hearts and minds of the former communist citizens, thereby reversing the corruption of communism. Memory is needed to protect and heal society: break the amnesia pact between the regime and the nation, a pact upon which communism rested. (Eyal 2004:21)

An objective representation of national history is

one of the most important political and symbolic demands of post-socialist museums. It is a widespread strategy: aim at a symbolic restoration of history, meaning the recovery and representation of missing historical experiences. History must be complete. Forgotten events and social groups are reinterpreted as central in the new, real history. For example, the work camps and personal stories of deportees have become the core of history. Truth and memory is seen as necessary to the therapeutic process and the recollection of past evils seems to be a crucial source of empowerment. The idea that memory heals through truth has provided the rationale for the new museums.

We can recognise here the psychoanalytic model of the impact of childhood trauma on the adult psyche: because it is too painful to remember, trauma is repressed. This is where museums find a new role for themselves: healing through truth and overcoming trauma, positions cultural historians as the transcendent pastors of civil society, whose conscience they must guide. Just as psychotherapy aims to help individuals recover by bearing witness to their suffering, so the museum helps to empower victims, and thus heals the nation's collective identity. Making exhibitions is a way of breaking the silence. Using museum representation as a therapeutic tool is a creative process which imposes meaning on an otherwise incoherent suffering. But a reconstruction of national memory in terms of victimhood may disempower people by institutionalising the position of victim.

Documentary texts – autobiographies, diaries, life story narratives, memories – are seen as a way of correcting or restoring manipulated history. They are not simply memories but testimonies. A testimony is a specific kind of memory, told by witnesses. The first person account has a certain kind of legitimacy and survivor testimonies are also known from Holocaust museums. Bearing witness has become a central obligation for moral museums. The stories of victims as well as victimisers are paid attention to. Their stories are transformed into nation-transcending experiences such as expulsion, terror and genocide. In this process of recognition, a new definition of victim has come into being which only rarely accords with the legal status of victim. Victim status is awarded based on the experience of politically-motivated injustice suffered in the past. Because the term *victim* captures the helpless psychological position of a subject during torture and terror, the construction of identity through this term enforces a continued victimisation role. The problem is, on the one hand, that this staging of victimisation may subject people to feelings of helplessness; and on the other, that the historical context and macro perspective vanish behind individual fates and particular lives, as Niedermüller points out. (1998:174) This opens up a biographical perspective on history. Rather than foregrounding social and political contexts, such privatisations emphasise the human being as an individual. One can debate whether this trend represents a gain in historical concretisation or promotes the depoliticisation of history. The experiences of the individual are reduced to a general human suffering, a universal victimhood. All the objects are ordinary everyday things; but displayed in the museum, they stand as testimony to the experiences of the deportees.

Another issue that is both emotional and controversial is the comparison of communism with Nazism. In the 1990s, politicians and scholars started to use such comparisons and applying the term terror to both regimes has become a successful and useful memory strategy. People are not encouraged to reflect on the specific content of the two ideologies. Thus putting the violent communist past into museums is a kind of cleansing. All the museums I have referred to are site-based, in former prisons or police headquarters with interrogation rooms associated with traumatic memories. Hence the emotional approach, predictable as soon as the audience enters the building.

Terror sites can be culturalised and packaged for tourists. Such sites have even become tourist attractions in the former Soviet states when they are marketed under the name *dark tourism*. Even the absence of something concrete can be eye-catching: the less that is left, the more the past can be imagined and felt. And the combination of terror and the paucity of material evidence left behind makes those objects which are seen all the more significant.

The places where traces are barely visible attract most attention, as pointed out by Williams: "there is something about remnant objects that remains, especially in the context of loss and destruction, little understood on a psychosocial level: they exist at the intersection of authentic proof, reassurance, and melancholia." (Williams 2007:50)

The idea of terror is inextricably linked with the notion of trauma, understood as a serious and enduring shock so severe that it induces a kind of numbing or blockage of feeling. There are a complex of theories that have made it possible to believe that bad events, especially if they are forgotten, act in potent ways on people's sense of themselves. (Hacking 1996:75)

This has resulted, all over the world, in what has been called *dark tourism:* museums as traumascapes, holocaust tourism, battlefield tourism, cemetery tourism, slavery heritage tourism and a new focus on difficult heritage.

Cultural history or curative history?

In 2004 a seminar on the role of museums in the politics of memory and the communist past was held in the German city of Weimar.[5] The important question was whether museums were political actors or instruments. Were museums being used as political tools? The consensus was that museums had strong symbolic power because they not only narrate but also materialise, visualise and ritualise the past.

It is a common feature of moral museums that they are both cultural history museums and sacred places for meditation, prayers, tears and emotion. The emotional, almost religious, way of dealing with the past is a common strategy in post-socialist museums. This mixture of historical and spiritual ambition is what distinguishes moral museums from more traditional museums.

One might discuss if these moral museums are undertaking cultural history when an understanding of power relationships and state organisation is distorted by evocative and emotional activities. Visitors' emotions are targeted and historical and social events explained as being due to evil individual actions. The assumption seems to be that visitors can only understand what happened by thinking how they would react in a similar situation – and that we can't contemplate the past without personal identification. This trivialises what happened, reducing the understanding of violence to a (bad) museum experience. Today's memorialising of suffering creates a vision of humanity as constantly at the mercy of arbitrary violence. All peoples are portrayed as victims of history, unable to change the cycle, forever weak and vulnerable.

When the past is remembered as genocide or terror, it excludes the opportunity to analyse and understand communism as a system, because any such attempt will inevitably be seen as a defence of genocide. This interpretation strategy is supported, not least, in the USA and is not exclusively an Eastern European phenomenon.[6]

And just to be clear... there have been great wrongs in the past, of course. And cultural history museums should set out to understand what happened – and why – and not be satisfied with museums which replace the history of events with theatres of trauma.

1. *This traumatic memory, with its preoccupation with victim status and suffering, counteracts the ongoing process of building a European Union on a common memory. It is seen as fundamental that the new narrative supposed to bring about European unity, includes the recognition of all victims. Since 1989 this has especially been about recognising the experiences of the East, in other words, about recognising its suffering. Former national legends and tales of heroism are being replaced by those of one's own suffering and victimisation. So, today there is a "clash" of memories, in the ongoing process of competing victim.*

2. *According to the legal definition of the UN Convention, genocide is "a systematic effort to eradicate the whole of or a large part of a group of people solely by reference to their group membership", whereby the elimination of individuals with regard to political affiliation or belief is not covered in the convention*

3. *The Ukrainian parliament has, as an example, adopted a law recognising the Holodomor famine in the country in 1932-33 as a genocide implemented by the Soviet Union.*

4. *http://www.terrorhasa.hu/index3.html*

5. *Knigge, Volkhard & Mählert, Ulrich (Hg.): Der Kommunismus im Museum. Formen der Auseinandersetzung in Deutschland und Ostmitteleuropa. Böhlau Verlag Köln Weimar Wien 2005.*

6. *American media and conservative organisations often repeat that 100 million died in the Communist holocaust against the 11 million victims of the Nazi Holocaust. Right-wing organisations in the United States, represented for example by the Heritage Foundation,*

THE POWER OF THE OBJECT

have encouraged the erection of a statue to commemorate "victims of communism, tragically numbering more than 100 million, struck down in an unprecedented imperial communist holocaust through conquest, revolution, civil wars , purges, wars by proxy, and other violent means". In 2007, such a monument – The Victims of Communism Memorial – was unveiled in Washington DC.

MUSEUMS AND WORLD WAR II

13

How Museums Speak

ESBEN KJELDBÆK

Head of the Museum of Danish Resistance

1940-1945,

The National Museum of Denmark

When The Museum of Danish Resistance opened on 15 October 1957, Børge Outse, editor of the former illegal newspaper, *Information*, wrote a leading article about the new museum. Outse, himself a member of the resistance, was sceptical about how well the exhibition, twelve years after the war, would be able to get its story across: "The things from real life will hardly say much more to the uninitiated than a pretty pebble does to a stranger about the beach where it was found on a lovely summer's day."

Strictly speaking, Outse has been proven wrong. The museum is still alive and has about 60,000 visitors a year. But his observation was acute. If a museum is primarily a collection of objects on public display, how are they made to speak. And what do they say?

In the Summer of 2008 I visited eight European war museums and, not for the first time, noted that museums seem to develop and show differences in age much as people do. Here is a museum that still looks very much as it did when it first opened; there a sparkling new exhibition whose roots in an older format are difficult to make out. But usually the roots are there, and I shall try to show how museums can be classified as belonging to one of three generations. Looking at some characteristics found in all museums, I shall build up a schema that tries to explain how objects work differently in these different surroundings. And how this affects the way the museum talks to its visitors.

The first generation museum

Perhaps you yourself have collected sea-shells or the kind of pebbles Børge Outse spoke about and kept them in the window sill of a summer house. Or maybe your family keeps a cardboard box full of old photographs, diplomas, memorabilia and other heirlooms. In that case you own a proto-museum, a collection that might eventually be displayed in showcases. Most first generation museums are really a collection of such collections. But they become museums because there is a collective will, a driving force, that claims them to be socially and morally important enough to merit public display. The Resistance Museum, for example, started out as a big exhibition in the Summer of 1945, in which members of the resistance showed how they printed illegal leaflets, how they produced home-made versions of the British sten-gun, and what the site of an illegal weapons drop looked like.

This grass-roots initiative aimed to show the large non-resisting majority of the Danes, as well as the world, that a resistance movement has existed in Denmark, and that it had contributed to the Allied victory. And when the museum opened twelve years later it was largely the same objects that were put on permanent display. So here a group, a movement made a bid to become part of history by, so to speak, putting themselves on display.

Thus the first generation museum tends to celebrate a victory won, a success achieved or wealth acquired by a person or by a class. Other examples from Denmark might be the Rosenborg Castle which shows the residences of the Oldenborg kings from the 17th to the 19th century (with the Danish crown jewels as a focal point); or The Open Air Museum consisting of farm buildings collected from all parts of Danish territory, established in 1901 following the political breakthrough of the farming class. You could add the Workers' Museum, founded by the Danish Trade Union Movement in 1971 at the height of Social Democratic success; or the Women's Museum in Aarhus established by feminists in 1984.

Sometimes you might get lucky and find a first generation museum that has not changed. In 1990 I visited the war museum in Calais. It was housed in a former German communications bunker, only partly above ground, and when you entered your first impression was the musty smell. Everywhere were hand-painted exhibition cases teeming with objects. Second-hand mannequins wore uniforms and stared back at you with confident grins. The subject was the fate of Calais during WWII. This included the engine of a German *Messerschmitt* that had happened to be shot down near the town. At the exit you could buy dud machine-gun shells for five francs a-piece.

The objects in the museum were still somehow available and not yet exclusive to the institution. Some of them might in theory have been picked up on the Invasion Beach, like pebbles. You half expected an old resistance fighter to enter with a gun, place it in a showcase and perhaps paint it in a better colour in the process! You had a feeling of being in a place with live roots.

The layout of objects in such museums may hark back to the collection of sea-shells in the window, in that they are displayed symmetrically. If you visit the new WWII exhibition in the *Musée Royal de l'Armée et d'Histoire Militaire* in Brussels you have to pass through an older section dealing with the Napoleonic wars, and here you might see sabres displayed in perfect rosettes as if they were still in an officers' club, or over the fireplace of a retired colonel.

What then happens is that members of the first generation museum's founder group will show up at the museum with new, important objects. They are usually a gift, but even though first generation museums are generally poor, they may sometimes obtain funds to buy an important object. You open the showcase and scoop some of the objects away to make place for the new one. The text you put next to it is short and to the point: Who, What, When, Where. And eventually the exhibition takes on a chaotic look. But that does not matter as long as the objects serve as proof and documentation of the group's right to a place in history. When eventually the founders are all dead and gone you are left with a monument to them.

In museums started as WWII exhibitions, there are some objects you are almost sure to find: they reflect the dangers faced and the efforts made to confront them: steel helmets, vehicles with combustion engines, rifles, Nazi paraphernalia (a great hit with private collectors), radio kits with enormous antennae, uniforms, black and white photographs (preferably professional, sharp ones showing how it was). And if the subject is the resistance: hand guns, illegal pamphlets and the typewriters that produced the stencils (perhaps with an illegal print-shop), cigarette-holders and handwritten notes from prisons and concentration camps, blurred but sometimes well-known (iconic), private photographs. Posters.

If we sum up the characteristics of the first generation museum, they look like this:

Type	First Generation Museum
Display	Symmetric/chaotic
Texts	W/W/W/W (short)
Role of objects	Proof/documentation
Funding	Money for things
Perspective	Rights of group
Function	A monument

The second generation museum

The development of a first generation museum into a second generation form is marked by the advent of the professional. The leader or curator is not personally part of the great story that the museum is commemorating but has instead a formal education, perhaps from a university. In the staff, which is being expanded, you now find teachers and other pedagogues. A new conservation department takes professional care of the objects, which are now being meticulously registered and safely stored.

This transition does not take place without argument. Every second generation museum has somewhere in its history a fierce battle between the founders and the reformers. In the case of WWII museums, veterans protest (sometimes successfully) against the new exhibitions of the professionals. But also in a local museum the priest, school-teacher and dentist, who founded the collection can feel dismayed by having their life's work taken away from them by a young academic. And they may start a campaign in the local paper to prove their point.

Usually they fight in vain. The museum is now financially supported by the local authorities, by the state or by a large corporation, and they expect a professional outlook and sense of responsibility from the institution. They also do not expect the institution to mount exhibitions that are deliberately provocative or in bad taste. It should now reflect the common values of the society.

Within the exhibition, information and education are now more important than having a mass of objects. Many of the objects are removed and replaced by texts and graphics in a standard format, and also by light and colour emphasising the points being made – those the education department is trying to communicate to visitors (many of whom are now school groups). The object is no longer on its own, but part of a story and within a planned route. It is much better explained.

In the second generation museum, graphs and enlarged photographs enter the scene, as does a new type of object: the professionally-made replica or model. And here the problem of authenticity arises.

The model may be instructive and beautifully made. Being three-dimensional it can take the role of an object in the exhibition. But as a historic artefact it only points back to the workshop of the modelmaker, his dexterity, the types of glue he used, and the knowledge of the mind that planned the model. But then, knowledge is important. Why not fill museums with models?

I think, because the model is only explanatory and, in a wider sense, the illustration of a world-view. In it you can only find what the maker – the teacher – put there. The model constantly empties itself of the information it contains, but has little more to offer. Its limits are clear. And the same goes for the replica. It can never contain more than its maker at a given time saw, understood and was able to reproduce in his copy. The model is authoritarian. Spiritually you are in a lower position, being talked to rather than being asked to reflect on what you see.

An example of a good second generation exhibition can be found in *Centre d'Historie de la Résistance et de la Déportation* in Lyons, France. It is housed in a former hospital which during the occupation functioned as the headquarters of the *Gestapo* under the notorious SS-man, Klaus Barbie. This is a black-box exhibition, where you walk through corridors made of plaster painted in grey, forming continuous "prison-walls". The exhibition is virtually without objects (or models either). It tells the story of occupied France and the resistance, through photos and texts mounted on back-lit acrylic panels, glowing in the dark, interspersed with videos. These panels are well laid-out with a clarity of arrangement that makes it easy to focus on whatever interests you. The text is heavy (in French and English), with 2,400 characters in the main texts. But as these are divided into four or five sections, they can be read. Dating from 1992, the historical explanations seem (to an outsider) informed by new research, so that opposing groups are differentiated – for instance, the fact that the resistance had roots both on the left and on the right. It points out the *Attentionism* of the general public, as well as the propaganda of the Pétain regime, and it tries to deal with the range of motivations to join the resistance, as well as its sociology. If you are interested, or at least a disciplined reader, you will leave the exhibition knowing more than when you entered. But even though the exhibition is housed in an "historic object" you notice the lack of objects, which the reconstructed living room or cattle-wagon (used for showing videos!) cannot compensate for.

But at the time of my visit there was a special exhibition in the basement that was almost worth the trip itself. Under the title *Objets de Résistance* the institution had created a small exhibition of Resistance Objects,

108 in all, borrowed from many small, French resistance museums. The objects were displayed in simple, purpose-built acrylic cases and had been grouped in one of eight categories. For example, *The Appropriated Object* showed examples of the Star of David which had been given another meaning with texts supporting the Jews or mocking the occupiers: *zazou*, *swing* or *Amis des Juifs*. *The Diffused Object* showed how alternative voices using pamphlets and posters worked to create resistance; while *The Mobilised Object* provided examples of how this was done: a bike, a typewriter, a pocket torch, a radio – all objects from daily life that had been put to different uses. *The Detention Objects* – small handmade objects and notes from concentration camps – were shown in an acrylic half-sphere like the ones you see in shops displaying cheap jewellery, but here giving the objects a moving glow. An example of how an institution with a fixed, permanent exhibition can circumvent its limitations. So let's sum up the characteristics of the second generation museum and compare them with those of the first:

FIRST GENERATION

Display	*Symmetric/chaotic*
Texts	*W/W/W/W (short)*
Role of objects	*Proof/documentation*

Funding	Money for things
Perspective	Rights of group
Function	A monument

SECOND GENERATION

Display	Planned route
Texts	Why (long)
Role of objects	Information
Funding	Money for staff
Perspective	Rights of society
Function	Official opinion

The third generation museum

To a museum professional, the second generation form is ideal, because it focuses on the skills he or she knows. But in real life it is unstable. It has a built-in propensity to expand. There is really no limit to the amount of objects it will try to collect, the hours of research that seem necessary to create the right texts, or the budget the conservation department will claim to preserve the objects. With its large staff there seems to be need for committees and sub-committees to hold meetings and produce reports on the museum's administration. The hours spent on this all add to the financial burden of the institution.

The exhibition is not designed to appeal to visitors'

THE POWER OF THE OBJECT

curiosity and their need to confront and interpret objects using their own experience. So the number of visitors may decline.

The organisation that supports the museum demands a better return on its investment, in terms of visitors, exhibitions, events and media exposure.

The museum must change into a third generation form and start making savings. Increasingly, staff will be hired only for special projects. A good café will be installed along with new rest areas. The institution will generally look after its visitors, who are not only coming to reflect on history or learn. They are also there to be part of an event and have a good time! In this sense the new museum is in competition with the shopping mall, the multiplex cinema and the fair, and influences from all these can be seen in the exhibition. Visitors expect to be able shop in the museum, as they do when on holiday, and they get a museum shop crammed with books, toys, scarves and replicas, because this, the commercial department tells you, is a money-maker for the museum.

In modern WWII exhibitions the objects are accompanied by a variety of other media. Graphics and large images appeared in the second generation museum, but now images take on a more prominent role – visual elements in themselves – and so easier to read than mysterious objects from a bygone era. Along too come films.

The WWII period was the heyday of black and white photography, where reportage and art mixed, making these artefacts particularly attractive visually. The period also witnessed the explosive growth of mass-communication in terms of radio and posters, which together with the film, could transmit news and propaganda much more efficiently than newspapers.

The photograph, the film or the soundbite can in many ways be treated as objects, but they have problems of their own. What, for instance, is the proper size at which a photograph should be displayed?

I have noticed that German exhibitions often prefer to show photographs as if they were indeed objects, at whatever size the museum collected them, still showing scratches from having been kept in a pocket, or stained with tea. With their small format, say 9x12 cm, they can be difficult to study in a showcase, but there is no question that their original function as part of someone's life comes across in this way.

Another way of using photographs can be seen in the *Versetzmuseum*, the Dutch resistance museum in Amsterdam. The exhibition, created in 1999, is clearly theatrical in its design of set-pieces forming a pathway through the history of The Netherlands in WWII.

THE POWER OF THE OBJECT

From this central pathway others branch out, describing the activities of the resistance. So you learn that, although war and occupation was the experience of all Dutch people, resistance was not necessarily so. The museum must have a very good photographic collection, which makes it possible to enlarge street scenes, so you see a lot of detail. But the museum also breaks the illusion that they are trying to create an illusion. On top of some of the street-scenes are mini showcases containing solid objects – a reminder that this is an exhibition, not an attempt to recreate history. Sometimes life-sized photographic figures stand in front of everything else, and it all works very well, because a lot of thought and planning has gone into making the – technically – rather simple set-ups. The museum was chosen as the best historical museum in The Netherlands in 2002 and 2003.

The difficulty of exhibiting photos and film is that they are modifiable.

When films were first introduced in museums they were shown in the way they were intended to be seen: by a whirring projector in a darkened space, where you sat shoulder-to-shoulder on hard seats. In the modern exhibition film is often used primarily to create atmosphere, as can be seen in the new WWII exhibition in the *Musée de l'Armée* in Paris. Here you might see film projected onto nine metre wide canvasses right in front of your nose. And since no film is that format, they will show up to three different films on the same canvass; and since this is digital projection, they might suddenly run the same scene of attacking German *Panzers* at the edges, while showing other scenes of fleeing civilians in the middle. Sometimes the original film is pushed beyond its limits to achieve these effects, so you get blurry, cotton-wool people acting out the war. Or you may see The Battle of Britain projected into a cone-like contraption in the ceiling, with of course very grainy pictures as a result. I have seen the same approach to film in the *Memorial pour la Paix*, in Caen, only here authentic films from the Allied invasion of June 1944 were mixed with clips from the war-movie *The Longest Day*! It seems that museums have not yet fully realised the limits and the dangers of electronics in exhibitions. It is as if we had suddenly discovered text and were pouring descriptive texts, argumentative texts, quotations, poems etc. in all manner of typography into our exhibitions, in an unintelligible jumble.

In the third generation museum, the design of the exhibition plays an important role, at times almost independent of the objects. The museum opens its doors to designers and planners in order to create meaningful, interesting displays.

THE POWER OF THE OBJECT

An example of this can be seen in the *Terror Hasa* (The House of Terror) in Budapest. At *Andrassy ut 60*, on one of the city's main thoroughfares, stands a building which housed the headquarters of the Hungarian Nazi-party, The Arrow Cross, and functioned as a place of torture from 1944-45. Under the Soviet occupation the same house became the headquarters of the political police of the new Communist regime and until 1956 remained a place of internment, torture and killings of the new regime's imagined or real opponents.

The initiative to form a museum, and perhaps some of the collections too, seems to have come from some of the civil rights groups that helped overthrow the Communist regime after 1990.

In 2002, under the right-wing government of Viktor Orban, the house was opened as a museum recalling the two successive occupations of Hungary (a perspective one can also find in museums in Estonia and Latvia). It must be the most heavily designed museum in Europe. The building itself has been given a giant "steel-collar" into which the word *Terror* has been incised along with the Arrow Cross and the Soviet star. The same two symbols are found on two polished slabs of marble in the entrance gallery, the red and the black colours forming a stark contrast with each other. You start your tour by going up to the second floor, from where the exhibition design, or the guards, guide you along the route of the exhibition. In the first room a double red/black wall with embedded videos shows scenes from the Nazi occupation, the fight for Budapest, and the victory of the Russians. Some of the videos are in slow motion, giving these scenes a strange blend of emphasis and distance. There is rock-music. You make your way along a black-polished corridor where shiny steel-letters reproduce a speech by the Hungarian Nazi-leader, Ferenc Nyilasi, to enter the recreated barracks of the Arrow Cross. Their black uniforms are on the wall alongside more videos, and at the end of a table, set for eight people, is the figure of Nyilasi standing, his voice booming out through speakers. His face is blank white but acts as a screen onto which his moving features are projected. He looks like something out of *Star Wars*.

In the next room you enter the era of Soviet occupation. A large room designed like a giant cattle-wagon tells of the Hungarian deportations. An enormous carpet shows a map of the Soviet Union where cone-shaped showcases have been set into the floor, marking the places of deportation. In the open ends of the cones small prisoners' objects are displayed: a necklace with a cross, a piece of barbed wire, cutlery, a handkerchief, letters in Hungarian – one of them dated 29

June 1967, a summer that, it will be remembered, has an entirely different meaning in Western youth culture of the time.

Numerous videos line the walls with people telling stories of deportation and loss (unlike the objects these videos have English translations). They are skillfully connected so that the narratives change place, sometimes with the same stories being told from two different screens. It all gives you the impression of hearing a sort of collective tale. The sound is a mixture of train noises and a string orchestra playing something that could be, but is probably not, Beethoven.

The next galleries take you through ever-changing designs that show aspects of the oppression during the Soviet occupation. The secret police and their Soviet "advisors" are of course prominent with pieces of their furniture, bugging devices, and personal belongings like hand-guns, papers and a truncheon – ostensibly belonging to Peter Gabor, head of three incarnations of the secret police. In these spaces you also find small, specially-crafted plaques in polished steel which indicate the theme of the room: in Gabor's case, a pair of scissors, referring to his original trade as a tailor. In another you are met by a big, black Volga, the Russian car of the elite. It is displayed behind a black lace-curtain and at intervals is lit up, the inside showing red plush. This display (which confusingly is in a gallery about population movements in Eastern Europe in the wake of WWII) could have been inspired by Salvador Dali's car in his museum in Figueres, Spain, where, intermittently, it rains inside it.

One problem in this museum is that you can never be sure which objects are authentic and belonged to a particular person or particular historical event – and which ones are merely of a type that could have been used, or are even replicas.

In the visitor's book I wrote something about the exhibition being impressive, which is quite true. A few pages earlier an American had written: "Arty-fartsy museum with no sense of authenticity... Total waste of time: (signed) Elvis Presley." Arrogant, yes, but he has a point. The obviously authentic Soviet pieces in the exhibition (paintings, posters and sculptures) were perhaps the ones that brought home to you the fact that these events really happened.

A case in point is that of the gallery dealing with the legal system. It is designed as a court-room with rows of (seemingly) authentic legal dossiers. You sit on wooden benches that the designer has pasted over with copies of legal papers, probably trial proceedings. All this is terrible. But what does work well is the video (with English subtitles) of the official Soviet propaganda movie produced about the trial of Imre Nagy (the real trial took place in secrecy). Here, you are seeing an authentic, brazen distortion of history, in which "witnesses" tell how he conspired with the Western powers… Again, this one authentic object – the film – is powerful enough to enable you to forget about the contrived surroundings.

Despite the inventiveness of the exhibition there are themes you miss, especially if you are not familiar with Hungarian history. How and why did Hungary end up as an ally of Hitler in the first place? How did the deportations of Hungary's more than 500,000 Jews take place? What was life like in post-1956 Hungary? To be sure, the population was oppressed politically, but how did the large number who were not actively persecuted cope with the situation?

The museum is an interesting place to visit. To my mind the heavy-handed symbolism of the design gets in the way of the story. In fact, this exhibition – which is dedicated to resistance and uprising – tells its story in a particularly authoritarian way. When you go down to the reconstructed cells in the basement, the lift travels extremely slowly, and you cannot escape listening to the lurid tale of how a hanging took place. You might want to know. But here you are forced to.

And this brings me to the odd conclusion that this

hyper-modern museum is perhaps not really a museum at all yet. Rather it is a modern updating of the kind of exhibition made shortly after a major historical event, and which only later may turn into a permanent institution providing a more balanced view, with shades of grey between the red and the black.

In the typical third generation museum, objects will play a different role from that in earlier types of museum. Since attracting visitors is important, it is also important to be able to present really interesting objects. There will be many fewer of them, but the museum will try to obtain iconic or striking objects which will fascinate visitors.

In the *Memorial pour la Paix* in Caen, for instance, they have an authentic block of stone from the ruins of Hiroshima! This trend is perhaps more obvious in the world of art museums. Here you find a smaller and smaller number of recognised masterpieces travelling the world, from special exhibition to special exhibition, where they attract huge crowds: Picasso, Monet, Velasquez, Turner, Warhol, Rauschenberg; whereas minor artists or young contemporary artists attract little attention. Fewer and fewer people go to real operas, but everyone wanted to get a ticket for the *Three Tenors* singing excerpts from popular operas.

In museums there seems to be a trend towards

displaying personal objects where the focus is on the fate of the individual. This probably has to do with the erosion of traditional ties to class or nationality. And behind it all is an increased interest in events rather than conditions, and in the individual rather than in his role as part of a group.

Of course, all WWII museums are basically about human rights. But in recent decades there has been a tendency to contretise Human Rights as a sort of over-arching ideology, which some museums aim to propagate explicitly. How this will eventually work out given the tougher economic conditions now facing museums, and the new conflicts resulting from globalisation is uncertain.

So let's compare some of the characteristics of the three generations of museum:

FIRST GENERATION

Displays	Symmetric/chaotic
Texts	W/W/W/W (short)
Role of objects	Proof/documentation
Funding	Money for things
Perspective	Rights of group
Function	A monument

Second Generation

Displays	Planned route
Texts	Why (long)
Role of objects	Information
Funding	Money for staff
Perspective	Rights of society
Function	Official opinion

Third generation

Displays	Scenographic
Texts	Videos, sound
Role of objects	Fascination
Funding	Money for events
Perspective	Rights of the individual
Function	Current trends

Rhetoric and museums

In 2007 I came across an article in the Danish weekly *Weekendavisen* in which two women in their thirties were discussing their experience of rhetoric. They had studied this suddenly popular subject at university in the 90s, and were familiar with modern trends and theories about how and why we communicate through speech. Since then, they had actually made a living from their knowledge, as communication advisors. They had kept in touch with the development of theories about rhetoric. But they agreed that, judging from their own experience, the only really valid theory was that of the Greek philosopher Aristotle, formulated more than 2000 years ago.

Aristotle (384-322 BC), arguably the greatest philosopher and scientist of his age, claimed that a speech must always contain three elements: that of ETHOS (as in ethical), that of LOGOS (as in logic), and that of PATHOS (as in pathetic).

For my purpose I shall define these as follows:
- ETHOS is who you are, where you come from, your history and thus the position you speak from, when you say something.
- LOGOS is your reasoning, the content of your speech and the arguments you use, when you say something.
- PATHOS is the feeling in your words, the way you express yourself, the tone of your voice, and your mix of pauses and emphasis.

The handling of these three aspects together determine how convincing your speech is.

I think it's obvious that you can apply these categories to how museums and their exhibitions speak. You could even do it negatively:
- Ignore ETHOS, and you have a fight with the

WWII veterans on your hands.
- Ignore LOGOS and you are laughed out of court by reviewers and academic colleagues.
- Ignore PATHOS and visitors won't come back.

I also think it's obvious that you could couple the three aspects of speech with the three generations of museums that I have tried to describe. It would seem that each generation is strong in one of the rhetorical aspects and weak on the other two.

The first generation museum, with its strong roots in the history of the special interest that created it, is clearly stamped by its ETHOS.

The second generation museum, with its dedication to teaching and rationality, is marked by LOGOS.

And the third generation museum, with its emphasis on design, the wish to follow trends and its focus on the needs of its visitors, is guided largely by PATHOS.

Thus we arrive at a final schema *(see table on following page)*.

How museums speak

This schema is of course mainly built on the experience of small, Western museums of modern history. But the three generations of museums are also visible in the types of exhibitions that are most commonly mentioned as precursors to the modern museum: the

THE POWER OF THE OBJECT

SPEECH	ETHOS	LOGOS	PATHOS
Type	First generation	Second generation	Third generation
Display	Symmetric/chaotic	Planned route	Scenographic
Texts	W/W/W/W (short)	Why (long)	Videos, sound
Role of objects	Proof/documentation	Information	Fascination
Funding	Money for things	Money for staff	Money for events
Perspective	Rights of group	Rights of society	Rights of individual
Function	A monument	Official opinion	Current trend

private collections of Renaissance kings and dukes from the 17th century that were showing the wonders of the world (first generation); the learned, taxonomic collections, like the Ashmolean, that were put on display to educate the public in the 18th century (second generation); and the great industrial exhibitions of the 19th century that linked the demonstration of technical progress with fairground appeal (third generation).

I do not know if this schema holds good outside traditional Western countries, or if it describes phases that most museums must go through. But as long as objects are at the heart of the museum it also says a lot about the institution how it treats them.

In any case, the schema could be a tool for analysis and planning. It could also be a guide when you have to decide what you want to do. It is possible to make a good exhibition almost without objects, as can be seen in the *Centre d'Histoire de la Résistance et de la Déportation* in Lyons, France. And it is possible to make an astounding exhibition, as in the *Terror Hasa* in Budapest, by letting your designer realise your aims.

But, as a source of inspiration, I would go for the first generation museum with its respect for the power of the object. An example of this might be the *Heeresgeschichtliches Museum* (Military Museum) in Vienna. On my visit there in 2008, a small special exhibition on the 70th anniversary of Austria's incorporation into Nazi Germany (the *Anschluss*) demonstrated that the museum has a very professional staff. But the permanent exhibition, despite efforts to modernise it, is still basically a first generation exhibition showing the remnants of an empire that no longer exits, the Austro-Hungarian empire that ended in 1918. And what treasures you can see there! Examples of the much-feared Turkish war-bow or an armoured cupola from the fortress in Prsmysl (now in Poland) reminds you that the Empire once defended borders far outside present Austria, that it once possessed a navy, and that it sent troops dressed in tropical white to the fighting in the Middle East during WWI. An object that could open almost any exhibition on the catastrophes of the 20th century is the very car in which Archduke Franz Ferdinand and his wife were assassinated in Sarajevo in 1914, after which WWI broke out.

Clearly, Austria still has problems with its history up to and during WWII. Technically Austria did not itself take part in the war, because it had been occupied by Germany. But in reality (as was noted in the special exhibition) large crowds greeted the advent of Hitler in 1938, and many army officers, one of them a Lothar Rendulic, welcomed the career opportunities that Greater Germany and a new war opened up for them.

But the section of the permanent exhibition that deals with the war is called *Republik und Diktatur* (Republic and Dictatorship), preferring to see the events from an internal angle. Here the objects give you a glimpse of reality. A painting from 1940 shows the spoils from the victory over France being displayed at the Heldenplatz in Vienna under the title *Sieg im Westen* (Victory in the West). A facsimile of the capitulation of *Heeresgruppe Ostmark* on 7 May 1945 is signed by its Austrian commander, SS-Generaloberst Lothar Rendulic with his pen, watch and glasses displayed on top of it. A painful episode of the 30s, the attempted Socialist (not Communist or Nazi) uprising of 1934 is recalled by the display of a field gun – about which the text says dryly that is was used against the inhabitants of tenement blocks in Vienna in 1934.

Now, the military museum in Vienna was hardly established by some oppressed group wanting to create a place in history for itself. But because it harks back to an empire now lost, it has some of the underdog attitude that you might find in museums created by members of the resistance, union members, suppressed ethnic groups, feminists or peace-activists. These exhibitions have no grand plan or explanation that they want to impress on you. Neither do they try to entice you with showy effects, as the third generation museum does. You might say that, whereas the second generation museum speaks down to you from above as if you were a pupil; and the third generation museum looks on you as a customer it wants to please; the first generation museum speaks to you straight from the shoulder, because it wants to convince you of the importance of its subject. That you can only do by talking to the visitor as an equal. And that is why – having tried to establish how museums speak – it is well worth noting, that it is in the traditions of the first generation museum, in its ETHOS, that you find the attitude that will also help you establish a dialogue with your visitors.

And that is not a bad purpose for a museum.

MUSEUMS AND WORLD WAR II

About the Authors

Christopher Addy is Collections Manager at Jersey War Tunnels, a privately owned heritage attraction, where his specialism is the gathering of oral testimony about the German Occupation of Jersey 1940-1945. He holds an MA in Museum Studies from Leicester University.

Heiki Ahonen has been Managing Director of Museum of Occupations in Tallinn since 1998. Prior to which he was director of the Estonian section of Radio Free Europe, active in the dissident movement, and Chairman of Relief Committee for Estonian Prisoners of Conscience in Stockholm.

Dr Hans Henrik Appel is Head of Education and Deputy Director General of the Association of Danish Museums. He was previously senior researcher at The Royal Danish Arsenal Museum in Copenhagen, where he was in charge of planning a new permanent exhibition. His special exhibitions include *The Danish-Swedish Wars 1563-1720* and *The Cultural History of the Machine Gun 1860-1920*.

Anne Godfroid has been working at the Royal Museum of the Armed Forces and Military History since December 2001. She is currently responsible for its paper collections (drawings, posters, photographs etc.) and in charge of the documentation centre and archives. As the Museum's expert on the Second World War, she has also been exhibition curator of its permanent exhibition about World War II.

Dr Oliver Benjamin Hemmerle is currently Visiting Professor at the Masaryk University, in Brno, Czech Republic, prior to which he held posts at universities in Chemnitz and Mannheim and was Research Fellow of the International Institute for Holocaust Research, Yad Vashem, Jerusalem.

Esben Kjeldbæk has been head of The Museum of Danish Resistance 1940-1945 (part of the National Museum of Denmark) since 1987. Has written books and articles about sabotage and the mental history of the occupation years, oral history and museology.

Dr Henrik Skov Kristensen is head of the Frøslev Camp Museum in Southern Jutland, part of the National Museum of Denmark. He is the author and co-author of a large number of books and articles on Denmark during World War II.

Dr Clemens Maier-Wolthausen is currently working as freelance historian in Berlin. After finishing his studies at Berlin's Freie Universität, he graduated at the European University Institute with a doctoral project on the politics of remembrance in Postwar Scandinavia. Since then he has worked for the Stiftung Neue Synagoge - Centrum Judaicum and other institutions in Germany. He is interested in representations of the past and the role of museums in the shaping of cultural narratives.

Dr Patrick Nefors was Head of Scientific Activities and Publications at the Royal Museum of Armed Forces and Military History until March 2009, having been acting director of the same institution from 2005 to 2008. Prior to that, he worked at the National Memorial of the Fort of Breendonk. He is an expert on the occupation of Belgium in the Second World War and has written two books (in Dutch) about the period, one on the question of industrial collaboration, and a second on the history of the Breendonk camp during the Second World War. Both books have been translated into French.

Lene Otto is Associate Professor in European Ethnology at the University of Copenhagen. She is a member of the Cultural History Board of the Heritage Agency of Denmark and author of numerous articles on the history of sickness and health, Eastern Europe, heritage, museology and material culture, and the politics of memory.

James Taylor is Head of Research and Information at the Imperial War Museum. He began his career as a curator in the German section at the British Library. He transferred to the Imperial War Museum in 1989 and worked as a researcher for five years on the Museum's permanent Holocaust Exhibition, and then as one of the team of historians on Imperial War Museum North in Manchester. He was Head of Research for the Churchill Museum at the Cabinet War Rooms, another of the Imperial War Museum's branches, which opened in 2005. His main interests are sites of memory relating to the First and Second World Wars, the Holocaust and the Strategic Bomber Offensive against Germany.

Marcel Wouters is an architect and designer. With Marcelwoutersontwerpers (marcel-wouters-designers), a team of enthusiastic and experienced employees, he creates exhibitions, educational concepts and software for museums in the Netherlands, Belgium and Germany. Short movies of many of their projects can be seen at www.woutersontwerpers.nl.

MUSEUMS AND WORLD WAR II

15
Bibliography

Agamben, Giorgio. (1999) *Remnants of Auschwitz. The Witness and the Archive*. New York: Zone Books.

Allgemeiner Deutscher Nachrichtendienst (ed.) (1962) *Tatsachen über Westberlin. Subversion, Wirtschaftskrieg, Revanchismus gegen die sozialistischen Staaten*. Berlin (East): Deutscher Militärverlag.

Andrew, Christopher and Noakes, Jeremy. (1987) *Intelligence and International Relations*. Exeter: University Press.

Anon (1960) *The Powers' Case*. London: Soviet Booklet.

Anon (1990) *Wir über uns. Reprint einer Anthologie der Kreisarbeitsgemeinschaft Schreibende Tschekisten*. Berlin: Haus am Checkpoint Charlie.

Anon (1990) *Das Kriminalmuseum*. Berlin: Heinicke.

Anon (2001) *Les Forces Spéciales Françaises en Action*. Paris: Raids.

Antse & Lambek (eds). (1996) *Tense Past. Cultural Essays in Trauma and Memory*. Routledge, New York.

Applegate, Rex. (1981) *Riot Control. Materiel and Techniques*. Boulder: Paladin.

Arbeitskreis Geschichte der Nachrichtendienste/International Intelligence History Study Group Newsletter [1993-1999].

Arnold, Dietmar et al. (2007). *Dunkle Welten: Bunker, Tunnel und Gewölbe unter Berlin*. Berlin: Links.

Bach, Christoph. (2008) *Der Regierungsbunker im Ahrtal*. Düsseldorf: Gaasterland.

Badisches Ministerium des Inneren (ed.) (1925) *Internationale Polizeitechnische Ausstellung, Karlsruhe.*
Bartel, Frank (1998) *Ausseichnungen der DDR.* Berlin.
Behrendt, Hans-Dieter. (2003) *Im Schatten der Agentenbrücke.* Schkeuditz: GNN.
Beil, Christine. (2004) *Der ausgestellte Krieg. Präsentationen des Ersten Weltkriegs 1914-1939.* Tübingen: Tübinger Vereinigung für Volkskunde.
Berckeley, Roy. (1994) *A Spy's London.* London: Pen & Sword.
Berlin-Brandenburgische Geschichtswerkstatt (ed.) (2006). *Prenslauer, Ecke Fröbelstrasse.* Berlin: Lukas.
Best, Stefan. (2009) *Geheime Bunkeranlagen der DDR.* Stuttgart: Motorbuch.
Beyrer, Klaus. (ed.) (1999) *Streng geheim. Die Welt der verschlüsselten Kommunikation.* Heidelberg: Umschau.
Blees, Thomas. (1998) *Glienicker Brücke.* Berlin: be.bra.
Boga, Bodan. Sighet Prison - we are made to forget. *Press Review,* www.siare.com, 22.10.07.
Brown, George A. (1991) *Commando Gallantry Awards of WW II.* Eastbourne: Naval & Military.
Bunker Museum in Vilnius. http://www.sovietbunker.com, 03/03/09.
Burleigh, M. (2001) *The Third Reich: A New History.* London: Pan Books.

Cameron, Duncan F. (1971) The Museum, a Temple or a Forum. *Curator,* 14 (1), 11-24.

CEGES. (1997) *Breendonk. Les débuts.* Brussels: Buch Edition.

Charman, Terry. (2008) A Museum of Man's Greatest Lunatic Folly: The Imperial War Museum and its Commemoration of the Great War, 1917-2008 in *A Part of History: Aspects of the British Experience of the First World War.* London: Continuum

Conquest, R. (2001). *Reflections on a Ravaged Century.* New York & London: W. W. Norton & Company.

Cornish, Paul. (2004) Sacred Relics; Objects in the Imperial War Museum 1917-1939 in ed. N J Saunders, *Matters of Conflict: Material Culture, Memory and the First World War.* London: Routledge

Crane, Susan (ed). (2000) *Museums and Memory.* Stanford University Press, California.

Crane, Susan A. (1997) Memory, Distortion and History in the Museum. *History and Theory,* 36 (4), 44-63.

Crouch, Tom. (2006) Legend, Memory and War. *Curator,* vol. 49, no. 4, p. 395-397.

Curvat, S. et al (eds). (2003) *Les Lieux secrets de la Resistance. Lyon, 1940-1944.* Lyon: Lejeune.

Danchev, Alex and Todman, eds. (2001) *War Diaries 1939-1945: Field Marshal Lord Alanbrooke* London: Weidenfeld and Nicolson.

Davies, Barry. (2001) *The Complete Encyclopedia of the SAS*. London: Virgin.

Dechow, Douglas R., Leahy, Anna. (2006) Not Just the Hangars of World War II: American Aviation Museums and the Role of the Memorial. *Curator*, vol. 49, no. 4, p. 419-434.

Dewar, Michael. (1987) *Weapons and Equipment of Counter-terrorism*. London: Weidenfeld.

Diester, Jörg. (2008) *Geheimakte Regierungsbunker*. Düsseldorf: Handwerk.

Dougall, Alastair. (2000) *James Bond. The Secret World of 007*. London: Dorling Kindersley.

Edwards, Grosden & Phillips (eds.). (2006) *Sensible Objects. Colonialism, Museums and Material Culture*. Berg: Oxford, New York.

Erfle, Manfred. (1993) *100 Jahre Kriminalmuseum Hamburg*. Hilden: Deutsche Polizeiliteratur.

Erler, P. and Knabe, H. (2004) *Der verbotene Stadtteil: Stasi-Sperrbesirk Berlin-Hohenschönhausen*. Berlin: Jaron.

Eyal, Gil. (2004) Identity and Trauma. Two Forms of the Will to Memory. *History and Memory* 16, 1: 5-36.

Eye Spy Intelligence Magazine [since 2001].

Eyre, Philip. (2002) *Those who dared. Gallantry Awards to the British SAS and attached SBS Units*. Honiton: Token.

Falk, J.H. and Dierking, L.D. (2002) *The Museum Experience*. Washington: Whalesback Books.

FBI (ed.) (2003) *Guide to Concealable Weapons*. Washington.

Feder, Klaus H. and Uta. (1996) *Auszeichnungen im Ministerium für Staatssicherheit der DDR*. Rosenheim: Autengruber.

Feldman, Jeffery D. (2006) Contact Points: Museums and the Lost Body Problem. In: Edwards, Grosden & Phillips (eds): *Sensible Objects. Colonialism, Museums and Material Culture*. Berg. Oxford, New York.

Finkelstein, Norman. (2000) *The Holocaust Industry*. Verso Books.

Foerster, Wolfgang (ed.) (1931) *Kämpfer an vergessenen*. Fronten, Berlin.

Fogu, C, & Kansteiner, W. (2006) The politics of memory and the Poetics of history. In: Lebow, Kansteiner & Fogu (eds): *The Politics of Memory in Postwar Europe*. Duke University Press. Durham and London.

Fowler, Will, 1996. Arms and Equipment of Special Forces, London: Greenhill.

Frankland, Noble. (1998) *History at War: the Campaigns of an Historian*. London: Giles de la Mare

Geheim [Journal, since 1985].

Gerken, Richard. (1965) *Spione unter uns*. Donauwörth: Auer.

Glasmeier, M. (1992) Vorwort. In Glasmeier, M. (eds.), *Periphere Museen in Berlin*. Berlin: Merve, 7, cited in: Kurilo, O. (2007) Der Zweite Weltkrieg im Museum: deutsch-osteuropäische Spiegelungen. In: Kurilo, O. Der Zweite Weltkrieg im Museum. Kontinuität und Wandel. Berlin: *Avinus*, 11-23.

Graaff, Bob de. (1994) *Duister Den Haag*. Den Haag.

Gresh, L.H. and Weinberg, R. (2008) *Die Wissenschaft bei James Bond*. Weinheim: Wiley-VCH.

Grote, Hans Henning Freiherr (ed.) (1930) *Vorsicht! Feind hört mit!* Berlin: Neufeld.

Gückelhorn, Wolfgang. (2009) *Die Geschichte des Bonner Regierungsbunkers*. Aachen: Helios.

Gumbrecht, Hans Ulrich. (2004) *The Production of Presence: What Meaning Cannot Convey*. Stanford University Press.

Hansen, Randall. (2007) The War Museum's Great Mistake. *National Post*. 31 August 2008.

Hartmann, C., Hürter, J. and U. Jureit. (2005) *Verbrechen der Wehrmacht. Bilanz einer Debatte*. München: C.H.Beck

Harwit, Martin. (1997) Über die Schwierigkeit, die Mission der Enola Gay in einer Ausstellung darzustellen, In Hins, Hans-Martin (ed.). *Der Krieg und seine Museen*. Frankfurt, New York: Campus, 127-145.

Heer, Hannes. (2006) *Vom Verschwinden der Täter. Der*

Vernichtungskrieg fand statt aber keiner war dabei. Berlin: Aufbau.

Hein, George E.(1998) *Learning in the Museum.* London: Routledge.

Hein, Hilde S. (2000) *The Museum in Transition. A Philosophical Perspective.* Washington, London: Smithsonian Institution Press.

Hemmerle, O.B. (1999) Genossen, Ihr werdet nicht oft besungen, nun ja, das wäre taktisch nicht klug…: Spionagedarstellungen in der DDR-Populärkultur. *International Intelligence History Study Group Newsletter* 7(2), 13-23.

Hemmerle, O.B. (2004) Wieviele Silberfäden wuchsen Dir…: Haare und Geheimdienst. In Janecke, C. (ed.), *Haar tragen. Eine kulturwissenschaftliche Annäherung.* Cologne: Böhlau, 177-194.

Hemmerle, O.B. (2009) Zwischen Völkerschlachtdenkmal und Mohyla Míru: Monumentalisierung und Musealisierung des Napoleonischen Zeitalters. In Hemmerle, O.B. and Brummert, U. (eds), *Säsuren und Kontinuitäten im Schatten Napoleons: Eine Annäherung an die Gebiete des heutigen Sachsen und Tschechien zwischen 1805/06 und 1813.* Hamburg: Dr. Kovac, 99-115 [in print].

Hemmerle, O.B (2004) *…für das Tragen der Orden bleibt oft nicht mehr die Zeit: Sur Repräsentation geheimer*

Dienste, Mannheim.

Herfurth, Dietrich. (1999) *Sowjetische Ausseichnungen. Ausseichnungen der Mongolischen Volksrepublik*, Berlin.

Hogg, Ian V. (1997) *Counter-Terrorism Equipment*. London: Weidenfeld.

Hooper-Greenhill, E. (1994) *Museum and Gallery Education*. London: Leicester University Press

Hooper-Greenhill, E. (ed). (1999) *The Educational Role of the Museum*. London: Routledge.

Hoorn, Melanie van der. (2003): Exorcising Remains. *Journal of Material Culture* 8:2.

Humphrey, Michael. (2002) *The politics of Atrocity and Reconciliation: From Terror to Drama*. London: Routledge.

Huyssen, Andreas. (2000): Present Pasts: Media, Politics, Amnesia, *Public Culture* 12.1: 21-38

Huyssen, Andreas. (2003) *Present Pasts. Urban Palimpsets and The Politics of Memory*. Stanford: Stanford University Press.

Ide, Robert. (2003). *Gedenkstätte Berlin Hohenschönhausen*. Berlin: Stadtwandel.

Imperial War Museum. Central Files A4/1 Press Notices 1917-19

Imperial War Museum. (1920) *Third Annual Report of the Committee of the Imperial War Museum: 1st April, 1919,* to 2nd July, 1919. London: HMSO

Imperial War Museum. (1939) *21st Annual Report of the Director-General to the Board of Trustees*. London: HMSO

Imperial War Museum. (2008). *Through My Eyes*. http://www.throughmyeyes.org.uk/custom/iwm/tme/

Ingemann, Bruno. (2002) See, talk, listen - the art of experience. *Nordisk Museologi* 2002/1, 31-48.

Institute for the Study of Totalitarian Regimes (ed.) (2008) *On the Cold War Front. Czechoslovakia 1948-1956*. Prague.

Intelligence and national security [Journal, since 1986].

Jacob, S. (2005) *Les Sept de Mons*. Brussels: Buch Edition - Willebroek: Mémorial National du Fort de Breendonk.

Jones, Simon. (1996) Making Histories of Wars. In Kavanagh, Gaynor (ed.) *Making Histories in Museums*, p. 152-162.

Jost, Walter and Felger, Friedrich. (1938) *Was wir vom Weltkrieg nicht wissen*. Leipzig: Andermann.

Journal for intelligence, propaganda and security studies [since 2007].

Jurado, Carlos Caballero and Windrow, Martin. (1985) *Resistance Warfare 1940-45*. Botley: Osprey.

Kaminsky, Anne (ed.) (2007) *Orte des Erinnerns. Gedenkzeichen, Gedenkstätten und Museen sur Dik-*

tatur in *SBS und DDR*. Berlin: Forum.
Kavanagh, Gaynor. (2000) Forgiving and Forgetting: Museums and trauma i Per-Uno Ågren (red.) *Museum 2000. Confirmation or Challenge?* ICOM Sweden, Swedish Travelling Exhibition and the Swedish Museum Association.
Kavanagh, Gaynor. (1996) Making Histories, Making Memories. In Kavanagh, Gaynor (ed.) *Making Histories in Museums*. Leicester, p. 1-15.
Kessler, Pamela. (1992) *Undercover Washington*. Washington: EPM.
Kierdorf, Alexander et al (eds) (2007) *Der Regierungsbunker*. Berlin: Wasmuth.
Kjeldbæk, Esben. (1984) Småsedler fra Theresienstadt - den uvirkelige ghetto. *Nationalmuseets Arbejdsmark 1984*, p. 68-79.
Kjeldbæk, Esben. (1998) Ting fra besættelsen - et museologisk essay. In Dethlefsen, Henrik, Lundbak, Henrik (eds.) *Fra mellemkrigstid til efterkrigstid*. København, p. 359-393.
Kjeldbæk, Esben. (1991) Idéoplæg til ændring af den faste udstilling på Frihedsmuseet. 25 January 1991, *Frihedsmuseets Bibliotek*, 37a.
Kjeldbæk, Esben. (2001) Post-Modernism and the Three Generations of Museums. *Nordisk Museologi*, pp. 119-26.

Knigge, V. and Mählert, U. (eds) (2005). *Der Kommunismus im Museum*. Cologne: Böhlau.

Knigge, Volkhard & Mählert (Hg.) (2005) *Der Kommunismus im Museum. Formen der Ausinandersetzung in Deutschland und Ostmitteleuropa*. Böhlau Verlag Köln Weimar Wien.

Kohn, Richard H. (1995) History and the Culture Wars: The Case of the Smithsonian Institution's Enola Gay Exhibition. *Journal of American History*, 82 (3), 1036-1063.

Kopf, Christine. (2001) Museum. In Pethes, N. and Ruchats, J. (eds.). *Gedächtnis und Erinnerung: ein interdissiplinäres Lexikon*. Hamburg: Rowohlt, 387-389.

Kristensen, S. and Nørskov Madsen Bar, D. (2000) *Frihedsmuseet - en analyse af den permanente udstilling med særlig vægt på formidlingen af oplysningen og mindet om frihedskampen* (thesis[speciale]), Roskilde: Roskilde Universitet.

Kunsten at tale godt (The art of speaking well), *Weekendavisen*, 7 September, 2007.

Kunse, Thomas. (2008) *Russlands Unterwelten*. Berlin: Links.

Lagrou, P. (2000) *The Legacy of Nazi Occupation: Patriotic Memory and National Recovery in Western Europe, 1945-1965*. Cambridge: Cambridge University Press.

Le Marec, Bernard. (1994) *Les Français Libres et leurs em-*

blèmes. Panasol: Lavauselle.

Lebow, Kansteiner & Fogu (eds) (2006) *The Politics of Memory in Postwar Europe*. Duke University Press. Durham and London.

Leggewie, Claus. (2006) Equally criminal? Totalitarian experience and European memory. *Eurosine* 2006

Lettow-Vorbeck, Paul von (ed.) (1931) *Die Weltkriegsspionage*. Munich: Moser.

Levy, P. (1971) *Le Fort de Breendonk*. 3rd ed. Willebroek: Mémorial National du Fort de Breendonk.

Light, Duncan. (2000) Gazing on communism: heritage tourism and post-communist identities in Germany, Hungary and Romania. *Tourism Geographies* 2(2):157-176.

Locken, Allan W. (1995) *Collector's Guide to the Fairbairn-Sykes Fighting Knife*. Winnipeg.

Lord, Cliff and Tennant, Julian. (1999). *ANSAC Elite. The Airborne and Special Forces Insignia of Australia and New Zealand*. Wellington: transpress.

Lundbak, Henrik (et.al.) (2005) Spærretid. Hverdag under besættelsen 1940-1945. *Nationalmuseet*, p. 99.

MacDonald, Sharon. (2006) *A Companion to Museum Studies*. Blackwell.

Macintyre, Ben. (2008) *For Your Eyes Only: Ian Fleming and James Bond*. London: Bloomsbury.

Magdans, Andreas. (2006) *BND. Standort Pullach*. Cologne: Dumont.

Maier, Charles. (2002) Hot Memory ... Cold Memory: On the Political Half-Life of Fascist and Communist Memory. *Tr@nsit* 22 online.

Maier, Clemens. (2007). *Making Memories. The Politics of Remembrance in Postwar Norway and Denmark*. PhD thesis European University Institute.

Marchington, James. (2004). *Special Forces. Weapons and Equipment,*. London: Brassey's.

Marr, Andrew. (2007). *A History of Modern Britain*. London: Pan Books

Medicus, Thomas. Helden, nicht Opfer sehen, *Süddeutsche Zeitung*. 23 March 2007.

Melton, H. Keith. (1996) *The Ultimate Spy Book*. London: Dorling Kindersley.

Minnery, John. (1990). *CIA Catalog of Clandestine Weapons, Tools and Gadgets*. Boulder: Paladin.

Mørk Hansen, Niels J. (1988) *En analyse af Frihedsmuseets permanente udstilling - med henblik på en diskussion af formidlingen af besættelsestidens historie*. (speciale [thesis]) Copenhagen: Københavns Universität.

Müller-Enbergs, Helmut (ed.) (1998) *Inoffisielle Mitarbeiter des Ministeriums für Staatssicherheit*. Teil 2, Berlin: Links.

Museums Association. (2002) *Code of Ethics for Museums*. London: Museums Association

Nefors, P. 2003. Het Fort van Breendonk. De Nazi-terreur in België. Besoekersgids. Willebroek: Nationaal gedenkteken van het Fort van Breendonk.

Nefors, P. (2003). *Le Fort de Breendonk. La terreur Nazie en Belgique. Guide de la visite.* Willebroek: Mémorial National du Fort de Breendonk.

Nefors, P. (2004) *Breendonk 1940-1945. De geschiedenis.* Antwerp: Standaard uitgeverij.

Nefors, P. (2005a) *Breendonk 1940-1945.* Brussels: Racine.

Nefors, P. (2005b) Das Lager Breendonk: vom SS-Auffanglager bis sum Mahnmal für Menschenrechte. *Gedenkstättenrundbrief* 127, 20-27.

Nefors, P. (2005c) Breendonk. Un Mémorial des droits de l'Homme. Espace de libertés. *Magazine du Centre d'Action Laïque.* 330, 13-14.

Nefors, P. (2008) Breendonk. Aron, P. and Gotovitch, J.(eds) *Dictionnaire de la Seconde Guerre Mondiale en Belgique.* Brussels: André Versaille.

Newark, T. et al (eds) (1998) *Brassey's Book of Camouflage.* London: Brassey's.

Ochs, J. (1947). *Breendonk. Bagnards et Bourreaux.* Brussels: Editions du Nord.

Otto, Lene (2009) Kommunismen materielle kultur. In: Damsholt, Mordhorst og Simonsen (red.): *Materialiseringer.* Århus Univeristetsforlag.

Pattinson, Juliette. (2001) *Secret War. A Pictorial Record of*

the Special Operations Executive. London: Caxton.
Pieper, Katrin. (2006) *Musealisierung des Holocaust*. Cologne: Böhlau.
Platt, Richard. (1996) *Eyewitness Guides: Spy*. London: Dorling Kindersley.
Poulsen, Henning. (1997). Denmark at War?. In Ekman, Stig, Edling, Nils (ed.), The occupation as History. Södertälje, 98-113.
Preute, Michael. (1984). *Vom Bunker der Bundesregierung*. Cologne: nachtraben.
PRO (ed.) 2001. *SOE Syllabus*. London: PRO.
Pugh, Harry et al. (2000) *Russian airborne, spetsnas and elite forces insignia*. Arlington: C&D.
Puvogel, Ulrike et al (1995/99) *Gedenkstätten für die Opfer des Nationalsosialismus*, 2 volumes, Bonn: bpb.
Reitan, Jon. (2005). Fra bruk til misbruk av et krigsminne? Falstad - Nazileir, landssvikerfengsel og nasjonalt minnested. In Sønderjysk Kulturarv. *Sønderjyske Museer 2003-2004*. Haderslev, 74-81.
Renseignement & opérations spéciales [Journal, 1999-2003].
Rottman, Gordon. (1989) *World Special Forces Insignia*. London: Osprey.
Rückel, Robert (ed.) (2006) *DDR-Museum*. Berlin.
Runia, Eelco. (2006) Presence. *History and Theory*: 1-29
Sakamoto, Akira. (1988) *Illustrated Spy & Scout Weapons*. Tokyo.

Schläger, Horst and Schwarzer, Wolfgang. (1998) *Top secret. Agenten- und Spionagefilme*. Berlin: Henschel.

Schmidt, Mária. (2005) Our Common National Commemoration Place - the House of Terror Museum. An interview with Mária Schmidt, *Diplomata* 20-10-2005

Schneider, Horst. (2005) *Das Gruselkabinett des Dr. Hubertus Knabe(lari)*. Berlin: Spotless.

Schwindt, Friedrich (2003) *Police & crime museums of the world*. Halle: Stekovics.

Seaman, Mark (ed.) (2000) *Secret Agent's Handbook of Special Devices. WW II*. London: National Archives.

Seifert, Heribert. Rückkehr der Texte. Die neue Wehrmachtsausstellung in Berlin. *Neue Zürcher Zeitung*. 29 November 2001. http://www.nss.ch/2001/11/29/fe/article7TIoA.html.

Skov Kristensen, Henrik. (2001) Fra fangelejr til museum og national mindepark - træk af Frøslevlejrens kulturhistorie 1944-2001. In *Sønderjyske Museer* 2001. Aabenraa, 81-101.

Skov Kristensen, Henrik.(2002) Frøslevlejren - fangelejr, museum, mindesmærke, efterskole og Foreningen af danske Eksportvognmænd. In *Sønderjysk Almanak* 2002. Aabenraa, 106-116.

Skov Kristensen, Henrik (2005a) Frøslevlejr og Fårhuslejr - samme sted, forskellig betydning. In Sønderjysk

Kulturarv. *Sønderjyske Museer 2003-2004*. Haderslev, 82-91.

Skov Kristensen, Henrik. (2005b) Det tyske mindretal og Fårhuslejren - retsopgøret på museum. In *Historie 2005*, 1, 54-110.

Skov Kristensen, Henrik. (2007). Eine Politik von grosser Tragweite: Die dänische Zusammenarbeitspolitik und die dänische KS-Häftlinge. In Hilfe oder Handel? Rettungsbemühungen für NS-Verfolgte. *Beiträge sur Geschichte der nationalsozialistischen Verfolgung in Norddeutschland 10*. Edition Temmen: Hamburg, 81-94.

Skov Kristensen, Henrik. (2008) The Museum of Danish Resistance and the Frøslev Camp Museum as Places of Danish Remembrance. In Bohn, Robert, Cornelissen, Christoph, Lammers Karl Christian (ed.) *Vergangenheitspolitik und Errinnerungskulturen im Schatten des Zweiten Weltkriegs. Deutschland und Skandinavien seit 1945*. Klartext Verlag: Essen, 169-180.

Souyris-Rolland, André et al. (1985) *Guide des Ordres et Décorations de la Résistance et de la Libération*. Paris: Public-Réalisations.

Spiegel, Gabrielle M. (2009) Presidential Address. The Task of the Historian. *The American Historical Review*, 114: 1-15 February.

Stiftung Haus der Geschichte der Bundesrepublik Deutschland (ed.) (2002) *Duell im Dunkel. Spionage im geteilten Deutschland*. Cologne.

Taylor, Peter. (2000) *Allied Special Forces Insignia*. Barnsley: Pen & Sword.

The Exhibitions Guide of The Sighet Museum. (upubl., u.å.)

The Falling Leaf [since 1958].

The Journal of Intelligence History [since 2001].

The Original Spy Tour of Washington(tm). http://www.coldwar.org/education/spy_tour.html, 03/03/09.

The United States Holocaust Memorial Museum. *Mission Statement*. http://www.ushmm.org/museum/mission/, (20/02/08).

Thompson, Leroy. (1985) *Commando Dagger*. Boulder: Paladin.

Thompson, Leroy. (1986) *Elite Unit Insignia of the Vietnam War*. London: Weidenfeld.

Thompson, Leroy. (1991) *Badges and Insignia of Elite Forces*. London: Weidenfeld.

Tolan, M. and Stolze, J. (2009) *Geschüttelt, nicht gerührt: James Bond und die Physik*. Munich: Piper.

Tucker, Louise. (1994) *Bewaffnung und Ausrüstung von Spezialeinheiten*. Stuttgart: Motorbuch.

Vedtekter for Norges Hjemmefrontmuseum vedtatt av konstituerende forsamling på Akershus 17. juni

1966 (Resolution on the founding of the Norwegian Resistance Museum at Akershus), cited in: Færoy, Frode, 1997. *Norges Hjemmefrontmuseum i stiftelsens år*. Oslo: Norges Hjemmefrontmuseum, 106.

Vergo, Peter. (1989) The Reticent Object. In, Vergo, Peter (ed.) *The New Museology*, p. 41-59.

Wahl, Günther. (1983) *Waffentechnische Kuriositäten*. Schwäbisch Hall: Schwend.

Wahl, Günther. (1996). *Kuriose Waffentechnik*. Melsungen: Jagd und Natur.

Walther, Klaus. (1993/94). *Uniformeffekten der bewaffneten Organe der DDR*, 2 volumes, Berlin: Ecotour.

West, Nigel (=Allason, Rupert). (1999) *Counterfeit Spies*. London: Time Warner.

Whitmarsh, A. (2001) We will remember them. Memory and Commemoration in War Museums. *Journal of Conservation and Museum Studies*, 7, 1-15.

Wilden, Joop van der et al. (1999) *Duister Amsterdam*. Den Haag.

Williams, Paul. (2007). *Memorial Museums, The Global Rush to Commemorate Atrocities*. Oxford, New York: Berg.

Worthington, Peter. WWII plaque an obscene summation. *Toronto Sun*. 22 April 2006.

Young, James. (1993) *The Texture of Memory: Holocaust Memorials and Meaning*. New Haven, Connecticut.

Zhurshenko, Tatiana. (2007) The geopolitics of memory. *Eurozine*.

Zolberg, V.L. (1996) Museums as contested sites of remembrance: the Enola Gay affair. In: Macdonald, S. and Fyfe, G., (Eds.) *Theorising Museums. Representing identity and diversity in a changing world*, Oxford: Blackwell, 69-82.

MUSEUMS AND WORLD WAR II

Also from MusemsEtc

Rethinking Learning: Museums and Young People
ISBN: 978-0-9561943-0-5
240pp

Inspiring Action: Museums and Social Change
ISBN: 978-0-9561943-1-2
324pp

The Power of the Object: Museums and World War II
Editor: Esben Kjeldbæk
ISBN: 978-0-9561943-4-3
424pp

Creating Bonds: Marketing Museums
ISBN: 978-0-9561943-1-2

Alive To Change: Successful Museum Retailing
ISBN: 978-0-9561943-3-6

The Science Exhibition: Curation, Design, Communication
Editor: Anastasia Filippoupoliti
ISBN: 978-0-9561943-5-0

Order direct from www.museumsetc.com

Published by
MuseumsEtc Ltd
Hudson House
8 Albany Street
Edinburgh EH1 3QB
www.museumsetc.com

Edition © MuseumsEtc Ltd 2009
Texts © the authors
All rights reserved

No part of this publication may be reproduced in any manner without
without written permission from the publisher, except in the context of
reviews.

ISBN: 978-0-9561943-4-3
British Library Cataloguing in Publication information available.

Text: Underware Dolly, 10/15pt

LaVergne, TN USA
22 September 2009
158571LV00004B/11/P